PLANTATION SILVICULTURE IN TEMPERATE REGIONS

PLANTATION SILVICULTURE
IN TEMPERATE REGIONS

with special reference to
the British Isles

PETER S. SAVILL

Lecturer in Silviculture,
University of Oxford

JULIAN EVANS

Silviculturist,
British Forestry Commission

CLARENDON PRESS · OXFORD
1986

Oxford University Press, Walton Street, Oxford OX2 6DP
Oxford   New York   Toronto
Delhi   Bombay   Calcutta   Madras   Karachi
Kuala Lumpur   Singapore   Hong Kong   Tokyo
Nairobi   Dar es Salaam   Cape Town
Melbourne   Auckland
and associated companies in
Beirut   Berlin   Ibadan   Nicosia

Oxford is a trade mark of Oxford University Press

Published in the United States
by Oxford University Press, New York

British Library Cataloguing in Publication Data
Savill, Peter S.
Plantation silviculture in temperate regions:
with special reference to the British Isles.
1. Trees   2. Plantations
I. Title   II. Evans, Julian, 1946–
634.9'56'0912   SD391
ISBN 0-19-854138-4

Library of Congress Cataloging in Publication Data
Savill, Peter.
Plantation silviculture in temperate regions.
Bibliography: p.
Includes index.
1. Tree farms—Great Britain.   2. Tree farms.
I. Evans, Julian.   II. Title.
SD45.S28 1986   634.9'0941   85-30622
ISBN 0-19-854138-4

Set by Dobbie Typesetting Service, Plymouth, Devon
Printed in Great Britain by
St Edmundsbury Press, Bury St Edmunds, Suffolk

Preface

This book is intended as an introduction to plantation silviculture for undergraduate and postgraduate students in forestry and related fields, though it is hoped that practising foresters and, indeed, all who work with trees will find it of value. In some senses it parallels, for temperate regions, an earlier book by one of us *Plantation forestry in the tropics* (Evans 1982*a*). Emphasis is on the biological principles which underlie silvicultural practices rather than the practices themselves. Principles do not vary greatly from place to place but economic, physical, managerial, social, and political conditions do, and influence the practice of forestry and attitudes to it. Where specific practices are mentioned, examples are drawn from throughout developed, temperate regions. Most come from Britain and Ireland. The principal reason for this is that most of our experience has been in the United Kingdom, but for plantation forestry this is no disadvantage since plantations make up a more significant part of the British forest estate than in most countries. Considerable efforts have been devoted to creating them since the 1920s, often on difficult land.

As public attitudes alter and scientific knowledge advances, approaches to plantation forestry change. Plantations are no longer exclusively places just to grow wood. Today, their values for recreation, wildlife conservation, watershed management, and other uses are widely appreciated though how to integrate these uses in an acceptable manner is not always so well understood. On a world-wide scale, as populations grow there are increasing demands for intensive production on the one hand and a more diverse and less intensive use of forest land on the other. Compromises can be difficult and conflicts of opinion are common. Though not addressing these problems directly, we have not been oblivious of these competing demands on forest land, including plantations.

The book is divided into four parts. Part A is intended as a general introduction in which the values and productive potential of plantations are discussed. Part B deals with the basic silviculture of plantations. We have inevitably concentrated upon coniferous plantations being grown primarily for industrial wood production since this is the main form of plantation forestry in the temperate zone. A deliberate omission has been any detailed consideration of forest nurseries because, in temperate regions at least, these are increasingly the province of specialized nursery managers rather than foresters. Part C covers some of the more specialized forms of silviculture with which foresters are sometimes concerned, and part D with aspects of protection and plantation design. The authorities for the scientific names of plants and animals mentioned in the text can be found in the index.

We gratefully acknowledge the help of several colleagues and others who have found time to comment on individual chapters of this book. In particular, we thank Len Leyton, Trudy Watt, Martin Speight, Colyear Dawkins, Richard Barnes, and Steven Libbey. Ken Eldridge of CSIRO in Canberra, John Worrall of the University of British Columbia, and John Matthews of the University of Aberdeen have also provided invaluable help. We have frequently adopted their suggestions though the responsibility for what is published here is entirely our own. The book also owes much to several generations of undergraduate and postgraduate students who have discussed many of the topics in tutorials and whose contribution is greater than they might have realized. We are also grateful to the British Forestry Commission and Northern Ireland Forest Service for permission to draw on unpublished material. Their pioneering work in all aspects of plantation forestry has created, not only almost one million hectares of new forest, but a wealth of knowledge and experience in the British Isles.

We are especially grateful to Carol Green and Felicity Awdry who have typed the manuscript and then, with good humour, put up with making seemingly endless adjustments to the text.

Oxford and *Alton*   P.S.S.
August, 1985   J.E.

Acknowledgements

We are grateful to the following who have given us permission to reproduce material:

The editor of *Forestry* for Figs 8.1, 8.2, 8.4, 9.2, 9.3, 9.5, and Tables 4.2 and 9.3.

The editor of *Forestry Abstracts* for Fig. 14.3 and Table 14.1.

The editor of *Irish Forestry* for Tables 4.3 and 6.1.

The editor of the *Quarterly Journal of Forestry* for Fig. 15.2.

The editor of *Scottish Forestry* for Table 8.4.

The Forestry Commission for Figs 3.3, 7.2, 9.10, and Table 3.1. Fig. 10.4 is Crown copyright and is reproduced by permission of the Forestry Commission.

Dr F. Olesen of the Danish Heath Society for Fig. 12.1.

Mr K. Taylor for Figs 6.3, 8.6, 16.2, and 16.3.

Dr K. Yoda of Osaka City University, Japan for Fig. 9.1.

Contents

Part A

Introduction

1. Introduction —
the role of plantations

Definitions

Plantation

A plantation is defined as 'a forest crop or stand raised artificially, either by sowing or planting' (Ford-Robertson 1971). To this may be added that some plantations are established by inserting cuttings, for example, many poplars and willows. The definition of a plantation may seem simple, but the word artificial or 'man made' needs further expansion. For example, when man establishes a new forest on grassland such afforestation is clearly artificial and may be termed a plantation. But, where an existing forest is regenerated by enrichment, though tree seedlings are planted, the general appearance is usually not very like a plantation, at least often not for many years. A full discussion of definitions is included in the *World symposium on man-made forests and their industrial importance* (FAO 1967), and some of the more arbitrary definitions noted below are derived mostly from this source.

Origins

Between the extremes of afforestation and natural regeneration of indigenous forest there is a range of forest conditions where man intervenes to a greater or lesser extent in regeneration. Five types are usually distinguished according to origin.

1. Planting bare land where there has been no forest for at least 50 years. All afforestation of grassland, such as the beech plantations on chalk downland in southern England and spruce planting in the uplands (Fig. 1.1), fall into this category. The somewhat arbitrary 50 years is used because most vestiges of the previous forest conditions, including the flora, and microflora and fauna will be lost during this period, especially if the land has been subject to arable farming, livestock grazing, or, of course, industrial or urban development.
2. Reforestation of land which has carried forest within the last 50 years but where the previous crop is replaced by an essentially different one. A frequent example in the past was where broadleaved woodland was converted to conifer plantation.
3. Replanting land which has carried forest within the last 50 years by renewal of essentially the same crop as before. This is not as common

FIG. 1.1. Dyfi forest in Wales is a typical upland area being afforested with spruce and pine in Britain, formerly used for grazing. (Photograph J. H. Williams.)

as the first two because one advantage of planting trees is the opportunity to introduce a new and more productive species. Examples include *Cryptomeria* plantations in Japan and, in Britain, much of the oak in the New Forest in Hampshire which has arisen from planting rather than natural regeneration, often in mixture with pine (Small 1982).
4. Forests established by natural regeneration with deliberate silvicultural intervention and assistance from man, for example many of the beech and oak forests of northern France and Germany.
5. Forests which have regenerated naturally without assistance from man, for example all the remoter conifer forests in north temperate regions.

In this book plantations are the forest types in the first three categories above, that is artificial regeneration is a basic criterion.

Shape

Plantations are mostly of regular shape with fixed and clearly defined boundaries. Land planted with trees is often only called a plantation if its width is at least 100 metres, but such a strict definition is not adhered to here.

Stocking

Stocking refers to the number of usable trees per unit area, and the very words a *forest* or *plantation* imply that land is reasonably well wooded. For a young plantation before it is first thinned a minimum stocking of 1000 trees per hectare or 75 per cent survival of the original planting is generally considered adequate. There are, of course, exceptions to this guideline, such as poplars grown for veneer, planted 7 m apart (204 stems ha^{-1}).

Naturalization

New plantations of exotic (introduced) species are obviously man-made and could not occur on the site naturally. But if, subsequently, the species proves well adapted to its new environment, sets seed freely, and can be regenerated naturally, for example sycamore and sweet chestnut in Britain and Scots pine in north America, it is sometimes said to be naturalized. However, such naturalized species are sometimes considered to be alien by many ecologists, even though they may have been present for centuries.

Mixed regeneration systems

Where enrichment planting supplements existing forest, the forest is normally classified as man-made if the planted trees ultimately form more than half the final crop.

Temperate regions

This book concerns plantation silviculture in temperate regions, principally in cool temperate climates. This broad climatic zone mostly lies between Mediterranean climates and the cool polar regions. It is characterized by a marked winter period when growth virtually ceases for one to several months because of mean monthly temperatures below 6 °C.

Cool temperate climates are in the zone of permanent westerly winds; to be more exact, they are in the path of the depressions which move eastwards from their origins along the polar front (Bucknell 1964). These affect the western coastal areas most and result in a strong maritime influence which leads to equable conditions of warm summers, mild winters, and year-round rain. Away from coastal regions conditions become progressively more extreme or continental with hot summers, cold winters and mainly summer rainfall. Plantation silviculture in cool temperate regions is dominated by conifers such as the Norway spruce, Scots pine and larches, several species from north western America, and trees from four angiosperm families — Aceraceae, Betulaceae, Fagaceae, and Salicaceae. Some reference is made to warm temperate regions where Monterey pine (*Pinus radiata*) has succeeded so well along with eucalypts and the Juglandaceae family with its valuable timbers and often edible fruit.

Silviculture

Silviculture is the art and science of cultivating forest crops. It is concerned with the growing of trees just as agriculture is concerned with the growing of food crops in fields. Apart from some of this introductory chapter this book is primarily concerned with silviculture and not in detail with issues of management, economics, policy, or harvesting.

Uses of forest

Plantations, though artificial, are able to satisfy most of the roles forests play (Table 1.1) though they are particularly well suited to providing industrial products.

Table 1.1   *The role of forests.(adapted from World Bank 1978)*

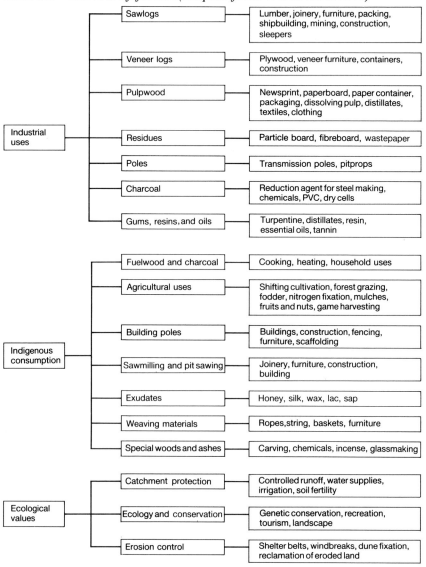

	Sawlogs	Lumber, joinery, furniture, packing, shipbuilding, mining, construction, sleepers
	Veneer logs	Plywood, veneer furniture, containers, construction
	Pulpwood	Newsprint, paperboard, paper container, packaging, dissolving pulp, distillates, textiles, clothing
Industrial uses	Residues	Particle board, fibreboard, wastepaper
	Poles	Transmission poles, pitprops
	Charcoal	Reduction agent for steel making, chemicals, PVC, dry cells
	Gums, resins, and oils	Turpentine, distillates, resin, essential oils, tannin
	Fuelwood and charcoal	Cooking, heating, household uses
	Agricultural uses	Shifting cultivation, forest grazing, fodder, nitrogen fixation, mulches, fruits and nuts, game harvesting
	Building poles	Buildings, construction, fencing, furniture, scaffolding
Indigenous consumption	Sawmilling and pit sawing	Joinery, furniture, construction, building
	Exudates	Honey, silk, wax, lac, sap
	Weaving materials	Ropes, string, baskets, furniture
	Special woods and ashes	Carving, chemicals, incense, glassmaking
	Catchment protection	Controlled runoff, water supplies, irrigation, soil fertility
Ecological values	Ecology and conservation	Genetic conservation, recreation, tourism, landscape
	Erosion control	Shelter belts, windbreaks, dune fixation, reclamation of eroded land

Brief history of planting

Man has planted trees for a long time; for example, many references to tree planting may be found in the *Old Testament*. In Britain the most famous early advocate of planting was John Evelyn who urged the repairing of the 'wooden walls' of England in his *Sylva* in 1664 though, in fact, 80 years before concern by Queen Elizabeth I over dwindling supplies of naval timber had led to some oak planting in Cranbourne chase. Comparable exhortations and examples can be found from the same period in Germany and France. Colbert, and later Pannelier, were instrumental in the establishment of several thousand hectares of new plantation in the Forêt de Compiegne in the seventeenth and eighteenth centuries. By the early nineteenth century most texts on forestry included many pages on tree planting and plantation establishment.

Up to the early nineteenth century nearly all planting was of native species in traditional forest areas; examples in Britain include the New Forest, the Chilterns, and the Forest of Dean. But increasingly from this time planting involved afforestation of bare land, for example *Pinus pinaster* in the Landes of France (Fig. 1.2) and spruce and pine planting on old fields in the Vosges, or conversion of broadleaved woodland to conifer. Many larch plantations and beech and pine shelterbelts in Scotland date back to this period. But it was in Germany that this new plantation forestry developed most rapidly, largely through the influence of Cotta, such as Norway spruce afforestation in Saxony. Silviculture in central Europe was, and frequently still is,

FIG. 1.2. Extensive afforestation, mainly of *Pinus pinaster*, in the Landes, S.W. France.

characterized by very close spacing (planting at least 5000 and sometimes 20 000 trees ha^{-1}), light thinning, long rotations, and a conservative attitude towards the use of exotics. Just as today, in the 1800s there were both misgivings about this kind of forestry (Jones 1965) and enthusiastic supporters such as Simpson (1900) who dubbed this silviculture 'the new forestry' and urged British foresters to adopt continental practices wholeheartedly.

Concurrent with the development of new ways of growing trees, and a multitude of silvicultural systems to achieve satisfactory regeneration — see all the examples in Troup (1955) — was a rigorous evaluation of introduced species as collectors sent seed and plant material to European countries from all over the world. With the minor exception of southern beech (*Nothofagus*), all the main exotic species used in British forestry today (Norway and Sitka spruces, Corsican and lodgepole pines, Douglas-fir, and Japanese larch) were first introduced more than a hundred years ago. In warm temperate regions this trial and testing of tree species gave rise to the phenomenal success of Monterey pine, particularly in northern Spain and the four southern hemisphere countries of Chile, South Africa, Australia, and New Zealand.

The present century has seen such an upsurge in tree planting that plantation forestry is becoming a major forestry activity world wide. In several countries, such as the United Kingdom, Ireland, New Zealand, and South Africa, it is the dominant form of commercial forestry (Table 1.2). Historically the first countries to embark on major plantation programmes were, naturally enough, those seriously deficient in natural forest cover having reached, as Sutton (1984) describes it 'the last resort to a country's wood supply'. Much effort was devoted to species selection, the relatively new challenge of tree planting on bare land, and protecting the expanding estate.

Recently other temperate countries, even those with still sizeable areas of natural forest have greatly expanded plantation programmes. The most notable example is Canada (Reed 1983) with its forest renewal programme. Many factors account for the ascendancy and dependence on plantation forestry, and these are discussed below. Today in temperate countries there are some 130 million hectares of productive plantations which are contributing an increasingly large proportion of total timber requirements.

Reasons for plantation forestry

Inadequacy of natural forest

All countries have experienced loss of natural forest cover as land has been cleared for farming and other uses. Although a balance has been achieved between forest clearance and forest renewal in temperate regions as a whole, in many countries the loss of natural or semi-natural forest continued long past the point where the remainder was able to satisfy most requirements for forest products. This was the principal reason why several countries embarked on vigorous plantation programmes. However, the total area of natural forest is not the only criterion. Remoteness, inaccessibility, and poor quality of the natural resource may make its working wholly uneconomic and thus indicate other reasons for establishing plantations. These conditions influence plantation policies in both Canada and the USSR.

Domestication

This term is used to describe the trend from simply using what forest there is, to growing and managing a specific forest crop that is wanted. The growing of certain poplar cultivars derived from a controlled genetic base, for veneer for match-making or vegetable crates is perhaps the most extreme example.

Plantations as an environmental influence

Considerable areas of tree plantations have been established where the primary objective is not production of wood, though of course this will be an added benefit, but to use the influence which trees and forests can confer. Examples include the role of tree planting in the rehabilitation of industrial waste, the shelter provided by windbreaks, stabilization of sand dunes, and, not the least today, as an amenity.

Problems with natural regeneration

On a world-wide scale, natural regeneration, whether planned or not, is by far the most common method of replacing forests. It accounts for 53 per cent of the reafforestation in the original nine countries of the EEC though less than one per cent in the British Isles (Kroth *et al.* 1976), where most establishment is concerned with the afforestation of formerly bare ground. Clearly, opportunities for natural regeneration hardly exist in such circumstances, though it is probable that as first rotations come to an end natural regeneration of spruce and other introduced species may become a viable alternative to planting in some parts of Britain.

Frequently, where opportunities for natural regeneration do exist, as in semi-natural woodland, the original species are replaced by planting more productive, commercially desirable trees. Sometimes adequate natural regeneration is cleared and replaced by genetically improved strains of the same species, as occurs with *Pinus radiata* in New Zealand (Clear 1976).

Methods of natural regeneration have the reputation of being less expensive than planting. They are especially appealing to owners of woodlands who do not wish to commit themselves to expensive replanting schemes involving clearing and a long period of weeding. Though it may sometimes be cheaper than planting, natural regeneration is not free. Seed years have to be awaited which sometimes necessitates longer-than-planned rotations. If regeneration is too prolific, respacing must be carried out, and if too sparse, gaps must be filled by planting.

Where natural regeneration is successful, establishment is faster than when trees are planted and it can benefit the stability of some crops in windy regions (see p. 76). Natural regeneration is also important for the conservation of genetic resources, or a particular woodland type.

Although natural regeneration of many species and forest types occurs widely and almost any site is eventually colonized with woody growth, if free of browsing, it can be difficult to establish a crop naturally at exactly the time it is wanted. In some places natural regeneration has come to be seen as an unreliable method of crop replacement. This is not a recent view since planting has been carried out for at least two centuries in much of the New Forest and the Forest of Dean in southern Britain, and the Forêt de Compiegne in France (Fig. 1.3). However, as many French and German forests demonstrate, natural regeneration is feasible provided there is no urgency to regenerate, and care is taken to ensure favourable stand and ground conditions.

FIG. 1.3. One-hundred-year-old planted oak and beech in the Forêt de Compiegne, France.

Survey of temperate plantations

Table 1.2 presents estimates of plantation areas for many temperate countries and also indicates the recent rates of new planting.

Table 1.2 *Estimates of total areas of closed forest and areas of plantations for predominantly temperate countries*

Region	Country	$10^{-3} \times$ forest areas (ha)			
		Total closed forest	Total plantations	Annual forest renewal	Annual planting
Europe	Austria	3754		21	5
	Belgium/ Luxembourg	682		19	
	Bulgaria	3328	312	50	
	Czechoslovakia	4435		37	
	Denmark	466	29		
	Finland	19885	3	158	
	France	13875		51	
	Germany (East)	2700			
	Germany (West)	6989		62	
	Hungary	1612		19	6
	Ireland	347	341	7	7
	Italy	6363	650	15	7
	Netherlands	294		2	
	Norway	7635		79	31
	Poland	8588		106	60
	Romania	6265			
	Sweden	24400	5000	207	173
	Switzerland	935		7	
	United Kingdom	2207	2052	31	25
	Yugoslavia	9100	64		2
USSR	USSR	791600	16000	4540	1323
North America	Canada	264100	2000	720	142
	USA	195256		1775	780
South America	Argentina	7670	717	38	38
	Chile	6250	887	50	50
Asia	China	125000	28000	4670	4489
	Japan	23890	9895	240	156
	South Korea	6275	2868	152	118
Africa	South Africa	1350	1095		8
Oceania	Australia	41658	818	62	36
	New Zealand	7200	989	43	43

Sources: Figures for total closed forest areas and annual forest renewal (i.e. natural regeneration plus planting) are mostly from FAO *Forest Resources 1985* and they refer to 1980. Others are from *World Wood* Vol. 25 (5) 1983. A number of estimates have been adjusted according to information in annual reports and other publications of the forest services concerned.

Throughout all temperate countries conifers have dominated plantation forestry with the three genera *Pinus*, *Picea*, and *Larix* being much the most important except in Japan where *Cryptomeria japonica* is the main species. In general the planting of broadleaves has been more localized, to continue a particular forest type or to grow specialized products such as are derived from walnuts, poplars, and willows. The main reason for the wide use of conifers is their superior growth on the kinds of sites available for plantations.

Plantation silviculture

Plantation life history

As indicated earlier under the heading of domestication, plantation forestry is, in essence, growing trees as a crop to yield a specific product just as in farming or horticulture. Though the time scale is much longer than these other branches of plant cultivation a definite sequence of events takes place in virtually all kinds of plantation developments. The main steps in the life history of a plantation are illustrated in Fig. 1.4.

Opportunities and benefits of plantation silviculture

Species

Planting enables a forester to select the species to grow, and be no longer dependent on the existing forest type. This is perhaps the greatest advantage which plantations bring in allowing the most productive use of a site and, at the end of each rotation, allowing further improvement through planting new species, provenances and genetically improved stock.

Stocking

By planting, a forester can ensure that the whole site is fully stocked for the whole rotation with the kind of tree most wanted. Thus full use is made of the land available.

Product uniformity

Many factors in conventional plantation forestry lead to great uniformity of end product:

(1) use of one or few species in a stand;
(2) raising a crop to form an even-aged stand;
(3) applying the same silvicultural treatment over a whole stand.

Yields

As a result of these three factors the productivity of plantation forests is almost always much greater than that of natural woodland, see Table 2.1 (p. 19).

Problems with plantations

The intensive nature of plantation forestry demands high levels of commitment, skill, research, and resources. If these are not available it may be more realistic to rely upon low input and more extensive systems based on natural regeneration if they can provide the desired species and products.

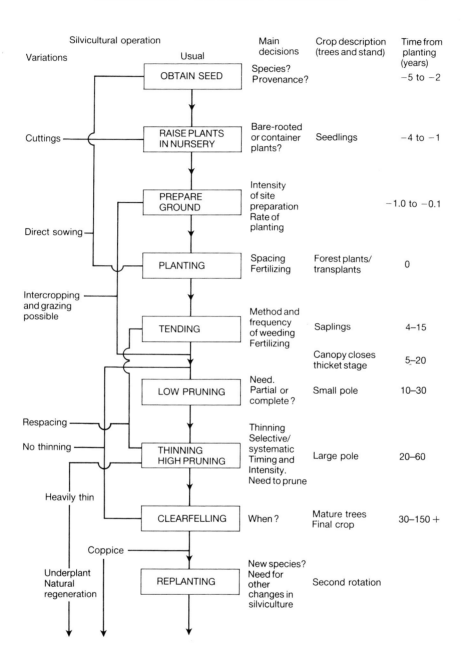

FIG. 1.4. Schematic representation of plantation life history. (Modified from Evans 1982a.)

These may be less productive but are more certain of providing a measure of success.

The uniformity of plantation crops brings possible biological risks and other disadvantages too, particularly aesthetic, and where one woodland type is superseded by another, loss in conservation value. Some of these disadvantages are discussed later in this book. But, where production is important, they are more than outweighed in most cases by the opportunities plantation silviculture afford of greater production of wood.

2. Primary production and long-term productivity in plantations

The attainment of high yields compared with those in natural forests is usually one of the aims of plantation silviculture. How these may be achieved and what risks may be involved in the long-term are among the most fundamental considerations in plantation forestry.

Definitions

The term 'primary production' is used to denote the turnover, expressed as dry weight, in a plant community: the annual production of wood, bark, leaves, flowers, fruits, and roots whether harvested or not. It may be expressed as *gross primary production*, representing total assimilation, including the proportion subsequently used for respiration in the dark, or as *net primary* production which is the amount of assimilated organic matter remaining after the requirements of respiration have been met. The subject has been discussed in detail by Jarvis and Leverenz (1983).

Gross primary production

Gross primary production is extremely difficult to estimate but in temperate forests it is largely determined by the amount of incoming solar radiation. In an analysis of many studies concerned with the International Biological Programme, Kira (1975) suggested that the highest rates of production may be about $120 \, t \, ha^{-1} \, yr^{-1}$ in the tropical rainforests of south east Asia. Rates decrease in tropical forests of the Congo basin and even more in the heavily clouded Amazon region (Brünig 1967). Gross primary production in the evergreen forests of the warm temperate zone is in the range of $40–85 \, t \, ha^{-1} \, yr^{-1}$. In the cool temperate zone, evergreen coniferous forests produce $40–50 \, t \, ha^{-1} \, yr^{-1}$ while deciduous broadleaved forests do not exceed $30 \, t \, ha^{-1} \, yr^{-1}$.

The effect of a long growing season on increasing gross primary production in the humid lower latitudes is therefore apparent, especially where shortages of water do not limit plant growth. However, the efficiency of solar energy conversion by photosynthesis to gross production varies much less in different climatic zones *during the growing season*, but whereas the growing season may be continuous in parts of the tropics, it may only be a few months or even weeks elsewhere. Environmental stresses, such as droughts, suboptimum temperatures, or lowered nitrogen availability, have a primary influence on the production of leaf area, and influence crop growth rates through their effects on the interception of radiation.

Net primary production

Annual net primary production is far less variable than gross primary production in forests. Over large areas in any stable ecosystem it is zero because production is entirely consumed or mineralized, and the system begins each year at the same level as the year before. Losses of dry matter are evident in leaf fall and somewhat less obviously from the fall of twigs and branches. Though rates of litter fall can vary widely, averages quoted by Jarvis and Leverenz (1983) are 3.7 and 3.2 t ha^{-1} yr^{-1} for evergreen gymnosperms and deciduous angiosperms respectively. There are also enormous but not well quantified seasonal losses resulting from the turnover of the fine root and mycorrhizal populations which may account for well over 50 per cent of annual photosynthetic production (see Persson 1982), and from grazing by insects and other herbivores. It has been estimated, for example, that 20 per cent more stemwood could be produced by sycamore (*Acer pseudoplatanus*) if heavy infestations of the leaves by aphids in spring did not occur (Dixon 1971).

Estimates of mean net primary production vary very widely (Leith 1975). In natural ecosystems they give little indication of the potential of managed forests because they ignore the effects of the removal of wood and other produce from the forest community. Net primary production is greatly influenced by removals, by the relative distributions of climax and early successional stages, and by other differences in forest structure, especially age. Generally, leaf biomass and gross primary production rates reach a ceiling value at the time canopy closes but total biomass and hence community respiration continue to increase with age (Fig. 2.1). Net current production therefore reaches a maximum value immediately after canopy closes when it often amounts to 25–35 t ha^{-1} yr^{-1} in *young, dense* stands with *fully closed canopies*, and thereafter declines. A common age for harvesting plantations is when mean net production reaches a maximum and this occurs a few years later (see Fig. 9.6, p. 122).

Estimates of the maximum levels of net primary production for various types of managed forest indicate that tropical forest communities are no more productive than some warm temperate evergreen forests. Upper levels of about 40 t ha^{-1} yr^{-1} are often quoted. Though gross primary production is higher in the tropics, the higher temperatures there cause a very marked increase in respiration which reduces net production. Kira (1975) quotes levels of net primary production of 35.5 t ha^{-1} yr^{-1} for young rubber crops in the

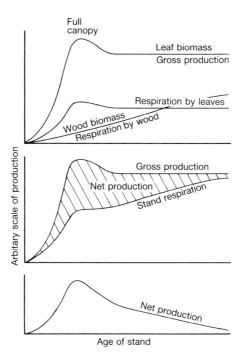

FIG. 2.1. Relationships between gross and net primary production during the development of an even-aged stand. (From Kira and Shidei 1967.)

tropics and similar rates for many parts of the temperate zone: 43.7 t ha^{-1} yr^{-1} for *Cryptomeria japonica* in Japan, 38 t ha^{-1} yr^{-1} for *Pinus radiata* in New Zealand, and 36 t ha^{-1} yr^{-1} in young *Tsuga heterophylla* in the Pacific North West of the USA. Yields substantially higher than 40 t are only found in some C4 plants. Napier grass (*Pennisetum purpureum*) can produce over 80 t ha^{-1} yr^{-1} (Loomis and Gerakis 1975) and among trees, rates of stemwood production of over 37 t ha^{-1} yr^{-1} are quoted for *Eucalyptus grandis* in Brazil (Zobel *et al.* 1983) indicating a level of net primary production of over 70 t ha^{-1} yr^{-1} if roots, branches, leaves, etc. are considered as well. Average rates of growth are, of course, much lower and the production of usable produce lower still, possibly about 40 per cent of net primary production.

Evergreen and deciduous forests

Over long rotations, deciduous forests are usually less productive than evergreen ones in temperate latitudes, but deciduous leaves are more efficient at converting solar energy than evergreen leaves. This apparent contradiction is discussed by Schulze (1982) who pointed out that deciduous leaves have higher photosynthetic rates per unit dry weight of leaf than the more perennial evergreen leaves found on many conifers (10–14 mg of $CO_2 g^{-1} h^{-1}$ compared to 4–6 mg of $CO_2 g^{-1} h^{-1}$). They are also less expensively constructed in terms of content of assimilated carbon so that a proportionally larger part of the carbon gain of the tree is available for the growth of the non-photosynthetic stems, roots, fruits, etc. Deciduous leaves can be most effective at promoting rapid growth if the growing season is long enough. This enables some species like birch, aspen, and alder to become invasive weeds in young conifer plantations, and pioneers in some natural successions and it accounts for part of their value as energy crops when grown on short rotations (Chapter 11). If the growing season is short the annual investment in new leaves may be much higher than in evergreens and such conditions occur as the length of growing season decreases due to reduced temperatures or light, and drought, which makes the habitat less favourable.

In such circumstances evergreen leaves are advantageous because they are retained for long periods, for example often around 5 years and occasionally up to 12 years in Norway spruce. The evergreen habit enables leaves which are already on the tree to contribute to photosynthetic gain. They can begin photosynthesis as soon as environmental conditions are suitable even if the new leaves flush relatively late. Because of leaf retention, there is often a much greater leaf biomass or Leaf Area Index, (LAI) in evergreen forests. For example, the LAI in deciduous forests in Japan is between 4 and 7 ha ha^{-1} whereas in evergreen conifers it ranges from 7 to 12 in pines and 15 to 20 in other species (Tadaki 1966). It has also been suggested that evergreens are at an advantage in environments where nutrients are scarce because the leaves act as storage organs for nutrients in short supply (Moore 1984).

The disadvantage of the evergreen habit is that carbon input is much higher than in deciduous leaves. This higher structural cost provides protection against heat, cold, desiccation, and possibly predation. It can be justified if the leaves serve for a long period as in the case of many conifers, but these trees have to accumulate leaf biomass over several years before fast rates of growth are achieved.

Thus, some evergreen trees are more efficient in temperate climates with a growing season restricted by winter cold and soils with low mineral resources where protection during the vulnerable early years is important (Bryant *et al.* 1983). They can also be very productive in climates with prolonged droughts such as in tropical monsoon and Mediterranean regions. Evergreens predominate in boreal climates but are replaced by deciduous trees where boreal forests give way to tundra, possibly because of the cost of maintenance during long dark winters, and the high risk of damage by snow and ice. However, the interaction of deciduous and evergreen species is not clearly understood in the oceanic arctic region and in continental boreal and alpine climates, where both forms are successful.

Production in plantation forests

Where production of industrial wood is an important objective, the most common plantation forestry strategy involves planting a single fast-growing species on a large cleared site, growing it until approximately the age of maximum mean annual increment (Fig. 9.6, p. 122) and then clear-felling the whole crop. This ensures high productivity and is simple to carry out. The system has the economic advantages of being cheap to establish, manage, harvest, and market. Whatever the biological arguments in favour of stands with a diversity of age classes and species, they carry much less short-term economic weight.

Felling an even-aged stand at the age when maximum mean annual increment is attained is analogous to harvesting a natural forest at the late pioneer stage of a succession when mean net annual primary production is at a maximum. For the six most widely planted species in the United Kingdom, maximum current values for production of stemwood lie in the range $6-12 \, t \, ha^{-1} \, yr^{-1}$. Mean values are about $4-8 \, t \, ha^{-1} \, yr^{-1}$. In the cooler, more continental temperate forests, values may be one-quarter of the UK maximum

Table 2.1 *Average growth rates of managed forest and plantation (stemwood volume to 7 cm top diameter over bark)*

Region	Growth $(m^3 \, ha^{-1} \, yr^{-1})$	Reference
Temperate		
Canada average	1.0	1
British Columbia	1.5–5.3	1
US average	2.6	1
Sweden average	3.3	1
UK average (conifer)	11.0	2
Sitka spruce	9–15	3
Douglas-fir	10–14	3
Larch	6–11	3
UK average (broadleaved)	5	5
Oak	3–5	3
Beech	4–6	3
Sweet chestnut	5–8	3
New Zealand pines	18–30	1
Tropics		
Moist tropical high forest	6–15	4
Tropical hardwood plantations	10–20	4
Tropical conifers and eucalypts	20–35	4

(1) Wood (1975); (2) Nicholls (1981); (3) Locke (1978); (4) Dawkins (1967); (5) Evans (1984).

(Jarvis and Leverenz 1983) and in warm temperate forests about twice these figures (i.e. $12–24 \, t \, ha^{-1} \, yr^{-1}$).

There is uncertainty about the relative productivities of even-aged and uneven-aged managed forests with comparable conditions of soil, climate, and species composition (Assmann 1970). However, the species composition in these two types of forest is seldom comparable in reality. Productivity depends far more upon the species that are grown than on any intrinsic qualities of a site because there are immense differences in efficiency of assimilation between species and even between genotypes on the same ground (Dawkins 1967). Hence selected conifers, especially pines, spruces, larches, and firs, or eucalypts are often favoured in plantations because, at least over long rotations, they produce so much more than most other species. Some comparisons are shown in Table 2.1. Exotic species often have particular attractions for the reasons discussed on p. 27.

Stand composition and long-term productivity

A major topic of speculation, debate, and research has always been whether the superior productivity of first rotation monocultures, especially of coniferous exotics, can be maintained without site-degradation, disease and serious losses of yields in subsequent rotations. The topic has been the subject of several reviews (for example, Evans 1976; Whitehead 1982; Helliwell 1982). It is frequently argued that extensive monoculture 'is tantamount to challenging the laws of nature' (for example de Gryse 1955), and so must be doomed to ultimate failure.

This is not necessarily so. Virtual monocultures are found often in nature. They occur in the pine forests of the eastern United States and in the Douglas-fir forests in the north west, as well as in many other coniferous forest formations. The dynamics and development of unmanaged forest in the north temperate zone have been reviewed by Jones (1945). The beech (*Nothofagus*) forests in New Zealand's South Island and in parts of south central Chile are also natural monocultures. Single-species even-aged forests arise in nature after catastrophes such as fire, windthrow, floods, landslips, and insect epidemics. Fire and windthrow occur so regularly in some parts of the world that climax forest formations are never achieved (see Chapters 14 and 15). The species which grow in them are, like most of man's crop plants, adapted to establishing themselves on open sites and in big gaps. They are known as light-demanding, pioneer or intolerant trees and have many of the characteristics of *r*-selected species (p. 173). Practically all the important plantation trees come from this group and their use in plantations is not as artificial as it might appear since natural conditions are quite closely simulated in extensive clear-felling systems. However, one potentially important difference is that plantation trees often have a much narrower genetic base than the wild populations of natural monocultures from which they were selected. Sometimes plantations are clonal. This makes them potentially more susceptible to pests and diseases (see p. 75).

At the other extreme, in regions where natural disasters are much less common, there are, of course, very extensive natural forests composed of intimately mixed species and ages. Tropical rainforests provide the most notable examples. Many of the trees are adapted to regenerate in closed forests or small gaps. They survive in them and eventually form understories beneath the canopies of more mature trees. These shade-bearing climax species or tolerant trees are able to compete in conditions of low light intensity, relatively low daytime temperatures compared with the open, and high root competition especially with subordinate vegetation (Shirley 1945). Climax trees are characteristically K-selected (p. 173) and are adapted to narrow niches in competition with many other species.

There is a continuum between the extremes of light-demanding and shade-bearing, and the degree of tolerance exhibited by particular species may differ with latitude or region. For example, Daniel *et al.* (1979) regard Sitka spruce as tolerant and noble fir as intolerant in the western USA, but in the British Isles the reverse is true. Furthermore individuals of most species become more intolerant with age.

In general, species adapted to regenerate in climax closed forests do not make successful pure even-aged plantation trees. They are more effectively managed by silvicultural systems which minimize clear-felling and which concentrate on mixed natural regeneration in small gaps for the reasons discussed on p. 28. For many purposes this can be a very appropriate form of forest management. Most mixed forests are made up of predominantly tolerant species and these sometimes have value in plantations for underplanting older crops to obtain forests with two distinct age classes. Many tolerant species of temperate regions such as *Abies grandis*, *Thuja plicata*, and *Tsuga heterophylla* are also most productive and successful in pure, even-aged plantations.

It is frequently argued that the introduction of some diversity into monocultures would result in the better use of the soil and less risk of pests and diseases. Some aspects are discussed in the next two sections.

Use of soil

Mixed climax forests use and conserve the resources of a soil in different, and probably more effective ways than those adapted to regular fires or other catastrophes. The recycling of nutrients contained in litter, for example, occurs efficiently in most mixed broadleaved temperate forests, whereas litter tends to accumulate under many natural or planted coniferous monocultures, where in nature much recycling is achieved by periodic fires or as a result of windthrow.

Differences between species in terms of potential root distribution and rooting depth will clearly influence the physical access of a plant to available nutrients and water, though limitations imposed by the soils themselves may sometimes prevent rooting potentials being realized (see p. 40). Less is known about the ability of species to use a source of nutrient that is physiologically unavailable or less available to companion species. Obviously leguminous and other nitrogen-fixing species are prime examples, gaining access to atmospheric nitrogen because of symbiotic relationships with various species of bacteria. The nitrogen can later be made available to non-fixing species through recycling of litter. Hall (1978) quotes examples of agricultural crop species differing in their utilization of various soil P fractions or differing in their degree of competition for P and K. Effects such as these between species of trees are sometimes exploited in plantations. In Ireland, for example, the growth of Sitka spruce has been improved on some sites by mixing it with larch (see p. 84).

The use of different soil resources by mixtures might ensure greater biological stability of the ecosystem. However, despite a considerable literature on the subject there is very little information about the specific requirements of different trees though it is known that, in general, broad-leaved species are more site-demanding than many conifers in that they require nutrients to be available in a particular form (Miller 1984). There is more information about the effects of different species on soil processes: some common plantation conifers, especially spruces and pines grown at close spacing with little or no thinning, have a long-standing reputation for causing soil acidification and, in susceptible soils, accelerated podzolization. This is accompanied by slow rates of organic matter decomposition and nutrient release and hence immobilization of nutrients in the soil organic matter. It is sometimes claimed that these processes reduce productivity in second and subsequent crops of the same species. A classical and much disputed case is the decline in the growth of spruce in Saxony (Wiedemann 1923). Most examples are confined to sites where the species is ill-suited or which are very infertile. There is circumstantial evidence of podzolization under spruce crops in Sweden (Troedsson 1980) and in Britain (Grieve 1978), though in these cooler temperate climates changes in productivity have proved difficult to detect (Holmsgaard et al. 1961). The most important warm temperate example is the decline of second rotation growth of *Pinus radiata* (Fig. 2.2) in South Australia where the problem is both serious and widespread, but not insoluble (Keeves 1966; Woods 1976; Boardman 1979, 1984).

By contrast, many broadleaved trees and a few conifers have reputations as mull-forming 'soil improvers' that can reverse the process of podzolization and improve the rate of litter decomposition. Birch, hornbeam, sweet chestnut, and larch are often noted for this. The effects of birch which has colonized heather (*Calluna vulgaris*) moorland have been investigated in

FIG. 2.2. Second rotation *Pinus radiata* at 4½ years of age in Mt. Gambier region of South Australia. The stand on the left is growing significantly more slowly than did the first rotation; the stand on the right is more or less equalling first rotation productivity following intensive cultural inputs described by Woods (1976).

Britain by Miles (1981). Heather has a similar reputation to spruce for causing podzolization. Miles notes that as birch crops age there is a considerable increase in numbers of earthworms which cause a gradual breakdown of the acid organic material derived from *Calluna*, and convert it to a mull-like humus. This is accompanied by a gradual mixing of the bleached podzolic horizon as the organic material and ferric iron are incorporated, thus tending to a podzolic brown earth. At the same time the rates of organic matter decomposition and nitrogen mineralization increase, as do pH, total phosphorus, and exchangeable calcium in the soil. It is believed that calcium may be essential for adequate earthworm activity (Cooke 1983). Birch has access to sources of calcium which are unavailable to some other species, heather in this case, because of deeper rooting and an ability to penetrate ironpans. Because such qualities are associated with many broadleaved trees it is commonly believed that mixtures might benefit the growth of conifers, yet the evidence for any benefit remains largely unconvincing. In most cases the application of fertilizers is likely to be more efffective.

Mixtures are not always beneficial. Some species can reduce the growth of companion species. Though it is difficult to find examples exclusively from forest trees, the phenomenon is illustrated by the effect of the dwarf shrub heather, on spruces and several other conifers. Heather can inhibit the development of spruce mycorrhizae and this results in very poor growth (Handley 1963) partly through unsuccessful competition for nitrogen. Certain species of walnut (*Juglans*) also produce chemicals from leaf secretions which reduce the growth of trees and other plants. Other examples are given on p. 25.

Diseases and pests

For a species to survive, grow, and reproduce, a set or range of values of a large number of environmental variables is required and it will respond to them in a particular way. Each species is adapted to exploit one particular range of these variables which ecologists describe as the 'fundamental niche' of the species (Hutchinson 1965; Harper 1977). Niches overlap since many resources are required by most species. Because resources are limited this overlap results in competition between species and prevents them reaching their full potential. Thus niches of newly planted trees commonly overlap with those of aggressive weeds and the trees' survival will depend upon the removal or suppression of the weeds. In natural ecosystems many species of both plants and animals have exerted adaptive pressures on each other over very long periods of time. This involves varying degrees of predation, competition and symbiosis but usually results in relationships in which none of the associates becomes dominant and so relatively stable ecosystems are ensured where fatal outbreaks of insects or diseases are unlikely. Managed semi-natural ecosystems are more at risk as shown, for example, by the frequency of spruce budworm outbreaks in the USA (p. 26). Plantations of exotics may be still more vulnerable because they have not benefited from interaction with other organisms in the system, nor has a set of parasites and predators of potential pests and pathogens had time to build up. Possible interactions between species therefore receive a great deal of attention in forestry. They determine the competitiveness of trees with weeds, pests, and pathogens and must not be ignored.

The trees which grow in mixed, competitive, and crowded habitats often have good defences to combat diseases and pests for, if they are seriously attacked, there is a danger of the species becoming extinct. Many of these defences depend upon complex interactions with companion species of plants and animals. Trees which grow in such forests tend therefore to be less prone to devastating attacks by predators and parasites, so long as they remain growing in an appropriate mixture. They are sometimes described as 'unapparent' plants and they have defences which are inappropriate for survival in monocultures (Feeny 1976).

The introduction of diversity into monocultures can sometimes aid the control of herbivorous animals and pathogens. For example, alders have a potential value for the biological control of certain pathogenic fungi such as *Poria* and *Armillaria* in mixed stands. This arises from their ability to fix atmospheric nitrogen which returns to the litter in nitrate rather than ammonium or amine form, and nitrates inhibit the growth of these fungi (Bollen *et al.* 1967; Li *et al.* 1967). Shea *et al.* (1978) have similarly found that there might be some potential for controlling the very damaging jarrah (*Eucalyptus marginata*) dieback disease caused by *Phytophthora cinnamomi* in Australia by encouraging an understorey of the leguminous species *Acacia pulchella*. However many of the more widespread and devastating outbreaks of plant diseases are recorded on trees in mixed climax communities (Quimby 1982). These often occur in forests which are well beyond the age at which they would have been harvested under intensive management regimes. The more dramatic losses of plantations are often associated with extreme climatic events or poor selection of species.

The widely held belief that mixed forests are exposed to fewer risks of attack from insect and fungal pathogens is not always correct. For example in western Canada, the spruce gall aphid (*Adelges cooleyi*) alternates its life cycle between interior Douglas-fir and spruce, and mixtures to these two species can lead to infestations of adelgids and reductions in the growth of spruce (MacLaren 1983). Another example occurs in mixtures of two needled pines and aspen (*Populus tremula*), where the rust fungus *Melampsora pinitorqua* alternates parts of its life cycle between the two, and can be very damaging to pines.

The risks associated with monoculture have been discussed in detail by Gibson and Jones (1977) who pointed out that many of the established constraints on local tree pests and pathogens may be removed in even-aged monocultures leading eventually to damaging attacks. However, few, if any of the most disastrous outbreaks can be attributed to the introduction of monocultures *per se*. Important diseases such as white pine blister rust (*Cronartium ribicola*), chestnut blight, Dutch elm disease, and the pine wilt disease in Japan have achieved their status through man's accidental introduction of exotic pathogens to regions containing appreciable populations of highly susceptible hosts. The existence of monocultures had little to do with the damage that was caused.

Difficulties arise in the prediction and identification of future pest and disease problems and these are compounded by the fact that their spread to new regions is still occurring (Gibson *et al.* 1982). Since 1950 one major 'new' pest has appeared about every five years on the principal plantation conifers in Britain (Bevan 1984). It seems probable that this may continue for many years both to indigenous species (for example Dutch elm disease) as well as to exotics.

Soil-borne diseases caused by wood-rotting fungi such as *Armillaria* spp and *Heterobasidion annosum* are also quoted as examples of diseases that have their origins in forest monoculture systems. In fact, they rely on the presence of infected stumps and root residues and so the time of origin lies more correctly in the history of the site before planting rather than its later use, though monocultures may influence their development. In parts of West Germany 10 per cent of potential annual production of many conifers is spoiled by rot caused by *Heterobasidion annosum*.

Among insects, there are also many whose origins as pests have been wrongly attributed to monocultures. The nun moth (*Lymantria monacha*) caused devastation to central European conifer plantations in the 1920s and earlier, and has been widely used as an example of the kind of disaster likely to follow the adoption of monocultures (e.g. Anon. 1923). However, this view ignores previous records of the moth as a major pest of natural conifer stands in Sweden and Germany, long before monocultures were widely used.

The spruce budworm *Choristoneura fumiferana*, which feeds on foliage, primarily of balsam fir (*Abies balsamea*) and white, red, and black spruces (*Picea glauca*, *P. rubra*, and *P. mariana*) in eastern north America, is an insect for which destructive attacks are traceable to 1702 (Sanders 1974), well before any intensive management or exploitation was carried out. Outbreaks are immensely damaging to north American forests and have become particularly serious during the course of this century. The reasons are not clearly understood but seem to be related to the increasing proportion of natural balsam fir which is now found in the forests (Prebble and Morris 1951). This is a tolerant species which grows naturally in mixed climax forests. Species other than balsam fir are preferred by many wood-using industries so, as exploitation proceeds, firs tend to be left standing. This, combined with the partial exclusion of fire from most managed forests, favours the regeneration and survival of fir, a marked shade-bearer, at the expense of other species. Here, the tendency towards monoculture may be making a natural problem worse. Similar results have been found in Douglas-fir forests in Montana and Idaho where mixed stands of Douglas-fir and ponderosa pine are damaged far less than almost pure Douglas-fir by the western spruce budworm (Fauss and Pierce 1969).

Though diversity itself is no safeguard against pathogens, monocultures can favour pests with a limited ability to spread, because of the close spacings used in plantations and the readily available food source with little genetic diversity. Risks from those with a wider dispersal range are also increased. That the disasters in plantations have not been more serious than the traditional foresters expected may, according to Gibson and Jones (1977), be attributable to two reasons. Firstly, foresters usually have a wide choice of species which allows for a good margin for avoidance of the obvious pest and disease problems. Secondly, the economics of intensive systems allow a much greater latitude for expenditure on protection measures. This was illustrated in Britain in the 1970s by the relatively cheap and effective control of the pine beauty moth (*Panolis flammea*) in its attacks on lodgepole pine (Stoakley 1979).

Exotics

At least part of the high productivity of exotics is explained by the absence of specialized grazing and of defoliating insects and diseases which enables more complete, and therefore more efficient, canopies to be maintained. This allows them to grow much faster than native species, at least until insects and diseases catch up with their hosts. This is discussed further in Chapter 13. Thus, in the more temperate parts of Australia the native eucalypts are trees of relatively minor significance in plantation forestry, yet several of the species are most important in other parts of the world. Instead, Australian foresters plant *Pinus radiata*, perhaps the most widely used of all exotics which, too, is insignificant in its native California.

The debate about the possible dangers of relying on exotic species is particularly strong in countries with a long history of forest management. In Sweden, several workers including Hagner (1983) have demonstrated that the north-west American lodgepole pine (*Pinus contorta*) is likely to be almost twice as productive and valuable as native *Pinus sylvestris*, yet such are the fears of eventual pests and diseases that legislation in 1979 limits the use of lodgepole pine until the possible risks are more clear (Persson 1980). However, in Britain and New Zealand where the native tree flora is either limited, or unproductive, or both, foresters have been less cautious about using exotics in plantations. It can sometimes be true that when planted away from their native habitats, exotics are temporarily safe from most pests and diseases, being only exposed to unspecialized forms. However, specialized pests eventually catch up with their hosts in exotic locations. For example, recent introductions of two pine aphids, *Cinara cronartii*, *Eulachnus rileyi*, and an adelgid, *Pineus pini* to South Africa have, together, proved so damaging to *Pinus taeda* that the Directorate of Forestry has suspended the planting of this species (Donald 1984) despite its widespread use since the 1920s.

Native pests also become adapted to the introduced trees, as shown by *Panolis flammea* with lodgepole pine, an insect normally associated with Scots pine. This illustrates a general principle that the risk of damage is much greater if close relatives of the exotic occur naturally in the host country. Thus exotic pines are relatively free from attacks by native pests in Australia and New Zealand, because there are no native pines there, but the introduction of exotic pines (*Pinus caribaea* and *P. oocarpa*) to south east Asia has proved risky because some of the pests of the native *Pinus keseya* have become adapted to the introduced trees with calamitous results (Speight 1985).

On sites where introduced species can co-exist with diseases and pests, productivity inevitably declines and this has often led to significant reductions in original forecasts of yields. In some situations a return to planting slower growing native species which are well adapted for survival may be justified.

Monocultures or mixtures?

Debates about the desirable composition of plantations will inevitably continue, especially in regions where native mixed forests are being replaced by monocultures.

To the extent that generalizations are possible or wise, accumulating experience suggests pioneers are better adapted to monocultures than successor species. They frequently prove successful plantation trees as long as the site is not limiting in some respect.

The tolerant trees characteristic of later stages in natural successions may be less successful. Though there are notable exceptions to this, some are difficult, if not impossible to manage in pure, even-aged plantations being especially vulnerable to attacks by pests and diseases once removed from the other species with which they grow in nature. The more impressive examples of this are found among tropical rain forest rather than temperate species. Many members of the mahogany family (Meliaceae), for example, can not be grown in plantations because of damaging attacks by a shoot borer, *Hypsipyla* spp.

Provided management is sufficiently intensive and careful, serious site deterioration does not occur in coniferous monocultures and declining yields in second rotations will be the exception. Sustained productivity is closely linked with the maintenance and recycling of organic matter. This can be achieved by maintaining a vegetative cover to prevent erosion but, at the same time, excessive competition for water must be avoided, by weeding, and by the retention of litter and logging residues (for example Farrell *et al.* 1981) and, if necessary, by fertilizing. A permissive attitude towards soil-improving trees may also be helpful.

One of the more serious threats to continued productivity results from the compaction of soils by heavy harvesting machinery (p. 60). The avoidance of this, or amelioration by ploughing or ripping can be important.

To counter resistance to epidemics, there must not only be careful matching of species to site (Chapter 5) but as much diversity as possible should be created in plantations through planting mosaics of different species and ages and retaining a wide genetic diversity. The use of mixed provenances may, for example, inhibit the development of resistance by pests. Barnes (1984) states that there seems little doubt that selection for pest and disease resistance will become increasingly important in fast growing plantation species, perhaps even on occasion to the exclusion of morphological and production characteristics. For example, new poplar breeding programmes in Italy and elsewhere have resistance to *Marssonia*, *Melampsora*, and *Dothiciza* as a first step in screening. Only as a second stage are the resistant families screened for growth habit, wood properties, and other characteristics. It is important however that the 'improved' breeding population has a sufficiently broad genetic base to have some prospects of retaining other resistance genes. This can be achieved by using multiple populations that are bred for a number of environments which will give both genetic diversity and the adaptation required to breed for resistance without loss of productivity.

In conclusion, it is clear that much has still to be learned about the biological stability and potential problems associated with monocultures. On most sites in temperate regions there appears to be little risk in planting them, but in certain conditions, some of which are known, there is a loss of productivity associated with soil deterioration and attacks by pests and diseases. Constant vigilance is needed to protect valuable monocultures but as knowledge and experience accumulates, so will unsuitable conditions be recognized with greater certainty.

3. Climate and site

An understanding of the nature of, and variation in climates and planting sites is central to silviculture because they determine the type and timing of operations and also influence many management and even policy approaches to forestry.

Climate

The main factors which determine the climates of different regions of the earth are differences in atmospheric pressure and consequent wind patterns, ocean currents and global position. These combine to influence temperature and rainfall, solar radiation, humidity, and other elements which make up a climate. They have been discussed in detail by Griffiths (1966) and Kendrew (1953). Temperature, rainfall, and wind are usually thought of as the most important elements of a climate for forestry.

In great simplification, temperature patterns are determined by ocean currents, by incoming solar radiation (which varies with latitude) and by atmospheric pressure systems. At low latitudes, the eastern seaboards of continents are warmed by ocean currents (see Fig. 3.1) which originate from the vicinity of the equator. For example, the east coast of the USA is influenced by the north-flowing Gulf Stream, and the east coast of Japan by the Kuro Siwo current, before these currents turn eastwards towards Europe and western north America respectively. On eastern seaboards the warm currents meet cold ones from the poles at about 45° latitude and the water is responsible for the cold summers of, for example, the Labrador coast and that of southern Argentina. Temperate western seaboards above about latitude 45° are, by contrast, warmed by currents from the west. By far the most significant is the voluminous North Atlantic Drift or Gulf Stream which has a major influence on temperatures in north-west Europe. The smaller North Pacific Drift or Kuro Siwo current gives to coastal British Columbia its mild winters. These west-flowing currents divide as they approach the western seaboards of continents and turn north and south. There is a distinct cooling to regions below 40° latitude as the relatively cold water moves towards the equator. Thus, the coasts of California, Chile, north-west and south-west Africa are all influenced by cool currents which bring cool temperatures, low rainfall, and much fog to coastal regions.

Temperatures in the interiors of continents are influenced by solar radiation and pressure systems. In winter, the pressure systems predominantly cause

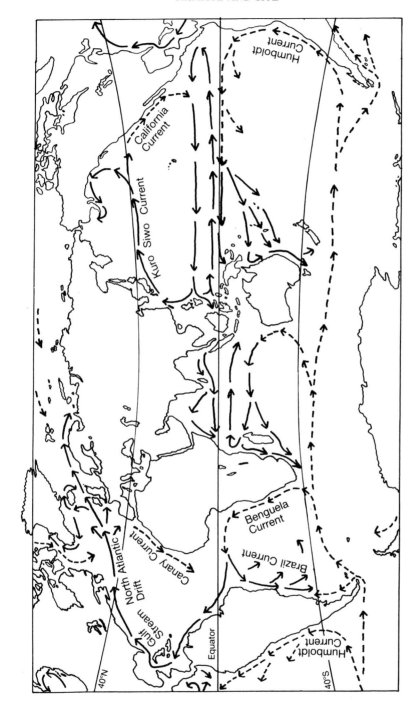

Fig. 3.1. Ocean currents which influence climate. ⟶ Warmer currents. ⟶ Colder currents.

a movement of warm air masses from oceans and cool air masses from continental interiors while in summer, when the oceans are cool in relation to continental interiors, the opposite occurs. The largest pressure system is in Asia and gives rise to the marked and complete seasonal change in wind directions called the monsoons.

Precipitation patterns are much more complex and depend ultimately upon the movement of moist air from oceans or other large bodies of water to the land. The type and extent of precipitation varies beween winter and summer. Most occurs along polar fronts in coastal temperate latitudes. In winter high-pressure systems over the interiors of continents block the movement of most rain-bearing cyclones from the west but as spring approaches the latter can break through, giving a spring or early summer maximum of rainfall. This short period may be an important one for establishing crops. In summer, fronts move towards the poles to 60°–70° latitude, and with them much of the rain. The interior of continents, in regions where there is a source of moist air, experience heavy summer showers, caused by the intense convection currents. Along eastern seaboards most rainfall is caused by moist onshore winds. Areas with uniform precipitation are generally very small and arid areas and deserts occur over wide bands of latitude.

Topography and the size of continents naturally cause innumerable variables in climatic patterns. The interior parts of north America and Asia, for example, are very wide at higher latitudes and remote from the moderating influences of oceans; they experience extremes of winter cold and intense summer heat for that latitude. The orientation and extent of mountain ranges has enormous influences. North–south orientated ranges such as the Rocky Mountains and Andes cause air from the tropics to sweep towards the poles in summer, while during winter cold polar air moves towards the equator. These ranges are also effective barriers, in temperate latitudes, to the prevailing westerly winds and their associated precipitation so that mountains near the Pacific receive a superfluity of rain while regions a short distance to the east suffer aridity and the extremes of temperature characteristic of a continental climate. In Europe, by contrast, the main mountain ranges (Alps, Pyrenees, Carpathians, and Caucasus) have an east–west orientation which results in much more gradual rainfall and temperature gradients from west to east. They also block excessive latitudinal movements of both tropical and polar air masses. Europe therefore has the great climatic advantages of relatively mild winters, warm but not hot summers, and well distributed rain. This ensures a relatively long growing season.

Major climatic regions are determined by these complex patterns of temperature, precipitation, and wind. Various systems of classifying them have been developed, such as those of Köppen (1923) and Thornthwaite (1948), and they have value in the search for homoclimes or regions of the world similar to the one in question, especially for such purposes of species introduction. Climate, in turn, influences soil-formation processes, the major vegetation zones, and levels of productivity. Thus along the eastern seaboard of the USA productivity increases from a maximum of 5 to 25 t ha^{-1} yr^{-1} dry matter moving southwards from the Canadian border to the Gulf coastal plain and, because precipitation is not especially limiting, correlates well with the increasing length of the growing season (Waring 1983). Moving westwards, productivity decreases from the Mississippi River to the Great Plains and increases abruptly in the maritime influence of the Pacific Ocean. The east–west variations cannot be simply related to length of growing season because regions of drought, infertile soils, and mild winter climates also play a part.

Local climates

While broad climatic patterns influence many regional approaches to forestry, climatic variations on a much more local even site scale can have a considerable bearing on practices. Some aspects are discussed below, largely in relation to the British Isles, and others are elaborated upon in Chapter 5, in relation to the selection of species.

The British Isles lie in a temperate, maritime region where polar, tropical, maritime, and continental types of air meet. The constantly changing relationships among these determine the character of the weather at any particular time, which tends to be extremely variable and unpredictable (Taylor and Yates 1967), and hence a constant topic of conversation.

Broadly, two patterns of variation exist at right angles to each other. One is latitudinal with decreasing temperature as the main influence on growth, from south to north. The other is an increase in oceanity from east to west. This leads to decreases in temperature range, radiation, and insolation and increases in precipitation, atmospheric humidity, and windspeed. The two gradients combine to cause a general increase in severity of conditions for plant growth in a north westerly direction, reflected in the downward shift of altitudinal zones of vegetation in the same direction.

However, altitude has a much more significant effect on climate. The uplands (land above 240 m altitude) which contain about 80 per cent of all forests are characterized by lower temperatures and increased windiness, humidity, and wetness. The differences between the climates of the major mountains and their adjacent lowlands are at least comparable in range with the more familiar contrasts between the climates of western Ireland and East Anglia or Cornwall and Caithness (Taylor 1976).

Growing season

The growing season is normally considered to start when an average daily temperature of 6 °C is reached and maintained, though this varies both between and within species. *Picea glauca*, for example, will grow when the mean daily temperature exceeds 1 °C (Armson 1962). The growing season varies in duration from 9 months or more in southwestern coastal areas of Britain, 7 or 8 months in lowland areas, 5 or 6 months in most of the uplands and as little as 4 months in the highest parts of the Grampians and the west Highlands of Scotland (Gregory 1976). The period between leaf expansion and leaf fall in deciduous woodlands in lowland England may vary between 190 and 240 days whereas in the deciduous temperate forests of central Europe and the central and eastern USA it is about 140–190 days (Jarvis and Leverenz 1983).

In very mild areas the critical temperature which initiates flushing of species able to take advantage of a long growing season occurs in early February, while in north Scotland it is not reached until well into April (Christie and Lines 1979). The effect of increasing elevation is more dramatic. The rates at which temperatures fall vary greatly according to region and site but are said to be among the most rapid in the world (Taylor 1976). Lapse rates are usually in the order of $0.6°–0.7°$C per 100 m increase in elevation. These cause an average reduction in growing season length of 13 days per 100 m (Fairbairn 1968). Regional variations to this figure result in variations in the productivity of forests with increasing altitude. It is impossible to quantify the effects of climate alone because soils and other factors also change with elevation, though Mayhead (1973*b*) has shown that in eight regions of Britain the yield class of Sitka spruce falls at rates ranging between 7.5 and $1.4 \, m^3 \, ha^{-1} \, yr^{-1}$ per 100 m increase in elevation.

Frost

A marked feature of the British climate is its variability over short periods of time. In the uplands, temperatures commonly oscillate across the 6 °C growth threshold, especially in spring and autumn, causing intermittent growth, and also across the 0 °C ground frost threshold in winter and at night throughout the year (Taylor 1976). Evergreen trees such as *Pinus radiata*, *Cupressus macrocarpa*, and some eucalypts, which are adapted to mild winter climates, can sometimes grow continuously in mild places such as the south-west of Cornwall and south-west Ireland but these species may be killed in severe winters.

Frosts during the growing season are more serious and can result in extensive injury or death to young trees of many species. In older crops frost can kill foliage, slowing the rate of growth and cause forking and crooked stems, though death is unusual except in very sensitive species.

Sites where frosts are most serious are hollows, especially on relatively level ground, where denser cold air collects. On such terrain, the depth of freezing air is often under 1 m and seldom exceeds 3 m, hence the most serious damage is usually confined to young trees (Day and Peace 1946). Many species become hardy to low temperatures in autumn, and midwinter temperatures as low as −40 °C may do no damage. This is achieved through physiological mechanisms during the dormant period which prevent water freezing within certain crucial tissues, either by supercooling, or by moving water from the cells so that extracellular ice forms (Levitt 1972; Burke *et al.* 1976). The same species may become susceptible to severe injury by frosts of only −2 °C in spring and many are especially at risk during the early period of bud burst and extension. In Britain, susceptibility to damage rises until the end of May or early June from when it remains more or less constant until October or November (Fig. 3.2), though differences of timing and degree occur between species and races. Late spring and early autumn frosts are also a feature of the climate of Canada and the northern USA, and they result in widespread damage to many agricultural crops which are not completely adapted to the region.

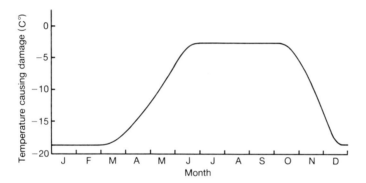

FIG. 3.2. Hypothetical relationship between season and susceptibility to frost damage. (Based on Day and Peace 1946.)

Precipitation and evaporation

Most upland areas of Britain and Ireland have at least 1250 mm of rainfall each year. By contrast most lowland parts of England and the eastern lowlands of Scotland have 750 mm or less. Areas between these two extremes are in the lower hill areas of the country (Gregory 1976).

Precipitation increases with altitude in an almost linear fashion up to a maximum of about 5000 mm yr^{-1} at about 1200 m and most afforested uplands are areas of major water surplus. Only in unusually dry summer spells and on south-facing slopes liable to soil drought may there be water stress during the growing season as rainfall is generally well-distributed in all months. The rainfall limit of about 1000 mm is usually considered by British foresters to be the lower limit for satisfactory growth of Sitka spruce and various other common conifers. In winter there is usually an excess of soil moisture everywhere and in areas of high rainfall this has resulted in leaching or gleying of soils. Many soils remain waterlogged and on these most trees are only able to root on the surface.

In the lower rainfall areas droughts and potential water deficits occur in summer and these can be particularly severe in the lowland areas of north-east, south-east, and eastern England. Though the frequency of rainfall is normally sufficient to prevent drought damage, especially in deep-rooted trees, some species are particularly sensitive to water stress and benefit greatly, when young from good weed control which reduces competition for water. Much of the reduction in growth potential can be accounted for by the effects of high vapour pressure deficits in closing stomata and halting photosynthesis.

Other parts of the world suffer much more seriously from droughts. In the USA the tract between the Rockies eastwards to 100 °W (for example to central Dakota and Nebraska) has a mean rainfall of between 300 and 500 mm which is very variable from year to year. The success of establishment can be critically influenced by taking advantage of the brief period when soils are charged with snow meltwater and the predominantly early-summer rain.

Snow

The occurrence of snow is closely linked to air temperature and so the frequency of snow falling increases towards the poles, towards the interiors of continents, and with altitude. The effect of a persistent snow cover is to reflect much of the incoming radiation and this results in a lowering of air temperatures. Soils are initially relatively warmer under snow but may eventually be deeply penetrated by frost which can last for long periods after the snow has melted.

Snow and frozen ground obviously preclude a number of silvicultural operations such as ground preparation and the planting season may be very short, having to be fitted in between the time of snow melt and the onset of spring droughts. If not too deep, it can assist other operations, especially harvesting. Breakage losses are reduced as snow cushions a tree's fall, and frozen snowy ground will support the weight of skidders and other machinery well, resulting in little or no damage to the soil. However too much snow can be a hindrance. It can cause machinery to clog, and in harvesting, the valuable part of tree boles can be buried. Much research is devoted to attempts to minimize these problems by, for example, using compacting or clearing machinery.

North America is the snowiest of continents north of 37 °N. Except on the west coast most of the winter precipitation falls as snow, and depths may be to several metres. In the British Isles, mean temperatures even in the coldest month are above freezing and snow cover is very variable and intermittent (Atkinson and Smithson 1976).

Tree lines

Towards the poles, and with increasing elevation, conditions become progressively less favourable for tree growth due to combinations of reduced temperatures, and day length near the poles, and excessive solar radiation, drought, exposure to high winds, and damage by snow and ice. Towards the north Pole, a point is eventually reached between 60 ° and 70 ° where the physiological cost of maintenance of tree tissue is too great, and trees cannot survive. The same occurs with increasing elevation though the height at which it occurs varies widely, depending on latitude among other factors. Thus, on mountains near the equator, such as Mt Kenya, the tree line is at about 3500 m, while in maritime regions such as Britain and Ireland it may be lower than 600 m. It rises progressively across Europe to over 2000 m in the Alps. The ecological and physiological reasons for the occurrence of timber lines have been discussed in detail by Tranquillini (1979). At high elevations most heat received by the soil and vegetation is by direct insolation rather than indirect warm air currents. Hence, there is a marked contrast between the vegetation of north- and south-facing aspects at the same elevation.

Wind

Wind damage to forests is a constant risk in many parts of the world, especially in maritime and mountainous regions. The British Isles are amongst the windiest parts of the world where commercial forestry is practised. Gales occur on from 20 to 40 days a year on northern and western seaboards but are less frequent in the east and inland (Shellard 1976).

In regions where wind damage is a serious threat to the viability of forestry, special forms of silviculture are often developed to minimize the risks of damage. These include shortening rotations, altering thinning regimes, and attention to the general structure and composition of forests (see p. 183).

Site

Even the best sites available for plantations, and most other forms of forestry in temperate countries are usually described as marginal for agriculture. Some are in regions where the climate is unsuitable for settled agriculture. Others usually suffer from one or more of the disadvantages of remoteness, difficult terrain, susceptibility to droughts or waterlogging, and infertility. These factors all impose varying degrees of limitation on silvicultural and management methods. Some, such as steep terrain or a drought-prone soil, are permanent while others such as waterlogging, infertility or incidence of luxuriant weed growth can be overcome to some extent by drainage and the use of fertilizers and herbicides.

Site classifications for use in silviculture

Whatever the form of management or silviculture, information is needed about the site, in terms of topography, soil, and vegetation, as an aid to successful practice. This is done by classifying sites.

Site classifications are required for a variety of purposes in forestry, as in other forms of land use. They are needed, for example, for estimating future yields from thinning and felling, and in helping to decide treatments such as species selection and the need for drainage and fertilizers.

Most classifications are based on assessments of either stand variables such as height and age or some other index of growth or site variables particularly climate, soil or ground vegetation, or a combination of both. Site productivity can be estimated directly, using stand variables. It is often expressed as site index (the height a crop achieves at a predetermined age), or as mean annual increment either at a fixed age, or the age at which mean annual increment is at its maximum. The latter is the basis of the yield class system used in British forestry (Edwards and Christie 1981).

Such indices of growth have little relevance, however, where the attributes of unplanted ground must be evaluated when assessments must be made on the basis of features with an integrated character such as soil and ground vegetation.

Soil

Soil classifications are commonly used to indicate the potential of forest sites (Hagglund 1981) since soil types often express nutrient status, or water-holding capacity and reflect many aspects of climate. Unless nutrient conditions are particularly difficult, as on many peats and sands, soil physical properties are more important than chemical ones for forestry classifications. The British classification, devised by Pyatt (1970), forms the basis for the delineation of types of ground for each of which a distinct form of silviculture may be appropriate. From it specifications can be given which aid selection of species and indicate the need for cultivation, drainage and nutrition. When exposure of the site has been estimated, it allows the assessment of windthrow hazard (Miller 1985). On the basis of the classification, several silvicultural guides have been produced for the twelve or so regions of upland Britain

Table 3.1 *Distribution of soil types in uplands owned by the British Forestry Commission*

Soil group	Percentage of Forestry Commission land	Attributes and limitations of soils
Brown earths	22	Free drainage; deep rooting usually possible. Fertilizers seldom needed. Vigorous weed growth can be a major problem in crop establishment.
Podzols	6	Free drainage; deep rooting usually possible. Strongly acidic often with surface accumulation of organic matter. Nutrient and water-holding capacities low. Characteristically carry vigorous *Calluna* which inhibits growth of some tree species, especially spruces.
Ironpan soils	14	Ironpan is a barrier to drainage and tree roots. Horizon above pan is waterlogged and anaerobic for much of the year. Organic surface horizon common. Strongly acidic. Considerable improvement possible if pan is disrupted by tining and cultivation giving good conditions for growth, similar to podzols. Application of phosphate often necessary. *Calluna* may be a problem.
Surface water gleys	39	Develop when vertical drainage is impeded by fine-textured, dense and structureless C horizon or where C horizon is indurated and impermeable. Organic surface horizon common. Strongly acidic on surface, but pH rises with depth. Perched water table leads to shallow rooting and instability in crops even after drainage for removal of excess water. Fertility levels vary widely but crops frequently benefit from phosphate.
Deep peats	14	Conventionally peats are classified as such only if deeper than 45 cm. Found in upland areas of high rainfall and low temperatures. Very acid. Rooting shallow, even after essential intensive drainage. Most peats very infertile, and require high inputs of nutrients. Species choice usually very limited.
Others	5	Include skeletal soils, sand dunes, and man-made soils, most of which have problems associated with shallowness and infertility.
	Total 100	

Sources: Pyatt (1970); Toleman and Pyatt (1974).

(Busby 1974) within each of which there is a narrow range of lithologic types, a characteristic range of terrain types, soil types, climate, and tree growth rates (Toleman and Pyatt 1974).

Emphasis is placed upon the soil properties which affect forest yield and which, though they may be modified by cultural operations, impose relatively permanent limitations on the use of soils. These include the natural drainage, available depth for rooting, the presence of compact or cemented layers, the texture and general level of acidity or alkalinity and the occurrence of peat. The main upland soil groups in Britain and some of their attributes and limitations are shown in Table 3.1.

Table 3.1 gives an indication of the type of land available for plantation schemes. Two-thirds of it carries soils which suffer from poor aeration due to periodic or permanent waterlogging. This is caused by the general excess of precipitation over evaporation which also promotes leaching of nutrients from the soil so that podzolization is widespread and there is a tendency towards the development of acidic surface horizons. Where topography also contributes to waterlogging of the soil, peats become the climax formation.

Soil, rather than vegetation, classifications have appeared the most useful form of site classification for silviculture in many places where bare land is being planted for three main reasons.

1. A large number of sites have been so extensively modified by agricultural practices and burning that vegetation is not always a reliable indicator of site conditions. This is particularly true in Britain in areas dominated by heather (*Calluna vulgaris*) and bracken (*Pteridium aquilinum*).
2. In establishing tree crops, many sites are so modified microclimatically and in terms of drainage, cultivation, and nutrition that the pre-existing semi-natural vegetation is profoundly changed.
3. Within a few years of planting the exotic species commonly used in plantations there is virtually no ground vegetation left. Most is shaded out and killed though the seeds of some species can live for decades in the soil and lead to rapid recolonization of a site late in the rotation and at re-establishment (Hill, M. O. 1979).

Ground vegetation

Though there is no causal relationship between tree growth and the composition of the lower vegetation, both are to a large extent determined by the same basic variables of temperature, light, water supply, soil aeration and fertility. None of these can easily be measured in practice. Where there is enough natural or semi-natural vegetation, it can be a remarkably sensitive indicator of remaining site variability in areas of uniform climate, soil and land surface (Kilian 1981). Classifications based on vegetation are commonly used in Europe and elsewhere. The main problem is that vegetation is often highly complex and difficult to sample objectively.

The basis of all systems is that various indicator plants or plant communities are used to give a guide to the productive potential of the site and other features of interest, such as drainage status or fertility. One of the oldest and best known classifications is that of Cajander (1921) in Finland who classified natural and thinned stands of Scots pine and Norway spruce, as well as treeless sites, using the dominant plant species in the ground vegetation. It enabled reasonably accurate predictions of site productivity to be made and the need for drainage is based on this classification today. On suitable sites in Britain and Ireland a ground vegetation classification is quite widely used as an aid to species selection based on the work of Anderson (1961); and in Northern Ireland vegetation on deep peats is used to indicate levels of fertility (Dickson and Savill 1974).

Multiple factor classifications based largely on vegetation, but also on the interrelationships between vegetation, climate, physiography, and soils are also widely used in Europe and Canada. At the lowest 'site unit' level, appropriate for mapping at a 1:10 000 scale sites have similar silvicultural potential and are prone to similar risks and have similar levels of productivity. These classifications are said to be 'often overcharged with specific academic objectives and do not meet the utilitarian requirements of foresters' (Kreutzer 1979), and are certainly more appropriate for use in semi-natural forests than where bare land, or highly modified land, is being planted with exotics (Jahn 1982).

Apart from its use in the classification of sites, vegetation is also of interest as a potential nuisance as weeds, or for its rarity value, as something which requires conservation, or for its potential in the management of domestic or wild animals as a source of food or shelter.

Terrain classifications

None of the ecological types of classification described so far takes account of factors like the steepness of slopes, ground roughness, and the occurrence of boulders, all of which have considerable practical importance to forest managers. Difficult terrain may present insuperable limitations to the use of some kinds of machinery, and also affect the output of the labour force. For this type of information, separate terrain classifications are usually prepared (Rowan 1977), often based on original Scandinavian classifications (Berg 1981).

Part B

Principles of plantation silviculture

4. Drainage and cultivation

One of the most important factors influencing the establishment and growth of a crop is the soil which must provide a suitable environment for the tree to anchor itself, and to obtain the water and minerals needed for healthy growth. In Britain, much of the land available for plantations requires some degree of drainage and cultivation to improve its suitability for tree growth (see Table 3.1, p. 39). The provision of adequate site drainage and the correction of restricted soil profile drainage are two of the most significant ways of achieving long-term improvements in site potential in forestry by:

regulating water movement;
improving soil aeration;
reducing compaction;
mobilizing nutrients, especially nitrogen;
reducing competition from the natural vegetation;
providing a planting position favourable to rapid establishment

Drainage is obviously practised to achieve the first two of these objectives while all are associated with cultivation. Drainage and cultivation are usually considered together in silviculture because appropriate practices can be a means of achieving both. Cultivation is also discussed in Chapter 6, p. 81.

Effects of waterlogging on tree roots

Some plants can tolerate the anaerobic conditions associated with poor drainage and a few compete successfully in such conditions but the majority of economic crops, including trees, require sufficient soil aeration to supply the oxygen requirements of the roots. Soil aeration is one of the most important determinants of soil productivity because, in most dry land plants, the internal transfer of oxygen from the above-ground parts to the roots cannot take place sufficiently fast to supply all the requirements of the roots. The soil must be aerated to allow adequate root growth, upon which trees depend for anchorage, water, and mineral absorption. Gaseous exchange must take place between soil air and the atmosphere at a sufficient rate to prevent a deficiency of oxygen developing. Soil micro-organisms also respire and, under conditions of restricted aeration, they compete with the roots of higher plants.

Measurements of rates of oxygen consumption by roots and soil micro-organisms have shown that soil aeration in the field can involve the exchange of approximately 10 litres of oxygen per square metre per day (Hawkins 1962). So, in a cubic metre of soil with air-filled pores comprising 20 per cent of its volume (and assuming the soil air contains 20 per cent oxygen and that the root zone is 1 m deep), the total root-zone content of oxygen is 40 litres. Hence the daily exchange rate must involve 25 per cent of the oxygen present (Hillel 1971). These figures indicate only an order of magnitude of requirements since, in actual conditions, the aeration rate and oxygen requirements of roots vary within wide limits. Also root growth and survival depend more upon the time of occurrence and duration of periods of oxygen deficiency than upon average conditions. For most species the length of the flooding period is critical only if it occurs during periods of active root growth.

The sudden flooding of a site can produce completely anaerobic conditions within a few hours as a result of gas displacement from the soil pores and the uptake by micro-organisms of the remaining dissolved oxygen. This can lead to a decrease or cessation of aerobic root respiration resulting in decreased growth, transpiration, and translocation and possibly the death of roots of some trees within a few days. In flood-sensitive species root tips are often damaged so that when aeration is restored, growth can only be renewed from regions nearer the stem. Even the most flood-tolerant trees must be flood-free for 55–60 per cent of the period when roots grow actively: all-year flooding is tolerated by some species only if it happens in occasional years and the upper limit is related to the need to regenerate younger absorbing roots every 2 years. Most woody species will therefore die in the third year after flooding (Crawford 1982). In general, broad-leaved trees show significantly greater tolerance to waterlogging than conifers although the ranges overlap (Gill 1970). Death is hastened by toxic compounds which are produced by roots of some species in anaerobic conditions, including ethanol and ethylene (Coutts and Armstrong 1976). Anaerobic conditions also cause the soil itself to produce substances which are harmful to plant roots, possibly more harmful than the lack of oxygen. These include reduced iron and manganese compounds, high concentrations of carbon dioxide and sulphides, and many freshly dug climatic peats smell very strongly of hydrogen sulphide.

In anaerobic conditions roots stop growing and may eventually die when submerged but many species of forest trees, like most herbaceous plants, can make good growth on moderately wet sites by surface rooting. Many, such as spruces, can quickly produce new roots in the upper layers of aerated soil when the lower parts of their root systems are flooded. Though roots cannot normally *grow* in the absence of a readily available source of oxygen those of some species can *survive* long periods of inundation and resume growth when the water table is lowered (Crawford 1976).

The mechanisms of tolerance of roots to waterlogging have been reviewed by Crawford (1982). They are commonly interpreted in terms of three different mechanisms, two metabolic and one anatomical (Coutts and Philipson 1978*b*):

(1) tolerance to toxic concentrations of substances produced in the soil;
(2) metabolic adaptation of anaerobic respiration to produce non-toxic products;
(3) internal oxygen transport to maintain aerobic respiration and to oxidize toxic compounds in the rhizosphere.

The two most commonly planted trees on wet sites in Britain, Sitka spruce and lodgepole pine show marked differences in these respects. In a series of experiments, Coutts and Philipson (1978*a,b*) and Philipson and Coutts (1978, 1980) have shown that the pine will penetrate more deeply into soils liable to waterlogging because, in constantly waterlogged conditions, large gas-filled cavities develop in the stele of pine roots but not in spruce. Similar enlargement of air spaces and relatively low soil oxygen demands are found in many other wetland species including poplars, willows, and mangroves and also Scots pine when grown under conditions of reduced aeration. These air spaces enable trees to transport their own supplies of oxygen internally.

Oxygen enters the stem and roots from the leaves in some species, but in most woody plants lenticels at the stem base or on roots in the top aerated soil horizons are more important entry points. Lenticels proliferate on parts of the root system above the water table in wet soils. Other mechanisms may also operate; for example in lodgepole pine live roots have been found as far as 1 m below the water table, which is in excess of published distances for internal oxygen transport. Other anatomical modifications found in trees able to withstand flooding and which may contribute to root aeration and ethanol removal include buttresses, pneumatophores, adventitious roots, and root branching (Crawford 1982).

With lodgepole pine (but not Sitka spruce) growing on peat, once growth has started and particularly after the canopy has closed and transpiration and interception losses increase, a process is initiated which may be progressive; growth improves and is accompanied by a rapid drying of the peat (Boggie and Miller 1976). Though the improved growth rate may not be sustained, the ability of lodgepole pine to dry peat often causes shallow, highly humified peat in the drier parts of Britain to shrink and crack. A network of deep fissures often develops and leads to permanently improved drainage (Pyatt and Craven 1979).

However, in peats and fine textured soils such as surface water gleys, whether a tree is relatively flood-tolerant like lodgepole pine or not, like Sitka spruce, root systems *even in drained areas*, are commonly shallow and severely restricted at about 10 cm below the surface due to lack of oxygen (Lees 1972) as Table 4.1 shows. This results in poor anchorage and crops are prone to

Table 4.1 *Percentage of roots at different depths in the soil*

Root depth (cm)	Sitka spruce[1]	Scots pine[2]	Lodgepole pine[3]
Soil type	Surface water and peaty gleys	Deep peat	Deep peat
Country	N. Ireland	Finland	Scotland
Litter	58	70 ⎱	62 ⎱
0–5	27		
5–10	10	20 ⎰	17 ⎰
10–20	5	10	12
below 20	0	0	9

(1) Adams *et al.* (1972); (2) Lähde (1969); (3) Boggie (1972).

windthrow. Nutrients and, paradoxically, during dry periods, water may also be in short supply.

Principles of soil drainage

Any consideration of drainage must take into account various hydrological and related factors of a site, including precipitation, infiltration capacity, which is the rate at which water will infiltrate from the surface into the soil, soil permeability, which is the rate at which water will move through a soil profile, and evapotranspiration. The importance of these in forests has been discussed by Leyton (1972).

The infiltration capacity of a soil is determined by the characteristics of the soil surface. When mineral soil is unprotected by vegetation, the impact of raindrops may break down the surface structure to form a seal which, by retarding water entry, promotes surface flow and can cause flooding and erosion. A vegetative cover protects the surface from such deterioration and the litter and organic layers of forests can provide considerable additional protection. Generally, infiltration capacities in forests increase with the age and density of a stand and in mature forests may reach maximum values of the order of 3–5 mm min^{-1} for saturated soils and higher rates for unsaturated ones.

However, infiltration cannot continue unless percolation through the soil provides space in the surface layers for the water. Percolation rates are greatest in soils with high contents of large (non-capillary) pores and those with high organic matter contents and where there is a good degree of aggregation in the surface soil. Characteristics which reduce the rate of percolation include high bulk densities and the presence of clay and silt in the subsoil. Most of these factors are interrelated and the superior properties of soils under forests are due to a generally higher non-capillary pore content as a result of the aggregation of soil particles by a high organic matter turnover. Forest cover therefore tends to improve the drainage characteristics, especially on fine textured clays and in the upper organically rich layers. Nevertheless, even after a relatively long period under forest cover, peats and clays in many places show poor drainage characteristics. They hold much water by capillary action and because of this, the movement of air into them may be extremely slow: often too slow to sustain tree roots because water within them is virtually immobile and can be removed only from a narrow band on either side of a drain (Stewart and Lance 1983). In some soils there may be no traces of oxygen at depths greater than about 20 cm, as was found by Armstrong *et al.* (1976) on a peaty surface water gley carrying a 23-year-old crop of Sitka spruce. Drainage of these soils can actually result in an increase in bulk density (Pyatt and Craven 1979).

Mull soils which typically develop on base-rich sites generally have better infiltration capacities than mor soils which are more characteristic on acid sites. The drainage characteristics of forest soils can easily be impaired by practices which destroy the surface organic layers or damage the surface structure, for example compaction by machines, burning or grazing.

Largely because of increased interception, evapotranspiration from forests can remove 400–450 mm a year from a site in most upland areas of the British Isles. This is possibly twice as much water as is removed by open moorland vegetation, particularly in areas of high rainfall (Anon. 1976). Forests are most effective at drying sites after the canopy has closed.

Effects of drainage on tree survival and growth

Until the importance of drainage was recognized most attempts at planting wet soils failed. There were many later failures too because the nutritional needs of crops were not adequately recognized.

A good experimental example of the effects of drainage of climatic peat on the growth of lodgepole pine is given by Boggie and Miller (1976). Their experiment was made up of five plots each 3 m × 30 m, isolated by perimeter ditches in which the water was maintained at different fixed levels. After fertilizing, trees were planted directly into the peat.

The results 12 years later (Table 4.2) showed that where no drainage had been carried out, mortality was high; what trees had survived had by chance been planted on hummocks. By contrast drained plots showed good or complete survival. All indices of growth including mean height and weight responded to the lowering of the water table, the lower the better.

These results illustrate the effects of lowering water tables alone but do not entirely represent forestry practice because, where drains are made, the material from them has to be put somewhere. It is usually spread in mounds or turfs when drains are dug by hand, or in continuous ridges alongside the drains when dug by machine. Young trees are planted *on top* of these ridges

Table 4.2 *Responses of lodgepole pine on peat to drainage (from Boggie and Miller 1976)*

Plot	Mean water table level (cm)	Survival (%)	Mean height age 12 (cm)	Weight of tree crop (t ha^{-1})	Apparent yield class (m^3 ha^{-1} yr^{-1})
1	0.2	38	65	2.5	<4
2	10.9	97	125	12.8	4
3	18.8	100	129	13.0	4
4	24.4	100	219	52.3	8
5	33.6	100	305	96.8	10

and benefit not only from a lowered water table but also from a raised and well-aerated ridge and the more fertile conditions of the sandwich of decayed vegetation between the ridge and ground surface. There is considerable evidence (for example Binns 1962; Jack 1965; Savill *et al.* 1974) that in ridges the availability of nitrogen and other nutrients is greater than in drained surface peat and that this incidental effect of drainage has far more influence on tree growth than the lowering of water tables as such. In general the deeper the drains, the more spoil is put on the surface and the better the growth of the trees. The additional growth reduces the time during which young trees are susceptible to hazards such as frost, grazing animals and grass fires besides having obvious economic benefits. Roots proliferate along the ridges but are virtually absent from the furrows, and the uneven root-plate which develops can lead to serious instability later in life (see p. 54).

Drainage and cultivation practice

At drainage intensities which are practicable it is difficult to maintain water table levels much below 30 cm in summer or below 10–20 cm in winter, or to control them at all for a distance of more than about 2 m from the edge of a drain. Little advantage is gained by deepening drains below 1 m on blanket peats because no measurable improvement is obtained in rooting depth (Taylor 1970; Burke 1967) though on some Finnish peats, Lähde (1969) found that for every additional 10 cm the water was lowered, the rooting depth was increased by 1 cm.

On upland surface water gleys, the problem is essentially similar, or possibly even more difficult. For example on gleys derived from carboniferous parent material in Northern Ireland, water table levels were scarcely affected by deep drainage except immediately adjacent to the edge of drains (Savill 1976).

For these reasons foresters no longer attempt to lower water tables in most wet upland soils over the site as a whole, as they did prior to the middle 1970s. Instead, modern drainage schemes only aim to aerate the more permeable and better structured surface layers by increasing the rate of removal of

FIG. 4.1. Deep central drain for collecting and removing surface water, with ploughed ridges each side on which trees will be planted (Beaghs forest, Co. Antrim, N. Ireland).

FIG. 4.2. Aerial view showing pattern of site drainage (by contour drains) and cultivation up and down slope — the top of the slope is at top centre of picture (Lough Bradan Forest, Co. Tyrone, N. Ireland).

surface water. They also provide *locally* better aerated raised patches or ridges of soil upon which the young trees can be planted. The water carried by drains is almost all surface water that cannot enter the still saturated soil.

It is useful to distinguish, at least in theory, between two different aspects of drainage on wet soils (Henman 1963*a*), sometimes referred to as site drainage and cultivation (Figs 4.1 and 4.2). In the field the distinctions are not always so obvious because the same ploughs are often used for both purposes.

Site drainage involves making a permanent drainage scheme which will function for the whole of the life of a crop and beyond. Drains either intercept ground water, where the water table is near the surface, or collect surface water from soils with a low infiltration capacity. These drains are normally aligned just off the contour, steep enough to give an adequate rate of flow but not so steep as to promote erosion.

Thompson (1979) gives a method of calculating the permissible maximum catchment area for cross drains which depends upon the velocity at which water can move without causing erosion after heavy rainfall. For most British conditions permissible catchments vary from about 5 to 8 ha depending upon the type of drain constructed. In practice, catchments are often much smaller.

Since about 1979 the British practice has been to taper depths of drains and eventually stop them 15–20 m from small water courses so that the water filters through the ground vegetation to prevent silting and consequent damage to fish spawning areas (Mills 1980). This practice may also have considerable value on some shallow soils of low buffering capacity in reducing acid runoff into streams.

Cultivation, by contrast, involves the disruption of pans and/or the provision of aerated ridges for planting. Ploughing is normally done up and down the slope to ensure easy movement of water and at intervals of 1–6 m, depending upon the type of plough and desired plant spacing. It is often referred to as 'spaced furrow ploughing' (Figs. 4.3 and 4.4). The furrows also initially act, to a limited extent, as drains and discharge some runoff water into the main cross drains. However, unlike cross drains, they are seldom kept clear of debris, partly for reasons of cost, but more because clearing them would damage tree roots. This loss of drainage benefit is at least partly offset by a reduction in water reaching the ground due to increased interception and transpiration as the canopy closes.

Drainage techniques

Before machinery was widely available it was necessary to drain wet sites by hand. This was done by cutting drains, usually between every fourth row of the proposed tree planting lines, and spreading the turfs cut from the drains into lines at square spacings of about 1.5 m and planting a tree on each

FIG. 4.3. Single mouldboard ploughing on a surface water gley soil at Kesh forest, Co. Fermanagh, N. Ireland. This method of ground preparation has now largely given way to double mouldboard or tunnel ploughing because it leads to windthrow.

FIG. 4.4. Double mouldboard ploughing on a peaty gley soil at Dyfi forest, Wales (photograph J. H. Williams).

FIG. 4.5. A large Finnish Lokomo drainage plough.

(4450 stems ha^{-1}). Because hand methods were so labour intensive little afforestation in this way was done until they could be replaced by mechanical ones. The machinery for doing this (Fig. 4.5) developed considerably during and after the Second World War.

Ploughing became virtually universal in Britain and other places where it was needed by the early 1950s. Although ploughs are continually being modified and improved, essentially two types are in common use: single mouldboard ploughs, designed to produce single ridges (Fig. 4.3) and leave furrows which vary from 45 to 60 cm deep and 35 to 45 cm wide at the base, and double mouldboard ploughs (Fig. 4.4) which produce furrows of similar depth, but 35–100 cm wide (Thompson 1978, 1984). The material from these furrows is split into two ridges, one being placed either side of the furrow at a distance determined by the design of the plough.

Modifications to ploughs have produced alterations to the shape of the ridge. Sometimes it is produced with a planting step to give early shelter and to enable roots to reach the more fertile ground of the vegetation 'sandwich' below the turf more quickly. In recent years ploughs producing deeper furrows and consequently bigger ridges were favoured because these resulted in better establishment.

The direction of ploughing is also important for species prone to developing leaning stems, such as lodgepole pine. If possible it should be in the same direction as the prevailing wind, to minimize this defect (Hendrick *et al.* 1984). By the early 1970s evidence was beginning to accumulate that the furrows associated with spaced furrow ploughing may seriously restrict rootplate development. A warning of this had been given as early as 1954 by Zehetmayr. Since rooting can never be deep on upland peats and gleys, crop stability must depend on widespread rooting in all directions. Furrows of any kind are likely to reduce stability, particularly if they have right-angled edges because roots cannot make sharp turns, about 60° appears to be the maximum angles they can turn (Eis 1978). For this reason single mouldboard ploughing was stopped in most areas by the mid 1970s and were replaced by double mouldboard ploughs. They, at least, give half the number of furrows per unit area and do not restrict rooting so much. At the same time more research was started to find methods of ground preparation, which would not involve the need for open furrows.

Among these is an Irish plough developed at Glenamoy, County Mayo, known as the 'tunnel' plough, which has proved successful on many deep peats (O'Carroll *et al.* 1981). It produces a closed drain, the bottom of which is about 75 cm from the surface and recent models give drain channels 36 cm high and 26 cm wide. The material from the channel is extruded on to the surface like a conventional planting ridge but there is no associated open furrow (Fig. 4.6).

Experiments show little difference between the growth of crops planted on tunnel-ploughed sites and on conventional single-mouldboard ploughing. However, water table depths, aeration, and bulk density of the peat are

FIG. 4.6. A tunnel-ploughed site on deep peat. Note the absence of open drainage channels (Beaghs Forest, Co. Antrim, N. Ireland).

Table 4.3   *Air content, bulk density and water table depth of peat drained by single mouldboard ploughing and tunnel ploughing (from Burke 1978; O'Carroll et al. 1981)*

Sampling depth (cm)	Single mouldboard ploughing (30 cm deep × 1.5 m apart)		Tunnel ploughing (60 cm deep × 1.5 m apart)		Undrained	
	Air (%)	Bulk density (kg/m³)	Air (%)	Bulk density (kg/m³)	Air (%)	Bulk density (kg/m³)
15	12.6	97	55.6	101	7.0	85
30	4.3	78	36.5	123	5.9	79
45	3.8	84	31.1	105	2.7	67
60	2.5	78	17.1	102	2.0	69
90	—	—	3.0	105	—	—
Water table depth (annual mean in cm)	43		80		—	

markedly better in tunnel ploughing (Table 4.3) resulting in much improved rooting. In conventionally ploughed treatments roots are largely confined to the planting ridge and ground surface between furrows, whereas in tunnel-ploughed areas a good symmetrical pattern is evident and roots are prolific down to 60–65 cm. This should result in more windfirm crops with fewer nutritional problems since the roots exploit a much greater volume of peat. Tunnel ploughs are now widely used on deep peats in Ireland.

On gleys and peaty gleys, similar attempts are being made to find a method of cultivation which does not involve open furrows. Among the most promising are variants of the agricultural technique of mole drainage (Hinson *et al.* 1970), which result in similar rates of tree growth as more conventional methods (Table 4.4).

Table 4.4   *Effects of various methods of cultivation on water table levels and growth of Sitka spruce on a surface water gley in N. Ireland (N. Ireland Forest Service, unpublished)*

Method of ground preparation	Distance between drains (m)	Winter water table depth (cm)	Mean height at age 10 (m)	Height growth in year 10 (m)
None	—	8.4	2.1	0.60
Turf planting	8.8	14.3	3.6	0.71
Double mouldboard plough	4.4	15.8	3.7	0.71
Single mouldboard plough	2.2	21.1	3.8	0.74
Mole drains	2.2	22.1	3.8	0.76

Trees planted as directly as possible over a mole drain show growth rates comparable to those on conventional ploughing, at least in the early years. The method needs more testing, however, because there is still some danger that mole drains may eventually become blocked by roots. This would result in a sudden rise in water level with potentially disastrous consequences. Also mole drainage is only appropriate for clay soils and it does not give the advantage of a weed-free site for planting. The creation of small planting mounds with scarifiers is also showing some promise (see p. 60).

A second approach (Read *et al.* 1973) has been to experiment with the ancient agricultural method of 'riggs and furrs', elevated, cambered 'riggs' separated by lower furrows or 'furrs', designed to improve runoff and drainage. While these show promise, they are extremely expensive to make and thus unlikely to become widely used.

A completely different and very specialized form of drainage is found in parts of the Netherlands and other places where land has been reclaimed from the sea. Such land is flat and lies below sea level. It requires an intensive network of drainage channels and associated pumping stations to maintain the ground water at an acceptably low and constant level. Reclaimed land is usually fertile and very productive in agriculture once the initial salinity problems have been overcome but tree planting for shelter and to provide some relief in flat and monotonous landscapes is also important.

Cultivation on ironpan and indurated soils

Ironpan soils are common on heaths in eastern Britain above 150 m in elevation. Ironpans at 30–40 cm depth can present impenetrable physical barriers to roots and to a lesser extent to water. Equally impenetrable indurated zones may underlie the pans. Shattering them by tining or deep ploughing often considerably improves aeration, drainage and rooting and the mixing of the superficial peaty horizon can also increase nitrogen and other nutrient availability. Bulk densities are reduced (Ross and Malcolm 1982) and oxygen levels in the soil are much improved by this form of cultivation (Pyatt and Craven 1979). In fact, these soils offer excellent prospects for improvement.

The technical problems of cultivation were difficult to overcome until machines were developed capable of withstanding the rough usage to which they are subjected on these wet, compact, and stony soils. In Britain the usual method on both ironpan soils and podzols is single mouldboard ploughing together with tining to break pans. This is much less intensive than methods used in parts of continental Europe where deep complete ploughing is often practised. However, the British practice may be safer in the long term because recent experience on complete-ploughed areas in Britain (Thompson and Neustein 1973) in the Netherlands (Leek 1979), Germany, and elsewhere has been that while early growth is greatly improved due to the rapid mineralization of the mixed organic horizon, once this has mineralized and largely been lost by leaching, serious nitrogen deficiency may then develop unless fertilizer nitrogen is applied.

There are still a number of technical problems to overcome on indurated soils where impenetrable cemented horizons also restrict water movement and root growth in a way similar to ironpans. The main problem is that the indurations are usually too deep for existing machinery, except at prohibitive cost. When indurations occur in upland clayey gleyed soils, rupturing indurations may give no drainage or rooting benefit.

Drought-prone sites

By global standards, aridity is not a problem in temperate regions but periods of drought are common and can be very damaging to young crops.

In many forest ecosystems water losses from leaves during the day exceed the amount absorbed by the roots, and trees tend to become dehydrated as absorption lags behind transpiration. Temporary water deficits caused by excessive transpiration are not serious when the soil is well watered because leaves usually make up the deficit at night. Many trees, including temperate species, can also store considerable amounts of water in the sapwood which can be used during the day. However, as droughts intensify, water deficits develop which result in reductions in growth, injury, and ultimately death. The stress imposed by drought can also make unadapted species more prone to diseases and attacks by some pests. Shallow soils and deep, coarse-textured soils are especially prone to drought. South- and north-facing slopes, in the northern and southern hemispheres respectively, can intensify problems.

Many species of tree exhibit various degrees of avoidance of drought damage through adaptations that retard water loss or increase water uptake. These include the ability to shed leaves to balance unavoidable losses of water. Leaf shedding occurs in dry summers even in the temperate zone and was very noticeable among many deciduous species in western Europe during the summer drought of 1976. Other adaptations to reduce water loss include leaf waxes which are common among the Mediterranean flora and the presence of few and sunken stomata in many pines. The ability to close stomata quickly in drying conditions explains why pines will grow and thrive on dry sites while species like Sitka spruce, which does not have this ability, will not. Trees adapted to very dry climates have much reduced leaf areas and a temporary reduction is also shown by most species soon after planting, until their root systems are functioning properly. Where the problems of drought are predominantly those of a dry atmosphere which causes high rates of transpiration, rigidly constructed evergreen leaves are best able to survive whereas deciduous trees are adapted to periods of severe soil drought. Trees which grow well on dry sites usually have fast-growing deep and extensive root systems which develop at the expense of stem growth. This enables them to reach water which is unavailable to surface-rooting plants like grasses, and ensures the prevention, or at least postponement of drought injury. Other species avoid drought by releasing chemicals, mostly organic acids, which inhibit seed germination and growth of competing adjacent plants.

From this, it is clear that the most important measure that can be taken to prevent drought damage is to select a species which is adapted to the anticipated drought conditions. In temperate climates, species of pines and, in warmer parts eucalypts are almost invariably the choice. In many dry climates, tolerance to alkaline or saline conditions may be an additional requirement.

Cultural methods to reduce water loss from the site and aid its water-holding capacity are secondary to those of species but can have important influences on survival and growth during the critical establishment stage. The most important of these is to control ground vegetation which competes with the young trees for water. Balneaves (1984), for example, found that control of grasses gave spectacular improvements in growth and survival of *Pinus radiata* in low-rainfall areas of New Zealand, not only in the year of planting, but in the subsequent 10 years. A mulch of litter and logging residues can help conserve soil moisture, reduce weeds and provide a more favourable habitat for root development in the surface soil horizons (Farrell 1984). Cultivation can be a valuable aid to establishment by suppressing weeds and, especially on compacted soils, it can improve soil texture, and hence the rate of infiltration and storage of water in the soil. In the Mediterranean climate of Cyprus, for example, it has been found that on some sites the soil moisture level is at wilting point to depths of 65 cm in summer on uncultivated slopes whereas on ground which has been cultivated by terracing, with associated removal of vegetation, the soil is above wilting point at depths below 15 cm, with obvious advantages to growth. Terraces are often constructed with a slope into the hill in order to retain the runoff water. Other measures include mulching, planting trees in 50–100 cm diameter concave pits, or at the bottom of ploughed furrows, both of which receive runoff water, and the roots, at the same time, are nearer to the moister, lower soil levels. Only in the most extreme circumstances can the routine use of watering or irrigation be justified in forestry. This is virtually unknown in temperate climates except in unusual circumstances such as promoting seed production in special stands in parts of the United States.

There are other means of ensuring good survival of newly planted trees in dry areas. Planting stock should be sturdy, bare-rooted transplants with a high proportion of root to shoot, and a high basal stem diameter (see p. 73) or grown in containers. Planting should be timed to avoid periods of desiccating winds and to coincide with a time when the soil is fully charged with water. This will vary according to region. In the western USA it is immediately after the snow has melted in early spring, and in the Mediterranean area it is just after the first heavy rain in autumn, when temperatures still favour root growth, and in Britain in November or February and March.

Second rotation sites

Ground preparation of second and subsequent rotation sites is difficult because machinery able to cope with the conditions among stumps and debris left from the former crop is not widely available. On wet soils it is rare for such sites to receive any treatment apart from renewing the permanent drainage system. Cultivation by using Scandinavian scarifiers which produce planting mounds, about 30 cm high and 50 cm wide, is now beginning to be seen as a cheap and effective method of preparing second rotation sites (Tabbush 1984).

Where debris creates a fire hazard, as in parts of British Columbia, and in many dry areas, 'broadcast' burning is a common method of site preparation. Fire also reduces the amount of competing vegetation, rodents, and potential insect pests. Apart from the risk of fire spreading to neighbouring stands, burning has the disadvantages of potential damage to the soil structure and loss of nutrients. It may increase the risk of some diseases, and may make steep sites liable to erosion.

Damage to soil structure

The heavy machinery used for harvesting can cause an increase in the bulk density and a consequent loss of porosity to soils, virtually without exception. Wingate-Hill and Jakobsen (1982) quote bulk density increases of between 2 and 40 per cent. The most vulnerable soils are wet ones, especially clayey soils, and compaction is most severe in the top 30 cm, where most roots grow. An increase in bulk density leads to reduced aeration, reduced rooting potential, and there is ample evidence that increment of trees on compacted areas can be reduced by amounts ranging from about 10 per cent to over 50 per cent. Soils do not recover quickly from such compaction which may last for decades and may even be cumulative from one rotation to the next.

In a study of damage in thinned areas caused by various common types of extraction machines in Oregon, Murphy (1982, 1984) found between 12 and 29 per cent of the area received some damage, the extent depending upon the type of equipment used, the intensity of thinning and the method of working. Similar results were found in Ireland by Boyle et al. (1982).

Damage can be minimized by using machinery with reduced ground pressures, covering tracks with branches, by the careful presentation of felled timber in rows for extraction and above all not logging when soils are very wet. Attempts at ameliorating damage by deep ripping and fertilizing have been tried but even where this is practicable growth does not compare with that on neighbouring uncompacted soils.

Apart from compaction, wheel skidding leads to reduced infiltration of water, to puddling of the soil surface, and the removal of litter and topsoil can reduce nutrient availability.

5. Selection of species

A correct choice of species is one of the most important of all decisions in forestry because a bad one can lead to many long-term problems or even the loss of a plantation. During the decades between planting and harvesting a forest the requirements of the tree must be well matched to the chosen site to avoid stress (see p. 171).

The long cycles of forestry rule out the possibility of taking risks which may sometimes be justifiable in agriculture since droughts, gales, and frosts will inevitably occur over a rotation of say 50 years. The species selected for planting should therefore be one whose requirements throughout life are likely to be satisfied by the site and climate in question. The suitability of the species in economic or other terms for the object of the plantation scheme is obviously important too, but must always be secondary to the basic biological considerations. There is usually a relatively wide range of species available

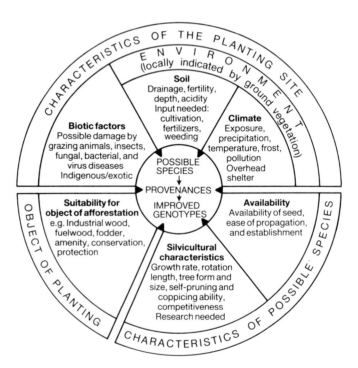

FIG. 5.1. Considerations in selecting species.

from which to choose, but if none suitable can be found it is better to abandon the plantation scheme or to locate it elsewhere than to risk a species that may not thrive on the site.

Essentially, the process of species selection requires a thorough assessment of the habitat factors and a knowledge of the responses of possible species to them. There are three stages (Fig. 5.1):

(1) determining the characteristics of the planting site in terms of soil, climate, and ecological factors;
(2) deciding which trees are likely to thrive in such conditions;
(3) deciding which trees, at the same time, satisfy the objectives of the planting scheme.

Decisions are made more difficult in regions where the native species are relatively unproductive or otherwise unsuitable because in such circumstances foresters usually rely upon exotics which are not naturally adapted to the new environments and, at least initially their requirements are less well understood. Even in countries with long-established forest industries based on native conifers, exotics may be attractive because of greater levels of productivity (see p. 27).

Site assessment

Many of the important climatic and site considerations in forestry are discussed in Chapter 3 and they have a bearing on species selection. The climate of an area limits the range of species which can be grown successfully. Thus, obviously, tropical species which require frost-free climates cannot be grown in cool temperate latitudes and though sub-arctic species might grow, preference is normally given to potentially more productive trees from regions with similar climates.

Failure to take adequate account of general climatic differences can lead to disasters, the recent examples of which come from more tropical, rather than temperate countries. For example, dothistroma blight (*Scirrhia pini*) of *Pinus radiata* is a disease of insignificant importance in regions which have dry summers, but plantations of the species in Brazil, in Zimbabwe, and in other parts of east-central Africa failed in the 1940s because the hot *moist* summers of these countries resulted in devastating attacks. Large amounts of effort and money could have been saved had those responsible for planting heeded the advice of pathologists who had warned of this danger (Zobel 1982). Of course, their advice seems wise now, with the benefit of hindsight. In New Zealand, although similar warnings have been given for decades, the current policy is to continue with the monoculture of *Pinus radiata* and to accept the cost of controlling dothistroma blight chemically, as well as to accept the risk from pests and diseases as yet not present in the country (Burdon 1982).

Even within quite a small geographical areas, climate can vary sufficiently to have a major influence on species selection. Within the British Isles some species, like Sitka spruce, need higher levels of rainfall than are found in lowland Britain; others like Corsican pine need higher temperatures than are found in the uplands. Corsican pine is near the limit of where it can successfully be planted in lowland Britain. On sites in the north and west that are too moist and cool, its resistance is lowered to attack by *Gremmenniella abietina*, a dieback disease. On marginal sites this disease is more serious on cooler north-facing than on south-facing slopes. Other species will not withstand severe late spring or early autumn frosts, exposure or atmospheric pollution.

In general, the more hospitable the climate, the greater the choice of species. Thus, in upland Britain where the climate is harsh and soils are poor, the number from which a choice can be made is limited to two or three whereas, on good soils in the better climate of the lowlands, a choice from about 20 may often be possible.

Exceptional climatic events can also reveal inadequacies in species' selection which may not be apparent in more normal periods and this is one reason why extreme caution is observed before a relatively untried but promising exotic is ever planted on a wide scale. For example, the very cold winter of 1981/82 in Britain killed much *Pinus radiata*, *Cupressus macrocarpa*, and some other species previously thought to be relatively safe on certain sites. It also eliminated many *Eucalyptus* spp. which were being tried experimentally, enabling future work to be concentrated upon the hardy ones (Evans 1983). Similarly, the prolonged drought over much of western Europe during the summer of 1976 caused a great deal of mortality to beech and larch which had been planted on unsuitable soils.

This was often caused by a lowering of the trees' defence mechanisms which enabled relatively weak pathogens such as *Armillaria* spp. and *Phaeolus schweinitzii*, which had previously been localized, to invade large parts of root systems and eventually kill the trees. A combination of two wet winters and a very dry summer is thought to have caused sufficient root death of lodgepole pine planted on an unflushed peat in Scotland to result in serious outbreaks of the pine beauty moth (Parry 1982).

Though soils can be modified by drainage, cultivation, and nutrition, many have a number of permanent limitations which restrict the use of some species suited to the local climate. Species liable to become stressed in conditions of soil drought, such as Douglas-fir from the British Columbian coastal regions, should not be planted on drought-prone sites, while many pines can tolerate drought well. Douglas-fir is also unable to produce an adequate root system in conditions of poor soil drainage and so, if planted on heavily gleyed soils, suffers from windthrow, while spruces can tolerate such conditions better. A few species such as some poplars and ash are very exacting and require high-fertility ample well-oxygenated soil moisture and little competition from weeds if they are to produce fast-growing crops. Other species thrive on a wide range of sites.

In many areas, and especially in hilly country, a detailed consideration of local topography and soils may dictate a change of species quite frequently to take account of local conditions. The composition of the ground vegetation is often used to indicate soil and climate within restricted geographic areas. It can be a valuable guide for species selection since changes reflect and integrate changes in the physical environment which can be difficult to measure in other ways. The main types of ground vegetation in the British Isles have been widely used as indicators for species selection since the time of Anderson's (1961) work on the subject though Gilchrist (1872) indicated the potential in Scotland well over a century ago. Evans (1984) provides a method for selecting broadleaved species based on various soil factors. He uses the potential of different soils according to pH, texture, rooting depth, drainage, and fertility.

Assessment of other ecological factors

Species selection can be influenced to varying degrees by many other physiological and ecological factors. An assessment of the predisposition of a species to damage must be made. Obvious examples are the palatability of species to large grazing mammals. Sheep, for example, seem attracted to various silver firs (*Abies* spp.) which, like many tolerant trees are slow at making early height growth and can suffer badly. Deer, squirrels, rabbits, and other animals can also cause damage which may influence species choice for example the prevalence of squirrel damage on beech, maple, and sycamore. Atmospheric pollution of various kinds can also be very damaging and this is a subject which is receiving great attention. The topic has been reviewed by Morrison (1984).

It is also possible to assess many of the more obvious risks from insects, fungi, viruses, and bacteria which have been discussed in Chapter 2.

Practice of species selection

Where locally native species are concerned, there is little difficulty in deciding what to plant. The problem becomes much more difficult with exotics. The practice of introducing trees into new homes is as old as civilization itself, but it is only since the middle of the 1800s that the formation of plantations, particularly of exotics, has come to be regarded as specially important. The period since the First World War has seen a rapid increase in both area and number of species planted. The history of many introductions to Commonwealth countries has been described by Streets (1962). They frequently follow a pattern of initial introductions to gardens and arboreta and then, if successful, perhaps half a rotation later, by small-scale planting on estates and by Government departments. Large plantations of the most promising species are established some 20–50 years after that. Thus, Sitka spruce which is the major plantation tree in the British Isles was introduced in 1831. It was established as one of the chief exotics in the early 1920s and by the mid 1950s it became the most widely planted tree. The history of *Pinus radiata* in New Zealand follows a similar pattern, being introduced about the end of the 1850s and planting started on a vast scale in the 1920s. Thus, a long period of trial, amounting to at least one and a half to two rotations is usually thought advisable before an exotic is widely planted. Introductions to many parts of the world, particularly the tropics, are still taking place and though guides exist for selecting species, based on climatic, soil, and other variables, there is still no substitute for extended trials before major schemes are started (Fig. 5.2). If there is no time for such trials, the decision makers must accept a considerable risk that their investment will not yield a financial return.

In many places today there may, however, be considerable past experience of which exotics will grow and how they will perform, either from former

FIG. 5.2. Southern beech (*Nothofagus obliqua*) is a species of considerable promise as an exotic in the British Isles, and is undergoing a period of extended trials on many sites before it can be considered for widespread use in plantations. The trees in this plot are 26 years old and growing at a rate of $19 \, m^3 \, ha^{-1} \, yr^{-1}$ (Micheldever forest, Hampshire).

crops of the same species on the site itself or from a nearby similar area. If such experience is lacking, species trials may sometimes give unexpected results. Lines (1984), for example, in a description of species experiments in the southern Pennine Hills of England concluded that Sitka spruce grew poorly where an experienced silviculturist would have been sure of good growth on apparently similar sites away from the industrial Pennines.

Further important considerations in selecting species are such practical ones as the availability of viable seed and the ease with which plants can be raised in nurseries and established in the forest. If such problems are present, they must clearly be resolved before the species is used on a wide scale however suitable it may be once established and growing in the forest.

Provenance

When dealing with exotic trees, it is not sufficient to decide simply which species to plant without considering the original geographic source of the seed as well, that is, the provenance. Some of the worst mistakes in plantation forests are the result of well-intentioned foresters importing seed from stands which look good but which are quite unsuited to the new environment (Lines 1967). In the north temperate zone, for example, seasonal fluctuations in day length and temperature control growth periodicity which is adapted to local conditions. The northward movement of birches, which are strongly adapted to their native photoperiod and temperature conditions, results in the risk of damage by frost because late-season growth does not stop soon enough. Movement of trees southwards or from continental to maritime areas results in early flushing and spring frost damage (Habjørg 1972).

The nature of variability within a species has been discussed by Callaham (1964), Burley (1965), and Perry (1979). There are always genetic differences between individuals of species which reproduce sexually, and differences also occur between local populations, which are often referred to as provenances. Population differences occur because the individual members of a population tend to breed with each other more than with members of distant populations. Genetic differences may be expressed in different morphological or physiological traits and arise because, under the pressures of natural selection, genotypes that are unsuited to the local environment do not survive, whereas the progeny of more fit individuals do survive. The population therefore becomes increasingly suited to the local environment in terms of such characters as adaptation to photoperiod, drought, frost resistance, and growth, besides less obvious features like mycorrhizal associations and enzyme production.

The extent of genetic differentiation between populations depends on the natural range of the species and the variability of the environment through the range. In most widely distributed species, patterns of genetic variation reflect patterns of environmental change, and discontinuities in one are commonly associated with breaks in the other. Thus, in species where there are no distinct populations but a continuous intergradation, there is a gradual change in the character under consideration. Ecotypic variation is the alternative and may occur between geographically separated populations, or populations on markedly different soil types.

Some species are relatively 'plastic' in that they have a good ability to adapt to conditions which differ from those of their native habitat; *Pinus radiata* and *Robinia pseudoacacia* are among the best known plastic species. *Pinus radiata* has a very limited native distribution of no more than 7000 ha in California and on two Mexican offshore islands, yet it is more widely used as an exotic than any other species. Species which lack plasticity but which have wide natural ranges (such as Douglas-fir and lodgepole pine) also prove widely successful only if the right seed origin is selected for each region. Conifers are normally favoured as exotics in temperate regions because of the wide demand for their timber, high productivities and also because of their general adaptability, hardiness and the ease with which they can be established. With the exception of eucalypts in warm temperate regions, and to a lesser extent poplars, hardwoods are much less successful.

It is widely accepted that the pattern of variation and growth within a tree species is continuous and is closely related to climate (Burley 1965). Individuals of a widespread species therefore show a continuous variability in response to photoperiod, temperature, and precipitation. Superimposed on this continuous pattern, discontinuities, such as abrupt changes in soil type, may lead to recognizable ecotypes. More complex circumstances may also be envisaged.

The selection of a suitably adapted provenance can therefore be critical when planting an exotic species with a widespread natural distribution, and a knowledge of the patterns of natural variation is of considerable practical importance.

The forester has much to gain by using the best possible seed source for raising trees for plantations. As a proportion of total establishment costs, seed represents no more than 1 per cent. Even if the cost is doubled, to 2 per cent, by buying the best available seed for the site in question, a negligible proportion is added to establishment costs but ultimate yields may be considerably enhanced. It is one of the falsest economies possible to buy cheap, inappropriate seed. By contrast, seed sources of native species which have been undisturbed by man are usually the best adapted for survival and reproduction in the local conditions. They are not necessarily the most productive however and one of the best known examples of this is with Norway spruce in Norway and Sweden. After the last ice age this species migrated to southern Norway around the Gulf of Bothnia, in a southerly direction and, on the way, became adapted to relatively harsh conditions. Non-native provenances often grow faster on some sites (Giertych 1976).

Provenance differences are best determined by experiments carried out in the region where the tree is to be planted. If the species exhibits continuous variation, it is theoretically possible, though seldom done, to predict the performance of an unknown provenance from that of two provenances at opposite ends of the cline. In ecotypic variation, prediction is restricted to within the limits of the ecotype.

Sitka spruce is a species which exhibits continuous variation and is widely planted as an exotic in the British Isles. It originates from a narrow (80 km wide) zone at low elevations along the Pacific coast of the USA and Canada across more than 22 ° of latitude from Alaska to California. In Britain, experiments indicate clines of decreasing vigour of growth, and increasing resistance to frost damage among provenances from Oregon to Alaska. Californian provenances generally do not survive in Britain. The choice of seed origin must attempt to compromise on these two characteristics. Seed from the Queen Charlotte Islands in British Columbia satisfactorily combines hardiness with adequate growth rates and often gives the best height growth on all sites (Lines 1979a).

Lodgepole pine (*Pinus contorta*) is a species, planted as an exotic in Britain and Ireland, which exhibits both continuous and ecotypic variation. It has a much greater natural distribution than Sitka spruce in north-west America, spanning some 33 ° of latitude, from Alaska to Baja California in Mexico, and 33 ° of longitude, from the Pacific coast to South Dakota. It covers a very wide variety of climatic and soil conditions. At least three interfertile races are usually recognized as subspecies which differ markedly in ecology and morphology. Subspecies *contorta* grows along most of the Pacific coast in bogs, on sand dunes and on the margins of pools and lakes. It is short, shrubby, and of poor form. This gives way to ssp. *latifolia* in the inter mountain systems from central Yukon to eastern Oregon and south Colorado, and to ssp. *murravana*, mainly on the Cascade and Sierra Nevada mountains in Oregon and California (Critchfield 1957). These two subspecies have better formed, slender, tall straight trees. The coastal ssp. *contorta* gives much the highest yields as an exotic in Britain and Ireland and a constant dilemma has been how far to compromise on form (Fig. 5.3), while retaining vigour. In Ireland the most vigorous provenance of ssp. *contorta*, from Oregon and Washington are almost exclusively planted (O'Driscoll 1980) while in Britain, slower growing, more northerly provenances from Vancouver Island and Puget Sound are favoured (Lines 1979b) besides some inland provenances of ssp. *latifolia* and intermediate ones between the two such as from the Skeena River.

There is also considerable variation within any natural population which cannot be attributed to differential selection along environmental

FIG. 5.3. Very poor stem form of a coastal provenance of lodgepole pine (*Pinus contorta.* ssp. *contorta*).

gradients: this may often be greater than responses to environment. It is frequently found that within-provenance variations are more than those which occur between provenances. A recognition of this type of variation is the basis of most tree breeding for increased productivity, disease resistance, and other attributes (Faulkner 1975).

Breeding programmes with selected species and provenances are now becoming common. Poplars (*Populus* spp.) are probably the trees on which most breeding has been carried out because of need to produce canker-free cultivars, the ease with which some species can subsequently be propagated vegetatively from cuttings, their very rapid growth and relative value in some markets. Poplars are one of the few genera where clonal selections for plantations are readily available in forestry. They can be used to illustrate the whole spectrum of considerations in selecting a species, provenance or hybrid and clone.

There are many species of poplars native to the northern temperate zones. Several have hybridized, both naturally, and artificially in cultivation and there is an increasing number of clones available for planting. Most grow best in regions of relatively high summer temperatures with long growing seasons. Thus France, Belgium, the Netherlands, and Italy are major areas for poplar growing in Europe. To grow well, poplars require sheltered sites and loamy soils with a pH above 5.5. They must have well aerated and moist soil and the water table should never be closer than 50 to 100 cm from the surface or further from it than 150 cm (Peace 1952). Alluvial soils in river valleys often provide the best sites. Apart from the normal considerations of selecting vigorous clones which are adapted to the local climate, the main criteria for deciding upon a particular clone include resistance to bacterial and fungal cankers and rust diseases of leaves, to which many poplars are susceptible. Stem and branch form are also very important considerations.

6. Plantation establishment

Next in importance to species selection in the management of any crop is how to establish it and how to replace it after harvesting. Artificial establishment is most commonly carried out by planting young trees which have been raised in nurseries or, more rarely, by direct seeding of the site.

Planting stock

The artificially raised plants used in establishment programmes can be:

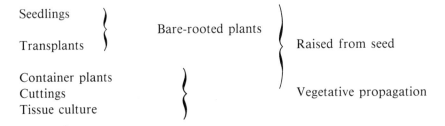

The aim is to produce plants which are cheap and have qualities and dimensions that make them suitable for use in the forest in terms of handling, survival, and growth. Plants must be big enough to be handled, not desiccate too quickly and with adequate reserves to make new growth and have root systems which will rapidly become established.

In most temperate countries the techniques for growing plants by any of these methods are now so specialized that they are the concern of nurserymen rather than foresters. However, it is important for foresters to understand the qualities and potential problems associated with different kinds of plants.

BARE-ROOTED PLANTS

The techniques for raising bare-rooted plants are described in detail by Aldhous (1972) and Duryea and Landis (1984) among others. Essentially, the nursery cycle involves sowing seedbeds in the spring and a year or more later the seedlings are transplanted into beds where they have more room to develop. The young plants are moved to their final position in the forest between 1 and 5 years after sowing the seed, depending on species, local climate, and the size of plants required.

An important aim of transplanting is to encouraging the formation of a root system which will ensure good survival and growth after planting. The root system should not be too spreading, and it must be possible to lift it reasonably intact. Sometimes seedlings or transplants are undercut at predetermined depths in the beds instead of being transplanted. The ratio of root weight to shoot weight is inevitably influenced by transplanting and is often lower than in natural seedlings of the same age, being about 1:2 at the time of planting compared to at least 1:1 and probably 3:1 in natural seedlings. In terms of root length to shoot length, ratios of 1:1 to 1:2 are common in nursery plants, whether bare rooted or container-grown, whereas 4:1 is more common in natural seedlings of the same age (Stein 1978).

Much work has been devoted to determining the nursery treatments which ensure good survival and growth after planting. These include spacing, fertilizing, and undercutting (see Driessche 1980, 1982, 1983, 1984). Many morphological standards of quality exist for bare-rooted plants (for example Chavasse 1979; Aldhous 1972; Kramer and Spellman 1980) of which the most useful indicator is a large root collar diameter. However, there is often a poor relationship between seedling grade and survival. This is at least partly because during the period between lifting from the nursery and planting, all the efforts and care taken to produce good-quality stock can be undone by neglect, resulting in desiccation during storage and transit (Leaf *et al.* 1978). The importance of care in these respects cannot be overemphasized. Physiological standards of quality, especially root regenerating potential (see p. 83), winter hardiness, and disease resistance are increasingly being recognized (Ritchie and Dunlap 1980; Ritchie 1982; Sutton 1979).

CONTAINER PLANTS

Since the 1960s there has been a trend towards raising trees in various sorts of containers in greenhouses. The initial development, outside the tropics and arid regions where it is a much longer-established practice, arose in the testing climates of Canada and Scandinavia where it can sometimes take 4 or 5 years to grow usable transplants in conventional nurseries compared with a year or less in greenhouses. There are many attractions in using controlled conditions to produce plants in containers.

1. It is possible to extend the planting season well beyond the normal limits for bare-rooted stock. This is of value to management if labour is scarce.
2. The short production period, of a few months to a year, makes a good match between plant requirements and plant production possible.
3. A high output rate per person is possible with container plant production leading to lower supervisory costs than in conventional nurseries (Low 1975).

4. Container plants usually suffer less from neglect and bad handling than do bare-rooted plants, though there is a danger of their being treated more roughly as a result.

5. If done properly, planting can be achieved in a highly consistent manner. There may therefore be less chance of damage from bad planting techniques.

6. Depending upon the size of container, survival can be better, and early growth improved, particularly with certain difficult species such as Corsican pine on drought-prone sites.

However, container plants are not without disadvantages. The main ones are that to compete in terms of cost with bare-rooted plants, containers must be small, so that handling and transport are not too expensive. This means that plants are also small, often much smaller than conventional transplants. They are therefore more susceptible to various sorts of damage, particularly from browsing animals and birds, frost heaving, and suppression by weeds. The establishment period is also longer. The roots of plants grown in some types of containers become deformed. Much is being done to improve container design and growing techniques to prevent this. However, bare-rooted plants commonly have serious root defects too. Finally, container seedlings are more susceptible to damage from low temperatures in the nursery because the roots, the most sensitive parts of the plants, are above ground.

Plants are grown in many different types of container, ranging from longitudinally grooved plastic tubes, paper pots, and a large variety of more solid containers through whose walls roots cannot penetrate.

VEGETATIVE PROPAGATION AND TISSUE CULTURE

It is normal practice to use rooted cuttings for propagating poplars, willows, some elms, and a few other species which are easy to root and where clonal material having disease resistance or exceptional vigour is important (Heybroek 1981). *Cryptomeria japonica* and other conifers have been propagated by cuttings for centuries in Japan (Toda 1974). Cuttings are used for propagating trees which do not produce viable seed, such as Leyland cypress which is an intergeneric hybrid, and occasional interesting cultivars of many species. They are also used to establish seed orchards of selected trees, such as *Pinus radiata* in New Zealand. There is growing interest in the use of mass propagation of cuttings of the more common plantation conifers. Mixtures of more than 1000 clones of Norway spruce are being raised from cuttings in Lower Saxony in West Germany, where the aim is to produce 30–40 per cent of plant requirements in this way. Gains in productivity of at least 10 per cent, and possibly much more, are expected compared with stock from seed orchard origin. The cost of plants is between 20 and 50 per cent greater than conventional seedlings or transplants, depending upon the age and size of plant required (Kleinschmit and Schmidt 1977).

Dormling *et al.* (1976) and Roulund (1981) have discussed many of the techniques and problems associated with vegetative propagation. Success at rooting is critically influenced by the physical conditions cuttings are subjected to, such as substrate, nutrients, humidity, temperature, light, and applied auxins, and also physiological factors, including particularly the age of the trees from which the cutting is taken, its position on the crown and its general health. Generally material which is less than 6 years old from seed is very much easier to propagate.

Tissue culture has even more potential for vegetative propagation through extraordinarily high rates of multiplication. The term is used to describe three areas of vegetative propagation: true tissue culture, which involves formation of undifferentiated callus before subsequent organ formation: organ culture, where organized regions of cells, usually bud meristems, are cultured but remain physiologically intact; and cell suspensions where the culturing unit is a single protoplast or plant cell with the cell wall removed. Techniques, especially for conifers, are difficult and though progress is being made, tissue culture in forestry is still in its infancy. The possibilities are discussed in detail by Bonga and Durzan (1982) and Dodds (1983).

The prospect of being able to raise clonal material in great quantities could enable the rapid replacement of forest crops by selected genetically superior trees in terms of vigour, form, wood properties, disease resistance, and other attributes which are thought desirable. Superiority is achieved by dominance or epistasis which may break down in sexual propagation. Clonal propagation has been practised for centuries with apples, citrus fruits, and rubber. These are relatively valuable crops on which expensive protection measures can be justified: timber crops are not. A disadvantage of single clones is that, if widely planted, they are likely to become exceptionally vulnerable to diseases and pests which are able to overcome any temporary resistance bound to one or a few genes. This has occurred in Japan with *Cryptomeria japonica*, and with poplars (see p. 28) in Europe (Mohrdiek 1983) and the problems associated with a narrow genetic base are very well known in various agricultural crops. These risks may be reduced by mixing numerous selected clones in plantations. Vegetative propagation is seen by many as a useful tool for studies in forest genetics but not a technique to be used on an extensive scale unless clones have undergone a long (two rotation) period of successful growth. The problems and possible advantages of clonal forestry are still being debated (for example Roulund 1981; Heybroek *et al.* 1982).

Direct seeding

Direct seeding can complement conventional planting and natural seeding when the needs, sites, and species are appropriate. Since repellants were developed for protecting seeds from birds, insects, and rodents the technique has been used with success in several temperate countries. For example about 10 per cent of afforestation in France is done by seeding (Kroth *et al.* 1976) and 5 per cent in the USA (Anon. 1981). Its main value in temperate countries has been in extensively managed areas, on difficult terrain, after large fires, in windthrown areas, and in forests devastated by insects. Seed is often broadcast from the air. Species appropriate for direct seeding must normally have small and easily available seed which germinates rapidly on the soil surface and then grows quickly. Among many species which have been seeded successfully in the USA and New Zealand are lodgepole pine, *Pinus nigra*, *Picea glauca*, and Douglas-fir. Direct seeding is not suitable for all situations without some preparatory work. For example, on many organic soils it may be necessary to burn or scarify first to achieve consistent success. The details of many of the techniques involved are discussed by Mergen (1981).

Root form of planted trees

The debate about the extent to which planted trees suffer from root deformations has been renewed every 20–30 years since the 1880s (Huuri 1978). The subject was recently given an airing at a symposium in British Columbia in 1978 (van Eerden and Kinghorn 1978).

Naturally established and direct seeded trees normally develop an array of sturdy lateral roots radiating from a well-developed tap root, which grows downwards to an extent which depends upon the nature of the soil. Some species, and especially pines, lose the capacity to initiate first-order lateral roots (which eventually become the main structural elements) early in their *first* season of growth (Burdett 1978, 1979) possibly within 60 days of sowing seed. Thus, the final configuration of a root system may be established very early in life and remain essentially unchanged with increasing age. Other species like Norway spruce are much more adaptable.

The number of roots, their growth, and branching habit control the shape, size, and symmetry of a natural root system. In spruces and some other species adapted to wetter soils, lateral and oblique roots take over the function of structural support as the growth of the taproot declines and the root system takes on a typically bell-shaped form, penetrating as far as soil conditions permit. In some pines and other species like Douglas-fir the taproot is relatively more important (Mexal and Burton 1978; Eis 1978). Natural root systems are normally highly effective anchorages for trees, as attested by the wind firmness and upright posture of most seeded trees.

Though asymmetry of the root system is sometimes a natural feature particularly of non-dominant trees and on stony and sloping sites (Eis 1978), the roots of many planted trees are generally much less adapted to the function of mechanical support at the outset. Root systems of bare-rooted plants are modified by pruning, lifting and transplanting and the roots of container plants are also shaped and pruned. All roots may be distorted on planting. Bare-rooted trees, *even if well planted*, are likely to have bilaterally compressed root systems. If, as is often the case, trees are not properly planted, all roots may be unilaterally distributed in relation to the base of the stem, or they may be bundled into a planting hole that is too small. Container-grown stock also has characteristic modifications. In some containers major lateral roots tend to lie parallel to the taproot for the first 10–15 cm of their length instead of growing in a more or less horizontal plane. Sometimes roots grow around the container walls in a spiral fashion, giving rise to the possibility of eventual strangulation of the stem by the roots.

Many authors express fears that these modifications will reduced anchorage for many years after planting and make trees more susceptible to toppling and windthrow. Burdett (1978) has demonstrated this in tree-pulling experiments with natural and planted lodgepole pine and he has also shown, with this species, that basal bowing is increased in planted trees, due to the young tree swaying and opening up an inverted conical gap around the root collar. This inhibits development of roots from the root collar area that are most effective in securing stability.

There is evidence that, with time, as the root system elongates, grows in diameter, and branches, mechanical stability may improve and that eventually a firm anchorage is achieved. But trees become more susceptible to wind damage as they increase in height, so permanent defects may again become apparent later in the rotation. Some foresters are pessimistic about the stability and growth of planted trees. There is general agreement that natural regeneration or direct seeding offer the best prospects for good root development and that bare-rooted stock offer the worst. Containers may lead to better root growth than bare-rooted plants provided roots do not get pot bound. If root systems in containers could be developed which grow in a similar way to natural roots, containers could be of special value. Some approaches are already showing promise. For example, it is possible to overcome the problem of root spiralling by incorporating vertical ribs on to container walls (Tinus 1978) and trials are being carried out with many forms of container design (Kinghorn 1978). These do not always prevent the downward growth of lateral roots though a chemical approach by Burdett (1979) is promising. His containers were coated with a root growth inhibitor, cupric carbonate, which prevents elongation upon contact with the container wall, but roots quickly resume growth after planting, in a similar way to those of a naturally established tree. Equally promising is the prospect of initiating more lateral roots by watering young trees with auxins (Selby and Seaby 1982).

While the pattern of root growth can be considerably influenced by nursery and planting practices the subsequent development of a root system can also be greatly affected by the soil and by cultivation and ploughing on the planting site itself.

Growth in relation to rooting characteristics

Many studies have demonstrated that in comparable conditions planted trees (both transplants and container plants) do not grow as well initially as naturally seeded material of the same age. Bare-rooted plants of most species may check during the year of planting, especially where there is much competing vegetation (Hellum 1978; Leaf *et al.* 1978). Spruces are particularly prone to this 'check'. Container-grown plants display a lack of root growth compared with top growth, and can have shoot to root ratios of over 25–30 per cent higher than natural seedlings of the same age after 10 years. This may be due to the difficulty roots have in some soils of moving from the medium of the container into the surrounding soil. The quality of plants produced by nurseries, especially the number of lateral roots, and the care taken in planting can both influence growth considerably (Grene 1978).

Size of plants

Variations in plant size in the seedbeds and transplant lines of forest nurseries, and in container plants, are usually obvious. It is desirable to know to what extent this diversity indicates inherent differences in vigour and how size might affect survival during the first few years after planting.

Work by Sweet and Waring (1966) with Japanese larch and birch suggested that early size variations found in nurseries arise by different rates of germination and variations in seed size as well as by genetic differences in vigour. They concluded that much of the normal size variation originates at the time of germination and is at least partly non-genetic in nature.

When outplanted in the forest, Pawsey (1972) showed that, within fairly wide limits, survival and subsequent growth in the field of different sized plants of *Pinus radiata* is essentially the same if the various size classes are planted *separately* but, where large and small seedlings are mixed together, the superior growth of larger plants can be maintained indefinitely by virtue of their original slight size advantage. He concluded that seedling size appears not to be a sufficiently reliable criterion of inherent vigour to warrant the rejection of small sized plants. However, in practice, mortality is often much higher with small plants owing to their more delicate nature, greater risks of desiccation, and susceptibility to weed competition.

Among conifers, bare-rooted transplants 30–40 cm tall are usually favoured but there are exceptions to this general rule on size, especially with some pines. For example the root system of *Pinus nigra* is particularly sensitive to damage during lifting from the nursery and transplants can suffer very heavy losses after planting. For this reason small sized container plants are often used even though they may require more weeding. With lodgepole pine large plants are very much more prone to basal sweep and early instability than small ones. With many broadleaved species, rather taller plants can be successfully used, and these often range up to 1 m in height, but sturdy transplants with at least a 5 mm root-collar diameter are usually the best choice.

Individual tree shelters

The establishment of broadleaved species is significantly helped by the use of individual tree shelters (Tuley 1983). These are plastic tubes, usually 1.2 m

FIG. 6.1. Tree shelter used for growing oak which, 3 years after planting, is already well over 1.2 m tall, about three times taller than unprotected trees (Bagley Wood, Oxfordshire).

FIG. 6.2. Five-and-a-half-year-old sessile oak (*Quercus petraea*) which were grown for the first 3 years in tree shelters.

tall with a cross-sectional area of about $80\,cm^2$ which enclose recently planted trees (Figs 6.1 and 6.2). During the critical first 3 years, height growth can be accelerated by three times in oak and several other broadleaved species: conifers are less responsive. This rapid growth reduces the period of susceptibility to weeds and frost damage. The shelters also give protection from smaller grazing mammals such as roe deer and rabbits and enable chemical herbicides to be used safely. On very weedy sites it is also possible to see clearly where the planted trees are.

Replacing dead plants

The replacement of dead seedlings (obscurely termed 'beating up' in Britain and 'blanking' in New Zealand) is often carried out as a routine measure after planting. It can be a very wasteful operation. The original crop has at least a year's start on the replacements which can fall far behind in growth; Chavasse *et al.* (1981), among other authors, state that they have a very remote chance of being included in the final crop. Nor, except at very wide spacings, does replacing dead seedlings normally have a significant effect on the original crop in terms of height or diameter growth or branch size. Unless failures are numerous, or planting very wide, or gaps very large, larger than the space occupied by one final crop tree (about 25 m²), replacement is not usually considered worthwhile. If it is necessary, then the plants used should be especially large and vigorous so that they are able to compete with the original trees. It is much better to try to ensure that the original planting is completely successful.

Planting methods

In spite of the fact that the way in which trees are planted is known to affect future rooting patterns, growth, and stability, planting is seldom given the care it deserves: tree planters are often paid according to how many trees are planted per day, not according to how well they are planted. It is well established, for example, that the growth of a tree after planting is positively correlated with the volume of soil disturbed. Mullin (1974) investigated how planting by two different squads affected the growth of red pine (*Pinus resinosa*). After 20 years one squad's planting produced a stand with 14 per cent more volume than the other's, indicating the long-term effect of bad planting.

FIG. 6.3. Planting trees in an upland forest at Eskdalemuir, south Scotland. (Photograph Ken Taylor.)

Many methods are used for planting bare-rooted trees and these often depend upon personal preference and experience. The simplest, and most common, is slit notching in which a single vertical cut is made with a spade (Fig. 6.3). The spade is then pushed backwards and forwards to break up the soil at the bottom of the notch and the plant inserted with the roots 'as well spread as possible' (Blatchford 1978). This inevitably leads to a bilaterally compressed root system, at best. The soil is then pushed back into position and firmed around the root collar without excessive compaction. On organic soils 'plugs' of peat are sometimes removed with semi-circular planting spades and then replaced after inserting the plant. On suitable terrain (usually relatively flat, stone, and stump-free sites), mechanical planting with modified agricultural 'cabbage planters', and other machines is sometimes practised.

The process of tree planting clearly introduces a measure of localized cultivation to the soil. It can vary from no more than opening a slit in the soil to digging a large pit in which the tree's roots can be spread. The much greater cultivation of the latter usually leads to better survival and, at least, initial growth, but these improvements are rarely considered justifiable because of the much greater costs involved. An experienced worker can, for example, plant about 200 trees a day by pit planting and up to 1000 by notching.

Position of planting

Planting positions are usually varied according to the method of ground preparation, expected competition from weeds, moisture regime, and exposure. On drought-prone sites, planting is often done in a ploughed furrow so the plants can benefit from the weed-free conditions and moisture at lower levels. On wet ground, by contrast, trees may be planted on top of, or on a step in the side of an inverted ridge, to benefit from drainage (see Figs 4.2, 4.3, and 4.5). Steps are used when the ridge is very thick or the site severely exposed. Where conditions are less extreme plants are inserted directly into the normal unprepared soil surface. This is also done on most second-rotation sites which are being replanted, where any form of ground preparation may be too costly, because of old stumps. On wet replanted sites, elevated positions beside old stumps are often sought, so the young trees will benefit from the slightly improved drainage.

Time of planting

The prospects for successful establishment are greatly improved if bare rooted stock is planted when it is dormant. The planting season in the British Isles where soil moisture conditions are seldom limiting and where snow and frozen ground is unusual can therefore extend from November to about the end of April. This season can be lengthened by up to 2 months if plants have been kept in cold storage (Brown 1971) thus, effectively increasing their period of dormancy. Container plants can be planted throughout the growing season if winters are not too severe and summer droughts unlikely.

With broadleaved and coniferous bare-rooted plants, opinion is often divided as to whether planting should be carried out in the autumn and early winter, or in later winter and early spring (Blatchford 1978). Sometimes there may be no choice because of the size of the planting programme and the labour force available to carry it out. Local preferences are often unconscious expressions of anticipated peaks of root growth potential (see next paragraph) for the area and species. This is particularly the case in Europe where the importance of root growth potential is less well understood than in north America. In Britain, spring planting tends to be favoured for conifers in upland forests, and in the lowlands autumn planting is generally preferred. In climates with a prolonged dry season and where winter snow and frost are normal, the planting season may be very short indeed if success is to be assured and it will vary according to the particular climatic conditions (see Chapter 3).

Survival is critically influenced by the root growth potential of newly planted trees; this is the ability to initiate, or elongate new roots shortly after outplanting (Ritchie and Dunlap 1980). Typically this potential increases during the autumn and winter months, peaks in late winter or early spring, and declines rapidly just prior to vegetative bud burst. There may sometimes be a minor increase in mid or late summer. It is also lower on sites suffering from drought. Survival is illustrated for one particular year on an upland site in Northern Ireland (Fig. 6.4), when March and April planting gave the

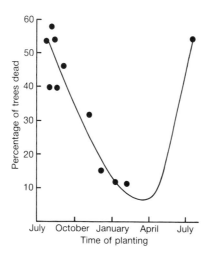

FIG. 6.4. Effect of the time of planting on mortality of Sitka spruce planted on deep peat in Northern Ireland (N. Ireland Forest Service, unpublished).

best results. Though this is commonly the case, very dry windy weather in early spring can, and sometimes does, result in high mortality.

Pattern of planting

Plantations are almost always established using regular spacings to ensure a reasonably uniform development of the crop. This involves planting in lines which can easily be followed, at least in one direction. It is most common to plant in a rectangular rather than square pattern, with the wider spacing of 2.2 m or more between rows to facilitate the passage of tractor-borne implements and to make such operations as chemical weed control cheaper.

The actual density adopted varies according to species, sites, and management intentions. It aims at the best compromise between establishment costs, the likely costs of future operations, and the expected value of produce. There are no definite rules but commonly close spacings are used to eliminate competing vegetation quickly, reduce fire risk and improve upward development in many broadleaved species. Wider spacings are more appropriate to fast-growing species, especially in areas which will never be thinned and where early thinnings are unprofitable.

Planting mixtures of species and 'nurses'

Pure even-aged crops tend to predominate everywhere that plantation forestry is practised due to their economic advantages. Management, work in the forest, harvesting, and marketing are all simpler. Mixed crops, and especially uneven-aged mixtures, have certain biological and aesthetic advantages, besides a few economic ones. For example, mixed stands may be more flexible in meeting market demands and mistakes with species selection are not so serious. However, the most common reasons for planting mixtures are for amenity and nature conservation, for providing early returns from a conifer, when a final crop of broadleaved species is intended, and for the 'nursing' effect of one species on another.

Nurses perform one or more of three functions. The first is to suppress competing vegetation rapidly. The second is to protect tender species from frost and exposure during their early years when they are particularly sensitive. Beech, several silver firs, and western hemlock may all grow better initially if mixed with a faster growing nurse or if planted under the canopy of a near-mature crop.

The third use of nurses is on impoverished sites where one species may benefit the nutrition of another. Nitrogen-fixing species, whether trees, such as many alders, shrubs, or even herbs are often used as nurses, but other trees can also benefit nutrition. For example, O'Carroll (1978) found that on a peaty podzol in Ireland, Sitka spruce, intimately mixed with Japanese larch or lodgepole pine, grew significantly better than spruce alone (Table 6.1 and Fig. 6.5) due largely to improved nitrogen nutrition caused especially by the larch.

How this improved nutrition is brought about is not clear but it may be by mobilization and rapid turnover of nitrogen by the deciduous larch. Similar effects have been reported on peat sites in Scotland by McIntosh (1983), and Evans (1984) gives several examples of the growth of broadleaved trees being improved by Japanese larch and Scots pine.

Table 6.1   *Effect of Japanese larch and lodgepole pine on growth and foliar nutrient contents of Sitka spruce (from O'Carroll 1978)*

Treatment	Mean height at age 18 (cm)	Height growth in year 18 (cm)	Foliar nutrient concentration (percentage dry matter)		
			N	P	K
Pure Sitka spruce	119	10	1.11	0.16	1.08
Spruce/larch	295	34	1.58	0.21	1.24
Spruce/pine	151	16	1.42	0.17	1.08
Least significant difference (LSD) 5%	23***	12***	0.23***	0.03***	NS

FIG. 6.5. Larch (left) in this mixture is benefiting the growth of the companion Sitka spruce.

There is also a growing interest in 'self thinning' mixtures for use on sites of high windthrow risk where thinning operations may be too dangerous (Lines 1981). These can be achieved by planting mixtures of species with different growth rates or by using fast and slow growing provenances of the same species, such as Queen Charlotte Islands (fast) and Alaskan (slow) Sitka spruce. The slow growing trees might limit the branch size and core of juvenile wood of the faster ones before finally being suppressed, leaving the stand effectively at a wider spacing.

Except for the last type, most mixtures are difficult to manage because the more valuable or long-term species is often slower growing. If thinning and liberation is delayed this species can easily be suppressed and lost.

FIG. 6.6. A planted mixture of oak (*Quercus petraea*) and Norway spruce (*Picea abies*). One row of oak alternates with three of spruce. These two species have very similar early growth rates and are often planted together in Britain. (Bagley wood, Oxfordshire.)

Planted mixtures are commonly made in alternating numbers of rows of the different species. In southern Britain one or two rows of oak are usually planted between every three, four, or five rows of Norway spruce (Fig. 6.6). More rarely oak is planted in groups of at least nine trees, within a matrix of the conifers. Such practices should be avoided on hillsides where they can result in unsightly striped or chequer-board effects. The important principle is, however, to ensure robust mixtures, that is mixtures in which a small amount of neglect will not irreparably impair the long-term potential of the final crop, and usually slower-growing species.

Some broadleaved species, most notably oak, require fairly dense stand conditions to ensure the development of a reasonably formed stem and upward growth. Growing oak in mixture with carefully chosen conifers, or using other naturally occurring woody growth such as coppice or naturally seeded birch, alders, or willows, should always be used if the only alternative, because of cost, is widely spaced planting of more than 3 m apart.

7. Weed control

A plant is usually regarded as a weed if it grows where it is not wanted and is a positive nuisance in some way. Weeding is necessary in forestry to eliminate or suppress undesirable vegetation during the early stages of a tree crop.

Weeds compete with young trees for light, water, and nutrients and hence retard growth. In areas which suffer from drought, or even mild summer water deficits, weed control may be critical for the survival of young trees and it can result in dramatic improvements to growth (Fig. 7.1). In an experiment in southern England Sitka spruce, which was kept totally weed-free, and also supplied with any deficient nutrients, is growing at a yield class of $32\,m^3\,ha^{-1}\,yr^{-1}$. This is 30 per cent more than the normal maximum of $24\,m^3\,ha^{-1}\,yr^{-1}$ (Rollinson 1983). Other examples are illustrated in Figs 7.2 and 7.3. Regrowth from stumps after thinning can also compete for resources. Such regrowth following the first thinning of *Pinus pinaster* plantations near Perth, Western Australia, reduced volume

FIG. 7.1. *Pinus pinaster* at Lowe, France. Disc cultivation for weed control has been carried out between lines on right and no cultivation on left. The improved growth on the right is probably due to better moisture retention in the soil during dry weather. (Photograph J. H. Williams.)

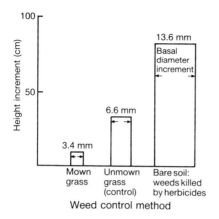

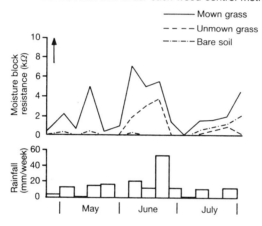

FIG. 7.2. First-year growth of cherry (*Prunus avium*) subject to three different weed control methods, and the effects of these methods on soil moisture between late spring and midsummer. (From Evans 1984.)

increment in the remaining crop by 16 per cent over 5 years through competition for limited soil moisture (Butcher 1980). Where water is not so limiting, it may still be necessary to control weeds to prevent them smothering young trees or to reduce the risk of fires.

Competition involves removal of an essential factor from the site, but some weeds are also allelopathic in that they form chemical compounds which are toxic to, or inhibit, potential competitors. Baker (1974) states that allelopathy of this sort seems to be proven in a growing number of cases.

Angiosperms provide the great majority of weeds though ferns such as bracken may also be important in forests. When disturbance first comes to

FIG. 7.3. One-year-old sugar maple (*Acer saccharum*) demonstrating the importance of good weed control. Foreground left — good growth in bare soil maintained by herbicide; foreground right — poor growth in dense clover; middleground right — very poor growth with mown grass sward.

an area of natural vegetation like woodland the weeds which appear are often species which are native to the area, whereas agricultural weed floras may contain a substantial proportion of non-native species as well. Weeds are nearly always present, at least in the early stages, in the life of a plantation. The main exception is on some man-made wastes. Though they lack the suddenness of severe outbreaks of insect and fungal pests, it has been estimated in the United States that agricultural crop losses due to weeds amount to 12 per cent of potential production. This is more than losses caused by all other pests combined (Worsham 1982).

Forest weeds are not wholly detrimental. Fryer and Makepeace (1977) state that they may, for example, provide habitats for predators of organisms which damage crop plants. (They may also be hosts for organisms that attack the crop: for example species of *Ribes* are alternative hosts for the fungus *Cronartium ribicola* which causes 'blister rusts' on five-needled soft pines.) Weeds, like surface litter in forests, can be useful in protecting soil structure, preventing erosion, and acting as a temporary 'reservoir' for nutrients in young crops, nutrients which might otherwise be lost from the site. In the sense that many woodland weeds may be part of a natural or semi-natural community of organisms, any reduction in the diversity of vegetation will affect nature conservation value of the site.

Species are not necessarily weeds throughout the whole of their ranges. Thus bramble, *Rubus fruticosus*, is a serious problem in many lowland British forests but not generally in continental Europe. The bracken fern, *Pteridium acquilinum*, is ubiquitous, yet is only recorded as a serious forest weed on acid soils in north-west Europe, and *Rhododendron ponticum* only becomes aggressive and very difficult to deal with in the wetter and milder western parts of Britain and Ireland where it is one of the few exotic forest weeds. Nor are weeds necessarily considered serious problems under all silvicultural systems within a particular area. Heterogeneous systems in both agriculture and forestry are often characterized by a lack of weeds, as well as pest and disease problems. Clear-felling and replanting usually cause the worst difficulties.

Characteristics of weeds

An 'ideal' weed has a number of the special characteristics listed in Table 7.1. Many are characteristics of '*r*'-selected species (p. 173). Fortunately no plants have all these features but those that have none, or very few of them, are unlikely to be weeds.

Table 7.1 *Ideal weed characteristics (adapted from Baker 1974)*

(1)   Germination requirements fulfilled in many environments.
(2)   Discontinuous germination (internally controlled) and great longevity of seed.
(3)   Rapid growth through vegetative phase to flowering.
(4)   Continuous seed production for as long as growing conditions permit.
(5)   Self-compatible but not completely autogenous or apomictic, though ecological races often found.
(6)   When cross-pollinated, unspecialized visitors or wind used.
(7)   Very high seed output in favourable environmental circumstances.
(8)   Some seed produced in a wide range of environmental conditions, tolerant and plastic.
(9)   Adaptations for short- and long-distance dispersal.
(10) If perennial, vigorous vegetative reproduction, or coppicing ability, or regeneration from fragments, and mechanisms that permit survival under temporarily unfavourable conditions, e.g. altering growth and development in response to changes in environment.
(11) If perennial, brittle, so not easily pulled from the ground, or unpalatable to grazing animals.
(12) Ability to compete interspecifically by special means (rosette, choking growth, allelopathic chemicals).

These characteristics lead to the problems which cause plants to be called weeds: they establish themselves without deliberate action by man; they are difficult to control because they are competitive, adaptable, and tend to form extensive populations.

Strategies of weed control

In forest plantations, crop trees suppress most competing herbaceous and many woody weeds once the crowns begin to touch. Weed control is normally only important before this stage. Unlike annual crops, if the growth of a forest plantation is somewhat slowed for a few years by competition with weeds, the economic losses are likely to be relatively small, provided that survival has not been badly affected. After the initial establishment period, crop trees at the thicket stage may sometimes need liberating from unwanted perennial weeds, often naturally seeding species of trees such as birch, and from climbers and coppice regrowth. This is done before, or at the latest, at the time of first thinning. The operation is usually called 'cleaning'.

The advantages of much enhanced early growth through nearly complete weed control are rarely realized in forestry because total control is very costly. Timber crops are seldom so valuable that they can carry the accumulated interest charges for intensive weeding operations incurred at the start of the rotation, to the time of clear-felling. Furthermore, many weeds provide a source of food for herbivores such as deer, voles, rabbits, and sheep. In their absence, the planted trees could be severely browsed and for this reason alone, complete control is not considered desirable. Until the advent of chemical herbicides it was only possible by mulching, regular hoeing or complete ploughing. Weeds also provide cover for rodents and a reduction in cover can prevent damaging increases in their populations. Traditionally, complete control has only been carried out with species such as poplars, which are grown rapidly on short rotations, or with allelopathic weeds, such as dense heather on sites planted with spruce though with this problem an application of a nitrogen fertilizer may be as cost effective, and occasionally where weeds are a major fire hazard.

Five major techniques of weed control are practised in forestry and effective and rational control involves a judicious mix of those appropriate for a given situation.

1. *Fire* is occasionally used to clear rank ground vegetation before planting, an example being heather burning. It is very cheap though risky in the vicinity of plantations.

2. *Chemical herbicides* provide a cheap method of weed control in plantations, though the use of chemicals may be forbidden by law in some places, such as British Columbia. Herbicides may act through:
   —leaves and only kill the parts of the plant touched, for example paraquat.
   —leaf translocation to kill whole plants, for example 2,4-D and glyphosate.
   —roots, via soil application, for example atrazine and hexazinone.

Herbicides are applied by:
— ultra-low-volume sprayers, especially controlled droplet size applicators which require very little water. They can only be used where spray does not drift much.
— medium- or high-volume knapsack sprayers.
— granules which indicate which areas have been treated.
— tree injection.
— surface wiping of foliage using a wick-like applicator.

Chemical treatments are relatively cheap and can be very effective for a long period but require skilled operators as the risks from using inappropriate chemicals, wrong dosages and spray drift are particular dangers to sensitive trees, where careful placement may be needed. Some chemicals are also highly toxic to man and animals. The timing of application and area treated around each tree are important attributes of success.

3. *Cultural control* methods are commonly used *before* planting in both forestry and agriculture, usually by cultivation to produce strips of temporarily weed-free soil for planting. After planting cultural methods include the use of:
— mulches such as peat, bark, polythene and felt which suppress weed growth. These are expensive and more commonly used in arboriculture than in forestry.
— hand control of weeds using grass hooks, scythes, and other cutting tools can be useful to supplement chemical or other practices and where weeds can be dealt with easily. The skill required is small, costs of equipment very low, but control is effected for short periods only. Risks to trees by cutting are slight and to operators, low.
— machine control, includes the use of portable hand-held machines such as brushcutters and clearing saws, pedestrian-controlled machines such as reciprocating cutters, and tractor-mounted machines including flails and cutting or crushing rollers. Mechanical treatments can be as cheap as chemical ones, but require somewhat less skill and are safe for operators. They are effective for a short period only because they do not kill the weeds and can involve expensive equipment. Risks to the crop are small if done carefully.
— grazing by domestic stock can be a valuable means of control in older plantations.

Much effort in weeding is often devoted to grass cutting. Insley (1982) has shown that in the British climate at least that, unless the grass physically smothers the trees, cutting alone does not result in significantly better growth than under free-growing swards and may even be positively detrimental (Davies 1984).

4. *Crop competition.* Shading out of weeds by the planted trees is an important constituent in weed control. It does not often eliminate a problem but can influence the extent and duration of serious competition. It is determined by initial spacing, size of transplant, rate of growth and choice of species among other factors.

5. *Biological control* with plant pathogens is not yet used on any significant scale, even in agriculture, but has potential. Examples of successful biological control includes the control of the prickly pear cactus (*Opuntia* spp.) in Australia by larvae of a moth introduced from Argentina. Inoculation of oaks with the oak wilt fungus, *Ceratocystis fagacearum*, has been used in Minnesota to convert marginal oak stands to pine. This was found to be cheaper and more efficient than the once conventional use of 2,4,5-T because of lower costs, easier application, greater mortality, and total lack of injury to other tree species. Though little spread of the fungus has occurred between treated areas and adjacent oaks, this technique met violent objections because of the possibility of oak wilt becoming epidemic (French and Schroeder 1969; Wilson 1969). Other examples of biological control are given by Templeton (1982).

The most desirable strategy of weed control, which can sometimes eliminate or greatly reduce the need for additional measures, is to ensure rapid establishment to harness the competitive ability of the trees themselves. Additional help can also be provided by cultivation which is, in Britain, the most widely used method of controlling grasses, herbs, heather, and sometimes bracken. Where the site is nutritionally impoverished and needs drainage, serious weed competition can be virtually eliminated by ploughing. The vegetation is buried under spaced, inverted plough ridges and by the time it begins to recover the tree crop is well on the way to occupying the site and has a lead which makes further control unnecessary.

On more fertile sites, especially second-rotation ones, there may be a rapid invasion of grasses, herbs, bracken and other ferns, and some woody weeds for which chemical herbicides are now the main counter. They may often be treated in the summer before planting. Weed tree species are seldom very numerous and are usually controlled by hand or machine cutting. More competitive weeds, including broadleaved coppice such as oak and birch, and *Rhododendron ponticum* are the most troublesome. Coppice regrowth is initially far more rapid than the growth of newly planted trees and, to enable the latter to survive, it is necessary to apply herbicides to cut stumps or to control shoots by frequent herbicide and/or cutting operations. This can cost several times more than the original cost of planting. Recommendations for Britain are described by Evans (1984). Though all the methods described have a definite place in crop establishment, expenditure on weeding has tended to decrease steadily since the mid 1960s. This is attributed by Holmes (1980) largely to the advent of chemical herbicides. Chemicals have often reduced the need for grass/herb weedings to one per season where two or three were necessary before. Similarly on sites covered with some woody weeds, only one chemical treatment may now be necessary in the life of the crop instead of many hand or machine cutting operations. A greater acceptance for environmental reasons of naturally regenerating native species among planted crops has also reduced the need for control, especially at the cleaning stage, as have reductions in the establishment period caused by more effective use of fertilizers, cultivation, and more appropriate sizes of planting stock and species.

Chemical herbicides

The discovery of the herbicidal properties of 2,4-D in 1944 and its subsequent widespread use heralded the rapid development of a large array of available

Table 7.2 *Common herbicides and their use in forestry*

Chemical	Weeds killed	Use
Ammonium sulphamate	Coppicing species	Applied to freshly cut stumps and regrowth. Not entirely effective.
Asulam	Bracken	Selective foliar spray. Many conifers and some broadleaved species unharmed.
Atrazine	Grasses and herbs	Selective pre-emergence spray for many 'soft' grasses. Most conifers not injured but broad-leaved species are, unless dormant.
Glyphosate	Heather, bracken, woody weeds and grasses	Foliar spray and useful for injection or application to cut stumps. One of the most effective of all herbicides. Many conifers unharmed, but only at certain times of year.
Hexazinone	'Coarse' grasses	Foliar and ground spray. Many conifers unaffected at certain times of year.
Paraquat	Grasses	Foliar non-selective spray. Kills green parts of most plants which it touches, but not roots. Very dangerous if inhaled.
Propyzamide	Grasses and some herbs	Applied as a spray to ground in winter to prevent regrowth. Many trees unaffected.
Terbuthylazine	Grasses	Selective pre-emergence spray, similar to atrazine but safe to use with broadleaved trees and sensitive conifers.
2,4-D	Heather	Selective foliar spray for many dicotyledonous herbs and some shrubs particularly heather. Should not be used on broadleaved crops but safe for many conifers.
2,4,5-T	Woody weeds	Selective foliar spray and useful for injection and application to cut stumps. Many conifers unharmed. Because of fear about dangerous contaminant (dioxin), now rather seldom used; largely replaced by glyphosate.

herbicides. Many are selective in that they only affect certain groups of plants, a feature of particular value in planted crops because this often makes it unnecessary to protect the crop from the chemicals, for example when killing grasses and broad-leaved weeds among conifers. Hence application is much faster and more economical. Selectivity is relative, not absolute, and means that under a given set of conditions certain species are killed or seriously injured whereas other plants are not injured. However, a given herbicide is selective only within certain limits of dose, environmental conditions, method, and season of application. It is possible to injure or kill the crop if the selective herbicide is not used properly. The chemical properties and mode of action of most currently used herbicides are described by Ashton and Crafts (1981), and recommendations for their use in particular circumstances by Fryer and Makepeace (1977, 1978) and in numerous other publications, including manufacturers booklets.

Future herbicide development seems likely to be through the use of placed applications, and enhancement of existing herbicides by surfactants which are chemicals to aid the penetration of the herbicide through relatively impermeable leaves and subsequent absorption, for example, control of *Rhododendron* by glyphosate has been improved by the addition of an oil-surfactant (Clipsham 1984), and mature bracken can be effectively controlled by asulam to which diesel oil and an emulsifier has been added (Preest *et al.* 1978).

The chemicals most commonly used in forestry are shown in Table 7.2.

8. Nutrition

Attitudes towards the use of fertilizers in forests have changed considerably during the course of this century, largely as a result of the great increase in planting. In the late nineteenth and early twentieth centuries the accepted view that 'almost any soil can furnish a sufficient quantity of mineral substances for the production of trees' (Schlich 1899) contrasts with the now commonplace use of fertilizers to correct deficiencies. Miller (1981a) contends that there is no great disparity between these outlooks: an understanding of nutrient cycling in forests has shown that while fertilizers can do much for forests *prior* to canopy closure, thereafter the nineteenth century concepts, which related to closed canopy forests, remain true. Such forests have efficient nutrient-conserving mechanisms but during the years before the canopy closes, while trees are accumulating nutrients to build a canopy, growth is dependent on the availability of soil nutrients. It is during this period that fertilizing and other practices developed in agriculture can be used to advantage by foresters. They have been discussed in detail by Bowen and Nambiar (1984).

Nutrient requirements of trees

Plant growth can be substantially reduced if there is an insufficient supply of any of at least twelve nutrient elements listed in Table 8.3 (p. 106). These exclude carbon, hydrogen, and oxygen, which are derived from the air and from water, and others such as sodium, silicon, and cobalt, which may be beneficial under some circumstances and for some species. The importance of each is discussed by Mengel and Kirkby (1978) among others. When a nutrient, or indeed any other factor such as soil water, soil oxygen, or light, is present in a critical concentration it can assume enormous importance and may far outweigh all other factors in determining the health and growth rate of a crop. A recognition of this led Mitscherlich (1921) to propound his 'Law of minimum' which, as stated by Baker (1934), is that 'by bringing any factor nearer to the optimum level will increase the yield of a crop, but increasing factors that are markedly deficient will increase the yield disproportionally.' It is helpful in silviculture, and especially in the field of nutrition, to look for such limiting factors when confronted with the many that are integrated together to produce a certain growth or yield effect since by modifying these the greatest improvements can be made.

Recent investigations of ecosystem processes, especially those that lead to the transfer, transformation or accumulation of nutrient elements have

Table 8.1 *Nutrient uptake in various crops and ecosystems*

Vegetation type	Uptake (kg ha^{-1} yr^{-1})			Source
	N	P	K	
Douglas-fir (2nd growth in USA)	39	7	29	Young (1967)
Corsican pine (pole stage crop in Scotland)	22	6	28	Miller *et al.* (1976)
Oak, hornbeam, beech (Belgium, 30–75 years old)	91	6	52	Duvigneaud and Denaeyer-de Smet (1970)
Oak, ash, hazel (Belgium)	123	9	99	Duvigneaud and Denaeyer-de Smet (1970)
Birch (on fen in England)	56	4	28	Ovington and Madgwick (1959)
Heather moorland	42	4	11	Frissel (1977)
Unimproved grassland	44	4	25	Frissel (1977)
Winter wheat	95	21	147	Frissel (1977)
Barley	57	11	40	Mengel and Kirkby (1978)
Potatoes (tubers only)	90	15	140	Mengel and Kirkby (1978)

contributed greatly to knowledge of forest nutrition. Few have contributed more to this than Miller (1979, 1981*a,b,c*) and his work is drawn upon here. It is now clear that annual rates of uptake of major nutrients in closed forest plantations are similar to those measured for other vegetation types, as shown in Table 8.1. Average rates of dry matter production are also similar (Jarvis 1981). However, an essential characteristic of most forests is the development of a distinct forest floor which results from the return, through litterfall, of leaves and other tree debris. Two-thirds to three-quarters of the nutrients absorbed from the soil and atmosphere each year are returned to the soil and they eventually become available for re-use by the trees. A detailed account of the various cycles within the ecosystem, whereby nutrients move between the living vegetation, the soil organic layers and the lower soil horizons is given by Miller (1979). He also describes the geochemical cycle in which nutrients enter a forest site in rainwater, as aerosols, and as dust trapped on tree surfaces, through absorption of gases and through biological fixation of nitrogen. Nutrients also move within a tree as a result of current nutrient uptake, moving recent uptake into temporary storage, and subsequently mobilizing it during the growing season or withdrawing it from ageing tissues.

Forest fertilizing — principles

As a result of investigations into ecosystem processes, Miller (1981*b*) has proposed three concepts relating to forest fertilization which have done much to rationalize the huge amount of sometimes apparently contradictory information on the potential role of fertilizers in forests.

(1) Generally fertilizers benefit the trees, not the site

Following application, fertilizer nutrients rapidly become distributed between the trees, the ground vegetation, the forest floor, and mineral soil horizons. A small amount may also be lost through leaching or, in the case of nitrogen, gaseous diffusion, but the forest floor and surface horizons are remarkably effective in retaining received nutrients, more so than under other forms of vegetation. If the trees are suffering from a deficiency of an applied nutrient, they will show a response, typically for a period of 5–10 years. Whether the additional amount of nutrient that promotes the improved growth in the years after application is derived from reserves stored in the tree or in the soil or is the result of a more rapid cycle between the two, is then important in relation to the nature and timing of fertilizer application.

There are normally two response patterns. The first (Figs 8.1 and 8.2) is shown by all fertilizer treatments and consists of a rapid increase in growth, followed by a slow and progressive return to preapplication growth rates.

In the years immediately after fertilizer application, the trees make no greater demands on the soil and organic matter than in unfertilized areas unless rooting is greatly enhanced. Improved growth is therefore normally

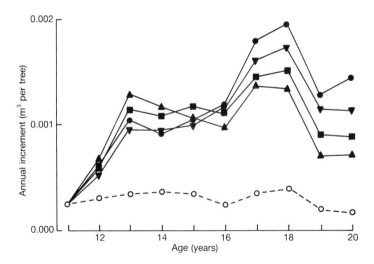

FIG. 8.1. Volume growth of *young* Corsican pine (before peak of current annual increment) showing that once response to fertilizer treatments (solid lines) has finished, growth rate remains *above* the level of unfertilized trees (dashed line). By age 20 nitrogen concentrations in foliage were no longer different between treatments. (From Miller 1981*b*.)

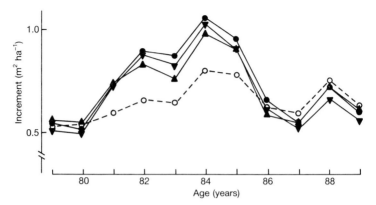

FIG. 8.2. Basal area growth of *old* Scots pine (after peak of current annual increment) illustrating that once response to fertilizer treatments (solid lines) has finished, growth rate falls *below* the level of that in unfertilized trees (dashed line). (From Miller 1981*b*.)

explicable in terms of nutrients accumulated in the tree's tissues immediately after fertilizer application in excess of requirements for growth. This explains why improved growth continues in the years after treatment, at least until the time when concentrations in the tree's tissues fall to pretreatment levels. Thus, it is the trees, rather than the site itself, which normally benefit from fertilizers. Applications should be timed to maximize both the rate of uptake and the storage within the trees. Because much of the storage occurs in foliage, it is important not to allow crowns to become too sparse before applying fertilizers.

Only in some heavily fertilized areas does the second pattern sometimes emerge in which growth remains consistently faster than in less heavily treated areas. In such cases, the amount of applied nutrient retained in the site is large in relation to its original capital. This results in a long-term response.

(2) Response to fertilizers is best considered as a reduction in rotation length

There is little to contradict the idea that fertilizer response can be adequately described using the simple analogy of an acceleration through time. This is because crops eventually rejoin the growth curve (Fig. 8.3) at a point commensurate with their development stage, or size, rather than chronological age. They jump several years ahead and eventually grow faster, or slower than a similar untreated crop depending upon which side of the growth curve is being considered. Depressions in growth of fertilized trees are commonly observed in older crops once the response period has ended (Fig. 8.2). Similarly in younger crops, growth never falls to the level of that of unfertilized trees on an age basis (Fig. 8.1) *but this does not mean that there is a continuing long-term response.* Apart from possible effects on wood

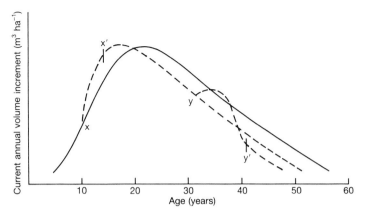

FIG. 8.3. Hypothetical growth curves illustrating that trees fertilized at points x and y will, once response to fertilizer has finished, follow growth patterns (dashed lines) parallel to, but ahead of, the curve for the unfertilized trees (solid line) from points x' and y'.

properties, for example a reduction in specific gravity (Heilman *et al.* 1982*b*), there is no evidence that a fertilized crop will differ significantly from one which has not been fertilized but grown over a longer rotation.

(3) Fertilizer requirements alter with development stage

There are several distinct stages in the life cycle of a plantation crop (Fig. 8.4). In Stage I the crowns are developing and need large amounts of all nutrients, little of which are returned through litterfall. During most of this period the trees are not fully using the site. Much of the soil volume and a large part of the nutrient input in rainwater is taken up by weeds. Although, in most soils, the amounts of potentially available nutrients are relatively large compared with the amount in the crop, and although the trees are able to obtain nutrients from fairly intractable soil sources, there are many soils, such as peats in Britain and Ireland, in which one or more nutrients may be in very low supply (Miller 1979). This is, therefore, the stage when the supply of available soil nutrients is likely to be the critical factor controlling the rate of crown development, and response to a range of fertilizer nutrients may then be expected.

By Stage II, which begins at the time canopy closes, immobilization is reduced and continues only in the trees' woody components. Although nutrient uptake rises to high values and tends to come to a peak shortly after the age of maximum current annual increment, most is recycled. During this period *nutrient cycling*, both within the ecosystem as litterfall, crown leaching, root death, and root exudation, and within the trees themselves becomes the dominant process. It is also the time when the capture by the tree crowns

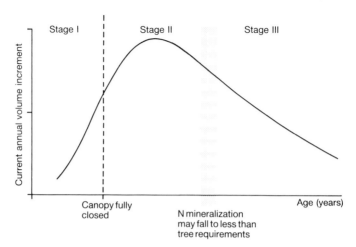

FIG. 8.4. The three nutritional stages in the life of a forest stand. (From Miller 1981*b*.)

and the retention of atmospheric nutrients from rainwater, aerosols, dust, and gas is most efficient. These natural inputs may balance losses from the mean annual removal of wood, at least for elements other than nitrogen and phosphorus (Miller 1979). Improved cycling of nutrients and enhanced input means that for many elements the demands made on the soil nutrient capital may be very low, often so low that supplies are usually adequate and hence responses to fertilizers are unlikely.

Anything in Stage II or later that reduces foliage biomass, such as thinning, causes a partial reversion to Stage I. A crop may therefore respond to fertilizing with nutrients originally found to be deficient in Stage I. So, even in Stage II which is generally unresponsive, fertilizers can be used on deficient sites to accelerate recovery from thinning or perhaps insect defoliation, though if there was no serious deficiency in Stage I no response to additional fertilizer would be expected.

During Stage III nutrient immobilization continues at a low rate within the trees but the increasing rate of immobilization in the soil organic layers may sometimes be well in excess of input, particularly beneath some species of conifers and on very acid soils. For nitrogen at least the quantity which is effectively removed from the cycle in this way can exceed the amount accumulated within the trees. This immobilization can lead, on sites of low capital, to nitrogen deficiencies later in the rotation. Eventually, at an advanced age, a crop's demands for nitrogen may fall below the rate of mineral nitrogen production and a natural recovery from a deficiency may be observed.

The time at which a crop enters Stage III depends upon the available nitrogen capital of the site. On sites where there is little it may set in soon after canopy closes with virtually no intervening Stage II. Where the nitrogen capital is higher, deficiency will appear much later, or even not at all.

A fourth Stage has been proposed by Heal *et al.* (1982) which occurs immediately after clearfelling. At this time, a high input of crop residues, cessation of tree uptake, and, initially, little uptake by a sparse ground flora allows decomposition processes totally to predominate. Nutrient retention is at a minimum through lack of plant uptake and increased runoff. Nutrient, and especially nitrogen, losses may be increased considerably, especially in areas favoured by high decomposition rates. A prudent forester takes advantage of these available nutrients by planting a successor crop as soon as possible after felling.

Thus, fertilizers are most likely to be useful before the canopy closes or towards the end of a rotation. During the early years when the trees are very dependent on soil supplies, almost any nutrient element may be deficient. Although tree roots are not exploiting the site efficiently and uptake and requirements are at their lowest, this is the time when judicious fertilizer application can most influence the subsequent development of a stand, perhaps cutting many years off the rotation length. Late rotation deficiencies are, by contrast, almost entirely of nitrogen.

Forest fertilizing in practice

Though fertilizers have been investigated and used to correct nutrient deficiencies since the mid 1800s in parts of continental Europe (Baule and Fricke 1970), it was largely in countries concerned with afforestation of poor sites with exotic conifers that advances were made. Thus, New Zealand, Australia, and the United Kingdom were among the first to apply nutrients on an operational scale, though forest fertilizing has been much more widely practised since the mid-twentieth century. In Britain, as in most other countries, it is almost wholly the major nutrients, nitrogen, phosphorus, and potassium that may be deficient, and of these, phosphorus is by far the most significant in improving growth during the early years of a crop's life. This is because many rocks and soils are naturally deficient in phosphorus. The most deficient soils are normally highly weathered, leached, and with thick surface organic horizons and peats. In extreme cases, as on many blanket peats, trees will scarcely grow at all without added phosphorus.

Though nitrogen is one of the most abundant elements in forest ecosystems, it is not contained in any soil minerals and most must be supplied from decaying vegetation. Deficiencies occur commonly in coniferous forests in cool climates where deep organic layers develop as a result of slow rates of decomposition. In Britain, serious deficiencies of available nitrogen occur on many peats. In very young crops they can be overcome temporarily by applying phosphate which increases nitrogen mineralization for a time, but from about the time canopy closes, frequent applications of nitrogen may be necessary to maintain growth (Dickson and Savill 1974) since recycling is not fast enough. The possibilities of at least reducing these problems by applying lime, to raise the pH to promote more biological activity and hasten mineralization are showing some promise on an experimental scale (Dickson 1977). In Germany, liming is also sometimes done to improve the biological properties of acid soils so that they are capable of carrying stands of broad-leaved trees rather than only conifers (Baule and Fricke 1970). Nitrogen deficiencies also occur on sandy heaths, especially well-ploughed ones where mineralization of organic debris is faster than the supply, and the most extreme problems are found on 'soils' such as sand dunes and some opencast mining sites where there is virtually no organic material present.

Potassium deficiencies become most obvious in vigorous young stands, especially where a nutrient imbalance has been created after applying nitrogen or phosphate. Frequently symptoms disappear naturally as the excess of other nutrients becomes reduced. Potassium enrichment to aid frost resistance has almost become a routine practice on pines in Thetford forest in eastern England.

Among other nutrients, magnesium deficiencies arise occasionally. Copper deficiencies are found on some sites where organic nitrogen mineralizes very fast, such as some cultivated heathlands and also on some peats (Binns *et al.* 1980). Douglas-fir is particularly sensitive to copper deficiency. Iron deficiencies occasionally appear on highly calcareous soils especially old arable sites, such as in pine/beech mixtures on chalk downland in southern England. Defiencies of other elements, such as boron, are known in many other temperate countries.

Very often deficiencies of more than one element occur at the same time, either because the site is deficient or because the application of one element may cause an imbalance and induce a deficiency of another.

Diagnosis of nutrient deficiencies

VISUAL SYMPTOMS

Serious deficiencies of many nutrients can be recognized by visual symptoms of colour or other features, particularly during the dormant season with evergreen conifers. The most common symptoms are summarized in Table 8.2 and have been described and illustrated by Binns *et al.* (1980) among others. The recognition of deficiencies in deciduous trees is more difficult and less well documented, partly because they tend to be grown on more fertile sites where nutrition is not a problem. Baule and Fricke (1970) illustrate some deficiencies of broad-leaved trees well.

Table 8.2 *Visual symptoms of some nutrient deficiencies in evergreen conifers*

Element	Visual symptoms
N	Usual dark-green colour of healthy foliage becomes *uniformly* paler, often yellow–green or yellow over the whole crown. Needles shorter and lighter in weight than healthy foliage. Height growth *suddenly* reduced. Leading shoot spindly. Form of tree unchanged.
P	No marked discoloration but needles dark, dull green. (P and N deficiencies often occur together in which case symptoms may be masked by N-deficiency symptoms). Needles are much reduced in weight and length; height growth reduces slowly and form of tree is unchanged except after prolonged deficiency when apical dominance may be lost.
K	With moderate deficiency in young trees, tips of needles at *top* of current shoots (or previous year's shoots in some pines) become yellow. In more severe cases, all needles on current year's shoots affected. On older trees, yellow tips are confined to older needles, often on lower branches only. Size of needles similar to that in healthy foliage. Growth not always significantly reduced except in cases of extreme deficiency and in very young trees. Form of trees unaffected, except in severe cases when apical dominance may be lost and a stunted, bushy habit develops, especially in very young trees.
Mg	Current year's needles become yellow from *base* of shoot upwards and yellowing spreads from needle tip downwards except in pines where all current needles yellow together. Often confused with K deficiency but transition from yellow to green is much sharper with Mg deficiency.

Sources: Binns *et al.* (1980); van Goor (1970).

Growth responses to an added nutrient can normally be obtained long before a visual symptom of deficiency is apparent, so prudent managers normally attempt to anticipate such serious conditions by other methods.

CHEMICAL ANALYSIS OF PLANT TISSUES

The concentration of elements within plant tissues can often reflect the nutrient status and health of a crop and is expressed diagrammatically in Fig. 8.5. Developing deficiencies can be detected by chemical analysis of tree tissues, using techniques developed by Leyton (1958). Conventionally, with evergreen conifers, samples of the youngest foliage from an upper whorl of branches are analysed. They are usually collected during winter, when foliar nutrient concentrations are fairly stable. There is less experience with deciduous species because they are more commonly planted on relatively nutrient-rich sites, but sampling is usually done in the middle of the growing season, July or August in Britain.

The concentration required for optimum growth varies between different parts of a tree and between species and even provenances. Optimum concentrations also differ according to which parameter of growth is being

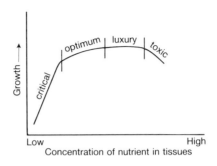

FIG. 8.5. Hypothetical relationship between concentration of a nutrient in tree tissues and growth.

considered. For example the optimum for height growth is often at a lower concentration than for volume growth. Concentrations also vary significantly with the size or age of the plant (Miller *et al.* 1981; Miller 1984). However, concentrations tend to be relatively uniform for a particular type of tissue, such as leaves, within a species at any development stage.

A deficiency may be considered to exist if the addition of an element to the soil–plant system in a suitable form and rate results in an increase in growth (Prichett 1979). However, it is not easy to define what critical or,

Table 8.3 *Ranges of nutrient concentrations found in some evergreen conifers (modified from Watts 1983)*

Element	Concentration of nutrient element (% of dry weight of foliage)		
	Severe deficiency	Slight/moderate deficiency	Adequate
N	1.0	1.3	1.5
P	0.08	0.13	0.15
K	0.3	0.4	0.5–0.8
Ca	0.05	0.07	0.1–0.2
Mg	0.03	0.06	0.12
S	0.05	0.14	0.16

	Concentration of nutrient element (p.p.m. of dry foliage)	
	Deficiency likely	Adequate
Mn	4	25
Fe	20	50
Zn	5	15
Cu	2.5	4
B	4	20
Mo	0.1	0.3

especially, optimum concentrations are, because levels which are adequate for tree growth in one set of nutritional and environmental conditions may become inadequate in others. Thus a critical concentration is an ill-defined value and may more accurately be considered as a narrow range of concentrations. Optimum concentrations tend to have a much wider range. An indication of the common ranges of concentrations is given in Table 8.3. It is also important that the concentrations of some nutrients should be in reasonable balance with those of others. If, for example, there is a radical departure from the ratios of N:P:K of 10:1:5, this might suggest nutritional problems.

SOIL ANALYSIS

Except in nurseries, equivalent techniques to those used in agriculture for detecting likely deficiencies by analysing samples of soil have proved difficult in forestry (Leyton 1958; Khanna 1981). This is partly because it is not possible to distinguish between *total* and *available* nutrient concentrations with current techniques, especially in organic soils which often predominate in forests, and in which deficiencies are common. Further complications arise because of soil heterogeneity and uncertainties about which soil horizons to sample because trees often root deeply and extensively throughout the profile. There is also a lack of information for interpreting test results in terms of tree responses to fertilizers (Prichett 1979). In spite of these problems soil tests, especially for phosphorus, have been developed and are being used in a few countries, including New Zealand (Miller 1981c), and the level of nitrogen in the humus has been suggested as a good measure of nitrogen status by Miller et al. (1977).

Fertilizer regimes

Experimental and other evidence of treating deficient sites has led to the development of recommended fertilizer regimes for different species and sites. The regime selected depends upon the finance available, among other factors, and if this is available, the growth rate at which the investment return is maximized may be selected. Examples of possible regimes and their effects on yield and rotation length of Sitka spruce in Scotland are given in Table 8.4.

Expensive high-input regimes necessitate relatively high and valuable outputs to justify the costs. There are frequent debates as to whether less expensive regimes based on lower inputs or less demanding and less valuable species might be more profitable especially where there are high risks to the crop from windthrow, fire, or grazing (Davies 1980; Lines 1980; Busby and Grayson 1981).

Table 8.4 *Three nutritional input options for Sitka spruce on unflushed deep peat (from Ogilvie 1983)*

Year	Low intensity	Intermediate	Extreme intensity
0	PK	PK	PK
3			PK
6			NPK
8		PK	
9		N	PK
12		N	NPK
15			PK
16		NPK	
18			NPK
21			PK
24			NPK
27			PK
Expected yield class ($m^3\,ha^{-1}\,yr^{-1}$)	8	16	22
Expected rotation length (years)	45	40	35

Types of fertilizers

Ideally, the fertilizers used in forests should be cheap per unit of nutrient, concentrated to allow low application costs from ground machines or the air, long-lasting, and unlikely to cause any pollution (Binns, 1975). Those used widely in forestry are shown in Table 8.5, with an indication of their relative costs. Detailed accounts of these fertilizers and their properties are given by Bengston (1977) and Prichett (1979).

Table 8.5 *Commonly used N, P, and K fertilizers and their costs*

Fertilizer		Nutrient element (%)	Cost tonne^{-1} fertilizer (£(1984))	Cost tonne^{-1} nutrient element (£(1984))
Nitrogen				
Urea	$(NH_2)_2CO$	46	125	272
Ammonium nitrate	NH_4NO_3	34.5	129	374
Ammonium sulphate	$(NH_4)_2SO_4$	20.6	76	369
'Nitrochalk' and similar materials (used in nurseries)	$NH_4NO_3 + CaCO_3$	26	103	396
Phosphorus				
Rock phosphate	usually $Ca_{10}F_2(PO_4)_6 \cdot x\ CaCO_3$	11–17	65	420–382
Superphosphate	$CaH_4(PO_4)_2 \cdot H_2O + CaSO_4$	8–9	85	1062–944
Triplesuperphosphate	$CaH_4(PO_4) \cdot H_2O$	19–21	149	784–710
Potassium				
Potassium chloride	KCl	50	101	202
Potassium sulphate	K_2SO_4	42	126	300

NITROGEN (N)

The two main choices among nitrogen fertilizers are between the large group of commercially available water-soluble fertilizers and the various so-called slow-release fertilizers. In current world-wide practice only two water-soluble fertilizers, ammonium nitrate and urea, are used to any significant extent (Bengston 1977). Both are concentrated and the cheapest forms of nitrogen per unit applied. There is evidence that in northern latitudes including Britain, ammonium nitrogen rather than nitrate nitrogen is the better source for getting nitrogen into the trees (Binns 1975; Bengston 1977). This could be because some mycorrhizal fungi can only utilize ammonium (Bigg 1982). In Britain the differences between the two in terms of response to equivalent amounts of N are small so in practice urea is usually favoured because it is cheaper and more concentrated, which makes it more economical to apply. It is quickly converted to soluble N by microbial activity. Slow-release sources of nitrogen such as urea formaldehyde and calcium cyanamide do not usually compare in effectiveness with water-soluble sources and they are generally too expensive to use in any case. Nitrogen is usually applied to crops at a rate of about 200 kg of element $N\,ha^{-1}$. If nitrogen is applied to young plants, care must be taken not to let the concentrated fertilizer touch the roots as this can kill the trees. There are, of course, also possibilities of using nitrogen-fixing plants to improve nitrogen nutrition, and use is being made of this technique in New Zealand, among other places (Miller 1981c).

PHOSPHORUS (P)

Phosphorus is usually applied at the time of planting at rates of between 50 and 125 kg of element $P\,ha^{-1}$. The choice is principally between water-soluble materials, such as superphosphate and triplesuperphosphate, and slowly soluble rock phosphate.

Rock phosphate, normally of north African origin, has proved to be of particular value on acid soils with a pH below 5.5 (Binns 1975) and is by far the most widely used source in Britain. Basic slag was once widely used on acid soils, but it is no longer available due to changes in methods of steel making, of which it is a by-product.

On soils with high phosphorus-fixing capacities, such as those derived from calcareous or serpentine rocks, rock phosphate becomes less available and so the more soluble and immediately available forms such as superphosphate are appropriate.

POTASSIUM (K)

Of the two common forms of potassium (KCl and K_2SO_4), only potassium chloride is used to any extent because it is cheap and easily available.

Potassium sulphate can be of value in rare cases where the absence of chlorine and/or the presence of sulphur are important, but few cases are known, and none in the British Isles.

MIXED FERTILIZERS

Extensive forest areas in Britain are often treated with both phosphorus and potassium and rarely with phosphorus and nitrogen (Binns 1975). Where P and K are needed together a physical mixture of rock phosphate and potassium chloride is normally applied. Granular fertilizers consisting of both materials have been made on occasions as they have better spreading qualities but are normally considered too expensive. Where urea and rock phosphate are required on the same area it is usually thought best to apply them in two separate operations, since their spreading characteristics are quite different. Elsewhere, for example in New Zealand, increasing quantities of high-concentration multi-element fertilizers are beginning to be used, in particular pelleted di-ammonium phosphate, 18 per cent N, 20 per cent P, (Will 1981).

SEWAGE SLUDGE AND ANIMAL SLURRY

Nutrients contained in sewage sludge and animal slurry can benefit tree crops in the same way as more concentrated natural or manufactured sources. There are several examples of successful trials in the literature (see McAllister and Savill 1977; Prichett 1979). Seattle in the USA, for example, puts all its sludge on nearby forest land but in general the enormous bulk of the material makes the costs of transport and application too high. It would require over 100 tonnes of slurry to supply the amount of phosphorus contained in half a tonne of rock phosphate which is the quantity commonly used per hectare on peats. With the same weight of rock phosphate 200 ha could be treated.

Methods of fertilizer application

Before the 1960s it was common to apply fertilizers by hand, as spot treatments in and/or around the planting holes. Subsequently it was found that broadcast applications over the *whole* of the site to be exploited by tree roots resulted in significantly better growth (Dickson 1971). Since then techniques, first for ground application by machines and later for aerial application (Fig. 8.6), improved and became much cheaper. By 1970 most fertilizer was spread by one of these two methods rather than by hand. Progress with aerial methods has been opportune because many young plantations are virtually impenetrable from the ground. There are still problems in obtaining acceptably uniform rates of spread from the air, though improvements in the form of fertilizers being used and the techniques of

FIG. 8.6. Applying rock phosphate from the air. (Photograph Ken Taylor.)

application are occurring. Will (1981) records that application rates in New Zealand have been reduced now that a relatively even spread can be assured in that country.

Season of application

Highly soluble fertilizers, including all commonly used sources of nitrogen and potassium, can easily be lost from a site by leaching if they are not applied during the active growing season. Though much still has to be learned about the timing of application, the normally recommended period is early in the growing season, between March and the end of June in Britain (Everard 1974), though Heilman *et al.* (1982*a*) found autumn applications of urea to Douglas-fir to be at least as effective. The time of application is not so critical with slowly soluble fertilizers such as rock phosphate which can be applied throughout the year.

Environmental implications

Indiscriminate application of fertilizers can result in the enrichment of drainage water and consequent eutrophication of streams, lakes, and reservoirs. In some circumstances algal 'blooms' may develop which can cause expensive blocking of filtering equipment from reservoirs; reduced oxygen levels can cause the death of fish and other aquatic life. Fertilizing of non-forest land can also enrich and destroy various habitats of rare plants, for example on boglands. Clearly guidelines for preventing such environmental damage should be followed and some have been given by Binns (1975). They include measures to minimize the contamination of water and sites of value, and avoidance of excessive soil enrichment by accurate and uniform application.

9. Spacing, thinning, pruning, and rotation length

The spacing between trees or stocking at which a crop grows affects the degree of competition in a stand. This influences mortality of trees, total production per unit area, the sizes to which individual trees will grow, and several aspects of wood quality. The value of timber, management practices, and costs are all affected by spacing. A clear understanding of the effects of possible spacing and thinning regimes on production is one of the most important aspects of silviculture since they influence the end use and profitability of a stand and, as with species selection, are directly under a forester's control.

Stand density relationships

MAXIMUM STAND DENSITY

In pure even-aged stands a site can only support a certain number of trees of a given size. Once it is fully occupied self-thinning begins to occur as individuals compete for resources. The maximum number which can be carried depends upon species and stage of development. Stand densities beyond a certain level can never be realized, however close the initial spacing may have been. As a stand becomes older and crown size increases, the upper limits of stand density become less.

At stand densities which cause tree mortality the relationship between average tree size and stocking can be represented graphically by a single line, irrespective of differences in age, site quality, or initial spacing. This can be interpreted biologically in terms of the relationships between crown area, stem diameter, and root competition which have a basis in physiological processes and which are genetically controlled. Though the environment can, and clearly does affect growth rate, it does not alter maximum average plant size for a given stand density, which is a phenomenon independent of age (Drew and Flewelling 1977).

Thus, Reineke (1933) found that the relationship between maximum number of trees and average diameter can be represented by a straight line when plotted on logarithmic paper and that for most species the slope of this line is constant, though its elevation (k) differs between species. Reineke represented the line by the equation:

$$\log p = 1.605 \log D + k \qquad (9.1)$$

where p is the number of trees per unit area, D their average diameter at breast height and k is a constant, which varies with species.

A very similar relationship has been found to be much more widely applicable than to trees alone by Yoda et al. (1963). They found that in all the plant species examined, including some herbs, the slope of the log weight–log density line to be nearly equal to $-3/2$ irrespective of the differences between species, i.e.

$$\log w = k * \log p^{-3/2} \qquad (9.2)$$

where w is average weight of surviving plants and p is density (Fig. 9.1). Though they used stand density as the independent rather than dependent variable, this equation is very similar to Reineke's if tree *weight* rather than diameter is considered. Tree weight is approximately proportional to the 2.5th power of diameter at breast height, so that Reineke's equation can be transformed to:

$$\log w = k * \log p^{-1.558} \qquad (9.3)$$

which is very close to the $-3/2$ found for other species.

The relationship given in equation (9.2) is found so universally among plants that is has been termed the *3/2 power law of self-thinning*. It is applicable to pure even-aged stands in which competition is severe enough for self-thinning to occur and is discussed in detail by Harper (1982).

A high stand density means that there are many relatively small plants per

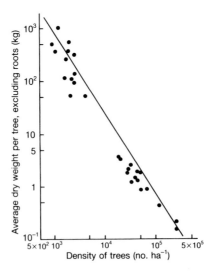

FIG. 9.1. 3/2 power law in natural pure stands of *Abies sachalinensis*. (From Yoda *et al.* 1963.)

unit area and a low stand density, few large ones. In forestry, as well as in agriculture and horticulture, it is usually undesirable to maintain crops at spacings which lead to mortality from competition. Thinning is practised with the result that if weight is plotted against stand density a point well to the left of the line is produced. It is never possible for a plant population to be represented to the right of the self-thinning line. In thinned plantations the steep slope of the 3/2 power line may never be reached, even though competition may be occurring. In spite of competition, as stands grow and fully occupy the site, the yield of dry matter *per unit area* rapidly becomes independent of the number of plants present; yield reaches a plateau over a wide range of initial planting distances, as illustrated in Fig. 9.2.

CROWN DIAMETER/BOLE DIAMETER RATIO

In considering the growth of individual trees rather than stands, the more space a tree has, the more it will grow in volume (but not in height, as is discussed below). Most intolerant trees maintain an almost constant ratio of crown diameter to bole diameter throughout the silviculturally critical part of their rotation. The ratio can slightly diminish with age, but has never been found to increase (Dawkins 1963). Thus, if the ratio is 20, a healthy tree of mean diameter d must, on average, have a crown $20 \times d$ across, and of course the same mean spacing between trees if it is not to become constricted. A knowledge of this ratio enables 'thinning regimes' to be drawn up quite easily, which depend on the diameter to be achieved, rather than age.

TREE HEIGHT/BREAST HEIGHT DIAMETER RATIO

The slenderness of a tree stem can conveniently be expressed as the ratio of total height to diameter at breast height (h/d). This ratio is relatively easily manipulated by spacing and thinning. The principle underlying the natural design of most trees is the maintenance of elastic similarity so when the curvature of a stem, caused by windsway or a branch by its weight, exceeds a specific threshold value, the stem or branch begins to increase in diameter. The mechanism which initiates this response is not known (McMahon 1975).

Thus trees in very crowded stands have much support from, and contact with, neighbours. They are thin and spindly and have high h/d ratios, usually of more than 100. Trees in more open-grown stands by contrast have much greater diameters for any given height, and hence lower h/d ratios. Similarly, slenderness decreases naturally among dominant trees and in thinned stands but not in unthinned stands, once competition has started. Any sudden exposure of trees in dense stands, for example by thinning, renders them far more susceptible to damage from windthrow and windsnap because they temporarily have an inappropriate h/d ratio.

HEIGHT/DENSITY RELATIONSHIPS

Unlike plant weight or stem diameter, the average height attained by the dominant trees in a stand is largely independent of density. Height, or conventionally *top height* which is the average height of the 100 largest diameter trees per hectare, has been found scarcely to vary at all with density in numerous coniferous species (Evert 1971). Slight decreases in height with decreasing stand density sometimes occur, especially with broadleaved species. Occasionally in over-dense stands on poor sites, height growth may also be depressed, but differences are small.

Spacing

From the relationships discussed above and in later sections the general effects of spacing on even-aged crops can be summarized as follows.

1. High densities result in the earlier onset of competition between trees and lead to higher mortality through self-thinning.
2. High densities are associated with greater total production per unit area than lower densities at any age since the resources of the site are fully used earlier in the life of the crop.
3. Once the canopy has closed in widely spaced stands and the site is being fully used, dry matter increment is essentially the same as in close spacings on the same site.
4. Low densities lead to greater volume production by individual trees because they are subject to less competition.
5. The height growth of dominant trees is little influenced by density.
6. Form factors increase and taper rates decrease in denser crops.
7. Wide spacings lead to larger branches, more knotty timber, a bigger juvenile core and, in some species, to wood of lower average density.

Since spacing influences total production and the dimensions of forest produce, it can have a profound effect on the value of a crop. It is important to know how stand density influences production and how it can be manipulated. This has now been worked out for most major plantation species. Many temperate countries have some form of production or yield models based on various spacing and thinning regimes.

In practice, there are two main aspects of spacing to consider: the effects of early or initial spacing and the effects of thinning. Initial spacings are sometimes the densities at which plantations remain (except for mortality) especially where thinning is uneconomic or leads to windthrow. In the British Isles planting spacings recommended for conifers have decreased from about 4500 stems ha^{-1} in the 1930s to about 2500 stems ha^{-1} in the early 1980s. The effects on productivity in a stand of Sitka spruce within and well below

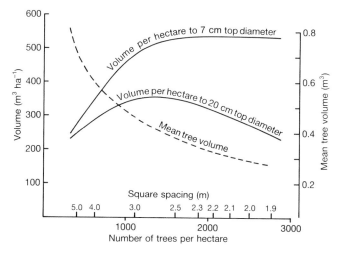

Fig. 9.2. Relationship between spacing and volume production and size distribution in unthinned Sitka spruce of 18.5 m top height. Total production (conventionally production to 7 cm top diameter) becomes independent of number of trees per hectare once densities of about 1500 stems per hectare have been exceeded. (From Kilpatrick *et al.* 1981.)

this range are shown in Fig. 9.2. In this example, when the stand was 18.5 m in top height, densities greater than about 1500 stems ha^{-1} gave very little additional total production of stemwood down to a minimum of 7 cm top diameter, but with fewer stems per hectare there was a rapid fall.

The fact that total production is not influenced by a very wide range of densities nor, as discussed later, by a wide range of thinning treatments and the fact that dominant height is independent of density led Eichhorn to infer that total production from a stand is a function of its height (Assmann 1955). This is the basis of practically all yield models for forecasting production.

Thus, by knowing the height of a stand and within a wide range of stocking levels it is possible to predict the total *cumulative* amount of timber produced since planting, i.e. the volume of timber standing plus any removed in thinnings. This can be done with acceptable accuracy whether the stand has been thinned or not, and irrespective of age. Total production is only one of the factors which influence value. The distribution of the volume in different size classes is often of greater importance because the size and number of stems influence the cost of harvesting and the markets to which the produce can be sold. Close spacing can result in reduced total production of the larger sized timber (Fig. 9.3) which is usually more valuable. Over long rotations, dense unthinned stands will give somewhat lower yields of usable timber than less dense crops due to mortality. This is illustrated in Fig. 9.7 (p. 123).

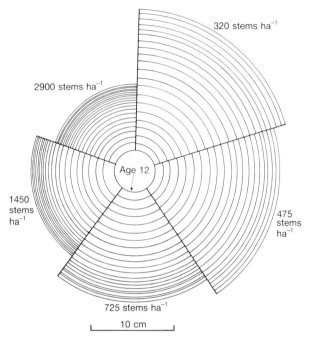

FIG. 9.3. Effect of spacing on mean tree diameter at breast height and annual ring
widths of Sitka spruce 32 years after planting. (From Savill and Sandels 1983.)

SPACING AND WOOD QUALITY

The faster growth of individual trees at wider spacings, especially among many
plantation conifers, causes an increase in the size of the core of juvenile wood.
Branches and hence knots are bigger and may be associated with more
compression wood. Fig. 9.4 shows how maximum branch size varies with
spacing in Sitka spruce.

A high wood density in conifers is usually associated with many desirable
characteristics, such as suitability for end uses requiring strength. In some species
like Sitka spruce and loblolly pine, which have strength properties close to the
lower limits for some industrial purposes, wide spacings may make the timber
unacceptable for uses which command high prices. Though spacing and thinning
both affect wood density in a stand, their influences are much less significant
than the genetic variation which exists from one tree to another. In both species
60–70 per cent of the total variability is associated with tree-to-tree variation
(Savill and Sandels 1983; Zobel et al. 1983). However, rapid growth in widely
spaced trees does result in relatively wide bands of lower-density earlywood being
formed, which alternate with narrow bands of higher-density latewood. The
uneven texture may make it unsatisfactory for some purposes, such as joinery.

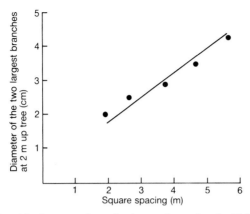

FIG. 9.4. Relationship between branch size and spacing in Sitka spruce. (From Kilpatrick *et al.* 1981.)

Table 9.1   *Effect of wider spacing on costs of operations (+ = higher costs, − = lower costs) (modified from Evans 1982*a)

Operation	Effect on unit cost	Effect on period of operation	Overall effect	Comments
Ground preparation	−		−	Wider spaced plough furrows, fewer pits
Planting	−		−	Fewer plants needed, fewer to plant
Beating up	+		+	Higher survival % more important
Tending	−	+	None	More opportunity for mechanization but fewer trees to tend though usually for a longer time.
Brashing			None	Fewer trees offset by thicker branches which take longer to cut
High pruning	+		+	Thicker branches
Fire protection		+	+	Delay in canopy closing lengthens period of risk from grass fires
Thinning	−		−	Fewer, larger trees can be removed to obtain similar volume
Harvesting (unthinned stands)	−		−	Fewer, larger trees to extract per cubic metre

OTHER EFFECTS OF SPACING

Because spacing influences the time when canopy closes, weed suppression is likely to be faster in closely spaced stands. This reduces weeding costs and fire hazard from flammable vegetation. Wider spacings require fewer plants which can save establishment costs. Spacing can also influence the period during which conditions for various animal and insect pests are favourable, and wide spacing will result in reduced natural selection or less opportunity for managers to select, and so possibly lower the genetic quality of the final crop. Spacing can also influence the costs of pruning, thinning, and harvesting as shown in Table 9.1.

Thinning

Thinning is carried out to reduce stand density and in so doing to reduce competition; the remaining trees have more space to grow and to put on increment. It is also normally done to provide the owner with some revenue though, if this is not possible, as with some early thinnings, it is carried out in the expectation of greater returns later in the rotation.

SILVICULTURAL CONDITION OF TREES

For many descriptive purposes and especially in thinning, it is useful to describe the silvicultural condition of a tree in terms of canopy position and tree form. In even-aged plantations the four position and three form categories shown in Table 9.2 are usually adequate, though in irregular forests and for certain types of detailed work, more categories may be needed.

Table 9.2 *Descriptions of silvicultural conditions of trees in even-aged plantations (adapted from Dawkins 1958, and Ford-Robertson 1971)*

Crown position	Definition
Dominant	Upper canopy trees with largely free-growing crowns exposed in entire vertical plan but usually in contact with others laterally.
Co-dominant	Upper canopy trees, similar to and often difficult to distinguish from dominants but crowns somewhat less free and more in contact with others.
Subdominant	Middle or lower canopy trees, partly exposed and partly shaded vertically by other crowns, but leading shoots free. Also known as intermediate or dominated trees.
Suppressed	Lower canopy trees entirely shaded vertically by other crowns. Also known as subordinate or overtopped trees.
Stem and crown form	
Good	Of good size and development, straight bole, circular crown.
Tolerable	Just in the satisfactory class, stem may not be quite straight or crown asymmetrical, or sparse.
Defective	Unsound individual rendered useless by some defect such as a bent stem, large fork, permanent stagnation or disease.

RESPONSES OF CROPS TO THINNING

Research into spacing, thinning, and primary production has indicated four main influences of thinning:

1. Provided a reasonably intact canopy is maintained, total production per unit area does not vary very much within a wide range of treatments. Hence, if there are relatively few trees, implying frequent heavy thinning, they will grow individually much faster in volume than where there are many (Hamilton 1976a, 1981).

2. The removal of suppressed trees, which may often be on the verge of death, has a negligible effect on volume increment per unit area but, if a proportion of the most vigorous trees are felled, there is an immediate reduction in increment because the remaining trees are not able to make full use of the resources of the site. Over a range of treatments, there is no permanent loss of increment; the stand not only recovers its normal level of growth, but also makes good the production lost when the increment was below normal immediately after thinning. The type of recovery pattern postulated by Bradley (1963) is illustrated in Fig. 9.5 and it can be seen that the length of the recovery cycle is proportional to the volume removed in thinning. The heavier the thinning, the longer the cycle. The reason for this pattern is not clearly understood but may be connected with the reduced level of stand respiration following the removal of some of the trees, making a greater net production possible for a period (see 3 below).

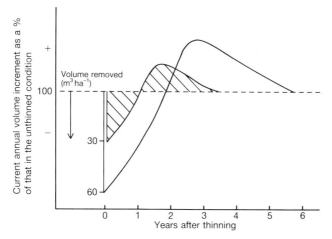

FIG. 9.5. Hypothetical relationship between volume per hectare removed in a thinning, and pattern of recovery of current annual increment. (Modified from Bradley 1963.)

3. If there is a large standing volume of timber and branches, as in a stand which has not been thinned, it will consume more assimilated carbon for respiration than where lower volumes are maintained through thinning, hence net production will be reduced in dense stands. The reduction will become more marked as the volume of standing timber increases.

4. There are two ways in which thinning practices can significantly reduce total cumulative production. The first is by consistently removing the most successful trees in the stand, the dominants, which are those most able to respond, and leaving the less efficient, smaller trees to grow. The second occurs if the intensity of thinning is so great that the site is not being efficiently used, when the crop cannot make up the lost production (Hamilton 1981). There may often be sound economic reasons for carrying out both these practices.

The precise effects of the interactions between the type, intensity, and cycle of thinning on *total* production have proved very difficult to determine with any precision over the range of treatments commonly used in plantation forestry. This is because differences are small and, for practical purposes, insignificant. The effects of these practices on the growth of individual trees are more clearly known and are of greater importance to managers.

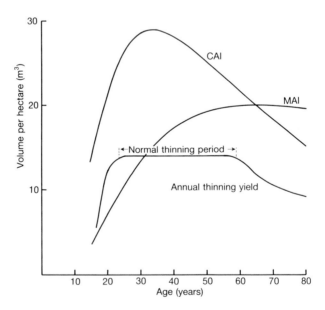

FIG. 9.6. Relationships between age, and mean annual increment (MAI), current annual increment (CAI), and annual thinning yields for yield class 20 m³ ha⁻¹ yr⁻¹ Norway spruce thinned at the marginal intensity. (From Hamilton and Christie 1971.)

THINNING INTENSITY

In an analysis of British thinning experiments by Bradley *et al.* (1966) it was shown that the proportion of growing stock which can safely be removed annually without decreasing future production is close to 70 per cent of the maximum mean annual increment over what is termed the normal thinning period. This period varies between species and between stands of different rates of growth within a species but occurs during the time when current annual increment is at its highest and ends shortly before the age of maximum mean annual increment. Annual thinning yields before and after the normal thinning period are lower. An example for a Norway spruce stand with a maximum mean annual increment of 20 m^3 ha^{-1} yr^{-1} is shown in Fig. 9.6. Here it is possible to remove 14 m^3 ha^{-1} yr^{-1} between the ages of 25 and 55 without prejudicing future production. If a stand is thinned at this 'marginal intensity', by the end of the rotation about half the total cumulative production will have been removed in thinning (Fig. 9.7). By contrast, in an unthinned stand of the same species, age, and growth rate, the standing volume will be about 10 per cent less than this cumulative total because competition will have caused some of the trees to die and hence some potentially useful production to be lost. In terms of basal area, 25 per cent

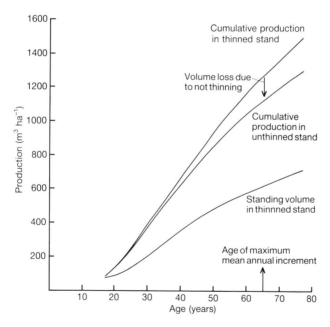

FIG. 9.7. Cumulative production in thinned and unthinned Norway spruce of yield class 20 m^3 ha^{-1} yr^{-1} and planted at 2500 stems per hectare. (From Edwards and Christie 1981.)

or more must be removed per hectare before any substantial increases in diameter will occur.

THINNING CYCLE AND TIME OF FIRST THINNING

The earliest a stand can be thinned without a loss in potential production varies in fully stocked stands between age 20 to 35 for most species commonly grown in Britain. At this time the total standing volume per hectare varies between about $70 \, \text{m}^3 \, \text{ha}^{-1}$ for light-demanding species, such as larches, to about $100 \, \text{m}^3 \, \text{ha}^{-1}$ for more shade-enduring ones.

After the first thinning, the cycle of thinning depends to a large extent upon the economics of the enterprise. A stand could be thinned every year but it is normally more profitable to obtain the benefits of scale, by thinning occasionally and heavily rather than frequently and lightly. Cycles are commonly adjusted to remove $40-60 \, \text{m}^3 \, \text{ha}^{-1}$ in a single operation. Thus a stand with a maximum mean annual increment of $10 \, \text{m}^3 \, \text{ha}^{-1} \, \text{yr}^{-1}$, thinned at the marginal intensity, can theoretically have $7 \, \text{m}^3 \, \text{ha}^{-1}$ removed every year. In practice it would probably be thinned on a 7- or 8-year cycle, to remove about 49 or $56 \, \text{m}^3 \, \text{ha}^{-1}$. In general, long cycles are associated with slow-growing crops and short ones with more productive stands.

If the cycle is excessively long, very large gaps will be made in the canopy and the site will not be fully used for several years. Losses in cumulative production will then occur even though the marginal intensity has not been exceeded.

TYPE OF THINNING

A certain intensity of thinning can be achieved in many different ways regarding the kinds of trees that are thinned. A useful indicator of the size of tree removed, and hence for describing the thinning type is the ratio of the mean volume of thinnings (v) to the mean volume of the stand before thinning (V). The types of thinning normally carried out may broadly be classified as follows:

		v/V ratio
1.	*Systematic or neutral methods*	
	line and strip thinnings	1.0
2.	*Selective methods*	
	Low thinning	about 0.6
	Intermediate thinning	about 0.8
	Crown, or high thinning	about 1.2
3.	*Combinations of 1 and 2*	
	e.g. Queensland selection thinning	variable

Systematic methods

Systematic thinning entails the removal of trees in a predetermined way, regardless of their individual size or quality. Complete lines of trees are usually removed, or strips which do not follow planting rows, though other systematic patterns are possible. The various types, techniques, and responses of crops to systematic thinning have been described by Hamilton (1976*b*, 1980).

Systematic methods are now very commonly employed as first thinnings which usually yield little income. Neither brashing nor selective marking of trees is necessary so costs are much lower. Also extraction routes for the first and subsequent thinnings are made (Fig. 9.8).

FIG. 9.8. A Lokomo forewarder using an extraction route made in a line thinning. (Photograph J. H. Williams.)

A disadvantage is that defective trees are not deliberately removed. The removal of a complete range of tree sizes, including some dominants, results in a loss of total cumulative production, often amounting to 6–8 m^3 ha^{-1} (Hamilton 1976*b*). If line thinning is only done once in the life of a crop, such losses are insignificant in terms of total production, amounting to about 1 per cent. However, even one line thinning may expose a stand to serious risks of windthrow (see p. 187), and to the development of some reaction wood on the exposed trees along the edges of lines.

Selective thinning methods

Low thinning is a selective thinning that particularly favours the dominants by removing trees progressively from the lower to the upper canopies. The

FIG. 9.9. Early selective low thinning in Norway maple (*Acer platanoides*) plantation; note spot marking of potential final crop trees.

first trees to be marked for removal are suppressed trees, then subdominants ($v/V = 0.6$); in heavy low thinnings some of the dominants may then be felled (Fig. 9.9). At the other extreme, crown thinning favours the most promising stems which are usually, but not necessarily, dominants. Theoretically trees from any canopy class which are interfering with selected trees may be removed. However, poorer quality dominants and co-dominants are usually removed and these have higher average volumes than in other types of thinning ($v/V = $ about 1.2).

The commonest type of selective thinning is intermediate between low and crown thinning ($v/V = 0.8$), but in all selective thinnings defective trees, especially defective dominants, are also removed. Included among numerous variations to methods, is the early selection of final crop trees in broadleaved stands, now widely practised in Britain and France (Evans 1982c). The best trees are marked early (Fig. 9.9) and favoured in subsequent thinnings. Because some inevitably become damaged, for example by squirrels, it is necessary to mark at the outset 2 or 3 times the number that will actually form the final crop.

The effects of the various types of thinning on crop productivity have been discussed in detail by Assmann (1970) and in the context of a classical British trial, the Bowmont Thinning Experiment of Norway spruce in Scotland, by Hamilton (1976a). At Bowmont four thinning intensities were applied, described as:

1. B grade—involving the removal of mainly dead and dying trees only, an extreme form of low thinning.
2. C grade—a moderate low thinning, intermediate between B and D.
3. D grade—a heavy low thinning in which only the best trees, mainly dominants, were left and given space for full crown development. It was somewhat heavier than the marginal thinning intensity.
4. LC grade—a moderate crown thinning, resembling D except that suppressed and subdominant trees were left to fill spaces between the best dominants. Defective dominants were removed.

The results (Table 9.3), 64 years after planting, in all treatments confirm the expected trends of larger individual trees being found in the heavier thinning treatments, but little overall difference in total production except in treatment B. As in wide spacing, the trees in the heavier thinning treatments tend to have lower tree height/dbh ratios.

Table 9.3 *Some results of the Bowmont Thinning Experiment (in Norway spruce) 64 years after planting (from Hamilton 1976)*

Treatment	No stems ha^{-1}	Top ht. (m)	Mean tree dbh* (cm)	Mean tree Vol. (m^3)	Volume per ha standing (m^3)	Cumulative crop yield to date Basal area ha^{-1} (m^2)	Cumulative crop yield to date Vol. ha^{-1} (m^3)
B	2204	19.6	21.7	0.333	733	109	861
C	1062	20.2	27.8	0.569	605	123	965
D	327	21.6	42.5	1.387	453	127	953
LC	691	20.9	30.2	0.641	443	128	924

*dbh = Diameter at breast height

The significantly lower production in treatment B, may partly be a result of a severe infestation of *Heterobasidion annosum* which existed, causing top dying. In Norway spruce and Scots pine, dense stands are more likely to be infected than those of low density (Belyi 1975; Tribun *et al.* 1983). It is also probably partly due to higher levels of respiration caused by the much greater volume of standing timber (p. 122).

Combinations of systematic and selective thinning methods

Where circumstances permit, there are attractions in combining some of the cost savings of purely systematic thinning with the ability to select for vigour and good growth form. The Queensland Selection method (Forestry Department, Brisbane 1963) is a combined method and was developed for treating Hoop pine (*Araucaria cunninghamii*) plantations in Queensland and has a wider potential for use in temperate forests.

It involves selecting dominant trees for retention and marking them in an obvious way, in Queensland by high pruning. The trees are selected by considering running groups of four trees (counting blanks as trees) on a row by row basis, for example:

S   S S S   S

1 2 3 4 5 6 7 8 9 10 11 12

Thus, the first group comprises tree numbers 1, 2, 3, and 4. Of these, 1 is the best stem and is selected and pruned. The next group is tree numbers 2, 3, 4, and 5, and of these 5 is selected. In the next group, 3, 4, 5, and 6, tree 6 is better than 5 and therefore the best in the group and is selected. In the next group, 4, 5, 6, and 7, tree 6 remains the best of this new group, so no additional tree is selected, and so on.

Selection can be done quickly by unskilled workers and results in about 40 per cent of the stems originally planted being selected, though the percentage can be varied by altering the size of the group.

Thinning rules can be applied equally simply in relation to the selected trees. For example, all trees which are equal in height or taller than the selected trees and adjacent to them may be removed in the first thinning.

PRE-COMMERCIAL THINNING

Thinning stands before trees are big enough to be sold is known variously as pre-commercial thinning, respacing, thinning-to-waste or unmerchantable thinning. It is often carried out at about the time canopy closes while access is still easy. The thinned trees may be killed chemically or felled and left in the stand.

In planted crops foresters have the options either of planting at the density required at the time of clearfelling or the first commercial thinning, or of planting more densely and carrying out a pre-commercial thinning. The arguments in favour of close planting and pre-commercial thinning have been discussed by Edwards (1980) and include more certain establishment, the opportunity for selecting the most vigorous trees, smaller branches, and narrow juvenile core. The disadvantages are mainly those of cost; establishment is more costly and the pre-commercial thinning itself is expensive.

Pre-commercial thinning is carried out in parts of north America and New Zealand where markets exist only for sawlogs. Foresters in the United Kingdom have similar difficulties in disposing of small sized material and there is an additional problem in crops established between the 1950s and 1970s. These were planted at rather high densities, in the expectation that normal thinning operations would be carried out. Subsequent experience has shown that many stands would succumb to windthrow if they were thinned, so a short-term problem has risen for ensuring that reasonable quantities of sawlogs will be available at the end of a rotation in which no commercial thinning can be done. Respacing is seen as one way of achieving this before crops reach a height at which they become susceptible to windthrow. The technique of chemical thinning and use of self-thinning mixtures are sometimes used, as well as conventional cutting of unwanted trees (see p. 188 and 86).

Pruning

Pruning may be done for one of two reasons:

1. Complete or partial low pruning (called brashing) to head height to provide access to stands, to make working easier and safer, and sometimes for lowering susceptibility to fire.
2. To improve the quality of timber by reducing the extent of knots.

The persistence of branches on trees varies with species and spacing. In similar conditions, tolerant trees retain living branches for much longer than intolerant species. Among the latter, the duration of retention of dead branches also varies considerably; larches and eucalypts self-prune well, while pines do not. Persistent dead branches can lead to the formation of loose or decayed knots. To obtain the economic advantages of clear pruned timber, the amount of knotty wood must be kept to a small core in the centre of the stem, usually no more than 10–15 cm diameter. Pruning such small stems necessitates the removal of living branches. If too many are removed in normal plantation conditions, the photosynthetic capacity of the tree is reduced and growth suffers. It is, however, possible to remove some branches from the lower crowns of trees without affecting growth because, in low levels of light, leaves on these branches may respire as much or conceivably more than they synthesize, and so contribute little or nothing to the tree. Wang *et al.* (1980), for example, found that removing 10 per cent or slightly more of the live crown of *Cryptomeria japonica* improved growth a little.

From a detailed survey of European and north American pruning experiments, largely in conifers, Møller (1960) concluded that the removal of up to 25 per cent of the live crown has no effect on the growth of most species. Removal of one-third of the crown reduces production by only a fraction of one per cent by the end of the rotation and in some species half or more can safely be removed. More severe pruning reduces both height growth, and even more markedly, diameter growth. Some species are more sensitive than others to increasing intensities of pruning. For example, Douglas-fir is more sensitive than spruces which, in turn, are more sensitive than pines (Henman 1963*b*). Excessive green pruning may sometimes lead to stress and all its attendant dangers of increased risks of attack by insects and pathogens.

Pruning young trees in very widely spaced stands may result in somewhat different responses. Funk (1979) found in 5-year-old black walnut (*Juglans nigra*) planted at 6.1×6.1 m that height growth increased over 3 years with increasing intensities of pruning (which ranged from no pruning to 80 per cent of the total length of the stem). Though volume growth did not differ among the various pruning intensities, increment was greater further up the stem in the more heavily pruned trees, making them more cylindrical. There were many more epicormic branches in the heavy pruning treatments.

Apart from eliminating knots, pruning may have other desirable effects on wood quality in some species. The removal of live branches can stop the formation of low-density juvenile wood in the pruned part of the stem of conifers. In *Pinus radiata* it leads to a temporary increase in wood density, by up to 7 per cent, for 2 or 3 years after treatment as a result of a greater proportion of latewood being formed. There may also be increases in fibre length and a decrease in spirality of the grain (Gerischer and de Villiers 1963). In some broadleaved trees, early pruning may also confine ring shake and discoloration to a small central core (Butin and Shigo 1981).

Where pruning is carried out it is normally done in up to four stages (Fig. 9.10) to achieve about 6 m of clear stem. Pruning in stages is necessary

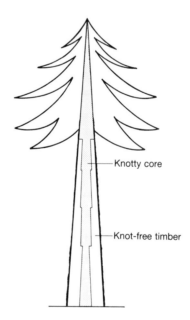

Knotty core

Knot-free timber

FIG. 9.10. Diagrammatic longitudinal section of a tree which has received four prunings at intervals of a few years. (From Henman 1963*b*.)

if the pruned core is to be kept small enough while sufficient crown is retained to maintain vigour. The first pruning often occurs when the breast height diameter of the tree is at a maximum of 15 cm and the stem is pruned to the point of about 10 cm diameter. The second occurs when the diameter at the pruned level has grown to 15 cm, and pruning continues up to 10 cm again, and so on. Detailed pruning schedules have been produced in some countries, for example in Japan by Fujimori (1980). It is difficult to manipulate even the longest pruning tools at heights much above 6 m, so if greater pruned lengths are desired ladders are needed which greatly increase the expense. It is seldom considered worth pruning unless the top diameter of the pruned section grows to at least 40 cm diameter over bark at the time of felling, hence only the number of trees likely to grow to this size, the final crop trees, is pruned. If selected trees are pruned heavily in dense stands, it will also be necessary to thin round them otherwise their dominance will be lost.

It is usually perfectly safe to remove live branches from trees without any undue risk of infection and decay, provided they contain no heartwood. This is especially the case with conifers. However, broad-leaved trees usually need pruning to prevent forking and heavy branching.

When trees are injured by pruning, or in any other way, wounds inevitably become infected, but trees are able to compartmentalize or wall-off the infected wound, confining it within the diameter of the tree at the time of wounding. Thus, if a tree is wounded when it is 10 cm in diameter, no more than a 10 cm core of defect may develop. The protective barrier zones formed have thin suberized cell walls which can become planes of structural weakness when stresses are set up. In highly susceptible species, notably oaks and sweet chestnut, they are thought to be a major contributory factor both to ring and 'star' shakes (Butin and Shigo 1981), defects which seriously reduce the value of the timber.

Apart from broadleaved species, where pruning may be essential if a stand of any value is to be obtained, pruning in the British Isles is practised comparatively seldom because there is little or no financial benefit. This is not so in parts of West Germany, where prices paid for pruned timber can be twice as high as unpruned. In some warmer temperate countries such as New Zealand and parts of Spain where growth is faster, pruning species like *Pinus radiata* may be a normal silvicultural operation because it is so profitable (Sutton 1970).

Rotation — clear-felling

The term rotation is used to describe the interval between successive crop regenerations. Rotations can be determined for technical reasons, for example growing to a specified log size, or for silvicultural reasons or for maximizing volume yields or financial returns. For some private woodland owners they may be determined by the need to realize capital or aid cash flow. Sometimes rotations are determined by force of habit or circumstances and they quite often remain undecided. However, in that plantation forests are usually established to fulfil a real or anticipated need, the tendency is usually towards short rotations (Fenton 1967).

The nineteenth-century concept of a 'normal forest' embodied the idea of an unvarying rotation (see p. 209). Today a fixed rotation could well be an obstacle to progress and the chocie of felling date is a subject for constant review, according to changes in the objectives of an enterprise or the circumstances which influence the method of attaining current objectives (Johnston *et al.* 1967). Management today is also more flexible because of opportunities for stand improvement, achieved through added fertilizers and tree breeding and other silvicultural measures.

Furthermore, the best time for felling a stand is usually considered in the light of what the whole of an enterprise has available and rotations are often varied from the best theoretical time so as to provide a measure of continuity of supply and of employment. It would clearly be unwise to fell large adjacent areas of woodland judged as overmature by current criteria as this might depress prices and have far-reaching amenity and conservation effects. In other circumstances, it might be prudent to fell some crops early to keep a new industry supplied. In many cases, when rotations are clearly laid down, they are simply rationing devices for allocating resources to wood-using industries.

Occasionally there are biological or silvicultural grounds for clearfelling at a particular time. For example, high windthrow hazard areas may be felled prematurely before windthrow sets in, and to achieve natural regeneration it may be necessary to fell during the period in the stands' life when it bears heavy seed crops, and in a particular year when seed has been produced.

Large forestry companies and state forest services usually consider the best time to fell is when stands yield either maximum net discounted revenue (NDR) or some other measure of profitability. In Britain, in the case of many conifers maximum NDR happens to coincide roughly with rotations of maximum mean annual increment, though in some cases rotations may be shorter by 10–15 years. For broad-leaved species like oak, longer rotations may be more profitable so that advantage can be taken of the sharp rise in value as trees move from the firewood/mining/fencing sizes to planking quality sawlogs or, for the very best trees, veneer.

In much of continental Europe quite different financial criteria are often used: the British use of NDR is considered inappropriate by continental foresters because it favours short rotations and consequently rather low-quality fast-grown timber. Continental forests usually have relatively well-distributed age classes. Foresters have not been primarily concerned with creating new forest resources by direct investment. For these reasons, crops are grown on longer rotations to yield maximum value at the time of felling. In northern Germany for example, high-quality valuable Scots pine is often grown on a 250 year rotation for joinery timber. On similar sites in Britain it is seen as more profitable to grow three or four rotations of Scots pine in the same period, or preferably four or five of Corsican pine, even though the sale price of timber at the end of each is considerably less.

Spacing, thinning, and pruning practice

In the words of Craib (1939), the purpose of most commercial forestry, and hence of manipulating spacing, pruning, and determining the length of rotations is 'the production of neither the greatest volume, nor the largest sizes in a given time, but the production of material which will most suitably fit the demands of the market, yielding, at the same time, the greatest revenue'.

Unfortunately, this is much more easily said than done. Many forest owners have a general idea of what they are trying to achieve but few know precisely what market demands will be decades ahead. Nor do they know the precise interdependence between growth and quality, and the effects of stand age, site and the costs of spacing, thinning, and pruning. The analysis and integration of numerous experiments is needed. A leader in this field is the New Zealand Forest Service which has developed an integrated modelling approach for *Pinus radiata* (Whiteside and Sutton 1983) able to predict, with great precision, the effects of almost any treatment on wood quality and subsequent value.

Practices differ very widely among countries. In some parts of Germany, Scots pine is planted at 10 000–18 000 trees ha^{-1}, 'a considerable reduction from earlier practice' (Otto 1976). Stands are thinned and pruned regularly and felled after rotations of about 250 years. In Britain, most conifers are planted at densities of about 2500 stems ha^{-1}. They are not always thinned because of risks of windthrow; pruning is seldom carried out and rotations are seldom longer than 70 years. At the other extreme, in New Zealand, where there is a surplus of plantation-grown timber for home demand, the main emphasis is upon producing high-quality knot-free timber for export. On some land, *Pinus radiata* is planted at densities of only about 200 stems ha^{-1}. Scrupulous attention is paid to pruning. Since canopy does not close until the end of the rotation, the grass growing among the trees is grazed or used for silage. Rotations are likely to be about 25 years with this regime, having been reduced from 40 years. It is clear that Craib was correct but regimes which achieve the best results differ widely, according to the economic and other conditions in a country and often according to the particular circumstances of individual owners as well.

Part C

Specialized forms of plantation silviculture

10. Plantations on derelict land

The artificial substrate and dereliction

A by-product of many mining and other industrial processes is the formation of much waste ground usually consisting of structureless material largely devoid of topsoil and subsoil. Such sites, epitomized by the colliery spoil heap in industrialized regions, are frequently ugly, may erode seriously, and become an environmental hazard. Quite apart from the loss of productive potential of the ground which has been spoilt, these other factors make rapid restoration an important priority. Experience has shown that the cost of restoring much of this kind of derelict land to agriculture is prohibitively expensive thus restoration, which for many is no more than the land being of reasonable shape and appearing green, is frequently 'solved' by planting trees. This brings more land under forest, especially in industrialized regions which often lack tree cover. However foresters should not welcome unreservedly the prospect of such planting. Derelict sites bring many problems and, even if establishment of trees is satisfactory on many kinds of sites, there is still considerable uncertainty whether a productive crop can be grown successfully.

Numerous kinds of industrial processes create waste land of which the principal ones are mining for coal and various ores, extraction of sand, gravel and clay, including china clay (kaolin), rock, and limestone quarries, and the deposition of waste products such as pulverized fuel ash and domestic refuse. The scale of dereliction relates not only to the kind of product being won but the way in which this is achieved. Deep mining yields tips and spoil heaps, opencast working in strip or surface mining involves removal and redistribution of large quantities of overburden, and accumulation of tailings in lagoons and rivers follows many metal extraction processes.

The greatest amount of dereliction occurs in industrial countries. Although usually less than half of 1 per cent of all land is degraded in this way such dereliction tends to occur in regions of high population thus magnifying the despoliation. As an example of the areas involved, Table 10.1 presents estimates for different regions of England and Table 10.2 the extent of land dereliction by opencast working in USA up to 1965 by causal industry.

Problems

The main problems on different types of derelict sites and the means of restoring a cover of vegetation have been described in detail by Bradshaw

Table 10.1 *Areas of derelict land in England (from Bradshaw and Chadwick 1980)*

| Region | April 1974 | | April 1974– March 1975 restored (ha) | April 1975– March 1976 restored (ha) |
	Derelict land (ha)	Justifying restoration (ha)		
North	9411	7757	498	700
Yorkshire–Humberside	5451	4635	256	313
North West	8015	7212	131	330
East Midlands	5171	4660	95	343
West Midlands	4667	4235	136	528
South West	6415	1762	56	39
East Anglia	1783	1280	26	61
South East	2360	1527	125	146
Total	43 273	33 068	1323	2460

Table 10.2 *Areas of derelict land in USA in 1965 resulting from opencast mining (from Bradshaw and Chadwick 1980)*

Type	Area (ha)
Coal	531 360
Sand and gravel	336 960
Stone	103 680
Gold	77 760
Phosphate	77 760
Iron	64 800
Clay	38 880
Other (mainly copper)	64 800
Total	1 296 000

and Chadwick (1980) and Fox (1984). The problems arise principally because the substrate to reclaim is almost always derived from mining or earth moving and is largely undeveloped subsoil or rock. That such conditions are inhospitable to plant growth are indicated by a virtual absence of natural colonization on many wastes (Fig. 10.1). This phenomenon is not exclusive to artificial substrates and can be found associated with volcanic lavas and ashes (Fig. 10.2), sand dunes, and along the course of retreating glaciers where development of soil structure may take up to 100 years. Time will eventually solve most of the problems, unless there is extreme toxicity, as the natural

FIG. 10.1. A reclaimed opencast coal-mining site in the south Wales coalfield, planted with Corsican pine 4 years previously. Note the almost complete lack of colonization by weeds of this shaley site.

FIG. 10.2. Experimental planting of lodgepole pine (*Pinus contorta*) in deep ash left after the Mount St. Helens eruption, Washington State, USA.

soil-forming processes take place, but the decades needed are unacceptably long.

The problems confronting successful afforestation are outlined below and fall into three main categories, those of soil conditions, exposure, and protection.

PHYSICAL CHARACTERISTICS OF THE SOIL

The physical conditions of many substrates arising from industrial processes are inhospitable for tree growth.

Structure and texture

The substrate is usually uniform shale, clay or hard rock with no organic matter and little biological activity to aid aggregation into a satisfactory structure. Such material, often made up of large solid particles, holds little water and where rainfall is intermittent, combined with the exposed condition of most sites, leads to rapid drying of the surface and consequent drought problems for newly planted trees. Another consequence of poor substrate structure and texture is the development of high temperatures at the surface, especially if the material is dark in colour. Lack of protective vegetation and a rapidly drying surface can result in surface temperatures well in excess of 40 °C on hot days.

In addition to these unfavourable inherent properties of many substrates is the effect of compaction caused by bulldozers and box-scrapers used in the early stages of restoration. Soils easily become compacted and consolidated and so present barriers to root growth and drainage. Compaction is a modern problem. Surface mining prior to the 1960s usually followed drag-line work and there was little modification or compaction to the rough topography that was left; good growth of many early plantings on such tips and unrestored ground is evidence of the very much more favourable rooting environment provided. Compaction not only affects the substrate but when topsoil is stripped and stored, often for many years while mining is in progress, and then respread on the surface it may not behave immediately as if it had never been removed. Storage in large heaps causes compaction, loss of structure, and loss of many of the organisms, such as earthworms, which aid nutrient cycling and plant growth. As is pointed out later in this chapter alleviation of compaction is an important stage in all reclamation work.

Drainage

The nature of the substrate, compaction, and poor reshaping all lead to problems of land drainage. Unless water can drain from a site, conditions for tree growth will be poor. However, the problem is not simply solved by ensuring adequate slopes and appropriately placed water courses for two reasons:

1. many substrates are easily erodible and rapid shedding of water can be a major hazard;
2. most water draining from derelict land has a high silt content and cannot be led directly into the natural drainage network of streams and rivers outside the site without first flowing into a pond to allow deposition of silt.

Stability

The physical composition of many waste materials combined with the lack of surface vegetation exposes them to erosion by wind and rain and the risk of landslips. The problem is worst on steep-sided tips and heaps but with some substrates even a slope of only 5 ° may slip under conditions of prolonged heavy rain as the material becomes more fluid. The Abafan disaster in South Wales bears testimony to this possibility.

CHEMICAL CHARACTERISTICS OF THE SOIL

Nutrient supply

Both the lack of organic matter and the unweathered state of much waste material can lead to nutrient supply problems. By far the commonest is a shortage of nitrogen: the total nitrogen content may be as little as 100 kg of N per hectare compared with figures of 750–1500 kg per hectare in normal topsoil. In addition to inherent nutrient deficiency is the lack of any effective pathway to aid nutrient cycling. Thus, until organic matter levels increase substantially, the successful establishment of tree crops depends on applying organic wastes, and to aid nitrogen enrichment, interplanting trees with legumes, using nitrogen-fixing species such as alders or *Robina*. The use of species which facilitate nutrient cycling such as the deciduous larches and broadleaved pioneers such as birches and willows is also important.

Toxicity

Some mining wastes contain high concentrations of elements which are extremely toxic to plants, notably copper, zinc, and lead. Even small amounts can be sufficient to prevent colonization while leaching of these elements can be a serious pollution hazard to rivers. Problems are worst on older mined wastes because methods of extraction were less efficient leaving more of the metal in the waste material. In Britain there are copper workings dating from Roman times where vegetation development is still sparse and there are many deposits and areas of land down wind from chimneys and flues polluted in the last century on which hardly any plant growth has occurred.

Acidity

The presence of pyrite (FeS_2) in some wastes, and especially the colliery spoils from deep mining, causes acidity as it weathers by releasing sulphuric acid. Low pHs of between 2 and 4 are inhospitable to many plants as well as leading to acidification of streams and rivers. The extent of the problem depends on quantity and particle size of the pyrite, but in serious cases it is sometimes necessary to wait until the pyrite has mostly weathered and the acid has leached from the soil.

   In arid climates, the oxidation of pyrite and other sulphates can result in accumulation of calcium and magnesium carbonates in the surface horizons. Sodium chloride in the ground water may necessitate the use of salt-tolerant plants. Salinity is not usually a problem in areas of plentiful rainfall where salts are leached from the soil. A few industrial wastes give rise to strongly alkaline substrates of pH 9 or more, for example pulverized fuel ash (PFA) and the waste from some soda ash processes. Once dumped, weathering takes place which will eventually lower pH to about 8, a level more amenable to revegetation.

Organic matter

Nearly all artificial substrates arising from industrial mining processes have very little or no organic matter. As has been mentioned this affects the biological, physical, and chemical characteristics of the substrate.

EXPOSURE

Trees planted on many derelict sites are frequently exposed both to wind damage and to airborne pollution.

Wind

The lack of vegetation on many sites and often the nature of the local topography on reclaimed sites leads to high exposure of the planted trees. As well as impairing growth and leading to poor form this causes two direct problems to newly planted trees. First, a common phenomenon is for young trees to socket in the planting hole. Where the substrate consists of large angular particles and stones such socketing or swaying in the wind can lead to abrasion and damage to the bark and cambium at the root collar. Secondly, the dry surface, so characteristic of many wastes, is readily eroded by wind exposing the roots while the fine gravel and sand whipped up will abrade the young trees.

Airborne pollution

Most reclaimed sites are in large industrial areas where atmospheric pollution is a common problem. Many trees, particularly conifers which bear their foliage all the year round, are more susceptible to airborne pollution than annual plants or deciduous trees. Sulphur dioxide emission from various industrial processes involving the burning of hydrocarbons is perhaps the commonest though not the only pollutant. This environmental hazard further stresses trees used in rehabilitation and affects the choice of species.

PROTECTION

Mammal damage

Trees planted on reclaimed waste are particularly susceptible to damage from rabbits, hares, and livestock, because there is very little other vegetation to browse. If such animals get on to the planting site their only food, often for many hectares of land, is the trees planted at regular intervals. Browsing by a few animals can devastate a young plantation in a few hours.

Fire

Although very young plantations on reclaimed sites are not particularly susceptible to fire damage because there is little other vegetation which is inflammable, once they have reached the thicket stage fires become a serious hazard. This problem is exacerbated because, as has been mentioned, many such sites are in industrial regions and areas of high population. Thus not only is the crop itself a hazard but the risk of a fire starting is high.

Restoration of sites for tree planting

RESTORATION PLAN

In the past, thought was seldom given to the restoration of a tip or opencast mine as it was being worked. This frequently led to the most inhospitable environments to work with. Happily this is rarely the situation today and plans for satisfactory restoration are prepared as part of the whole operation. Thus the organization undertaking the extractive mining or spoil deposition becomes responsible for the condition of the site afterwards and it is very much in their interest to leave the ground reasonably shaped and as suitable for revegetation as is practicable (Fig. 10.3). Agreeing the need to conserve topsoil, planning site drainage, avoiding high walls where cliffs are left exposed, and ripping compacted surfaces can all be included in the plan.

FIG. 10.3. The entire area in the photograph is restored land following opencast coal mining in the upper Neath valley, south Wales. Note gentle slopes, sympathetic landforms, and ripped cultivation lines ready for planting. Fencing is essential to prevent sheep browsing of young trees.

SITE PREPARATION

All site preparation has three aims:

(1) to leave a safe and stable substrate;
(2) to shape the restored ground in ways which blend with the local landscape;
(3) to make the site hospitable for trees.

This section is principally concerned with the third of these aims.

Retaining topsoil

The difficulty of revegetating many wastes and derelict areas is caused by the extremely unfavourable physical characteristics of the substrate. This is most simply and easily overcome by respreading a layer of topsoil, or subsoil, once reshaping operations are finished. Ideally topsoil should be respread to a depth of 50 cm or more. A greater depth may be necessary where the soil is also being used to bury toxic wastes or deposits in the underlying substrate. The most obvious source of such soil is from the ground before it is worked. An important part of the operational plan of any mining activity should be to provide for removal and storage of topsoil and subsoil for subsequent respreading when restoration begins.

Microtopography

It is clear that the physical condition of many substrates can lead rapidly to extremes of drought or waterlogging. This can be substantially alleviated by ensuring that there are no flat areas or large depressions where water will accumulate. Gently rolling ground with slopes of 3–5 ° are ideal.

Recent work in Britain has demonstrated the value of shaping the ground into a system of ridges about 30 m wide (Figs 10.4 and 10.5) and with the top 1–1.5 m above the intervening furrow (Binns and Crowther 1983). The line of the ridge itself should also slope gently.

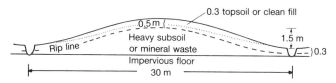

FIG. 10.4. Landform for restoration over impervious materials. (Vertical scale ×2 horizontal.) From Binns (1983).

FIG 10.5. Restored opencast mining site showing ideal ground configuration of long low ridges which slope gently both lengthways and either side down to the 'gully' between the ridges.

Alleviating compaction

Restoration of a site to an acceptable landscape form and creation of the appropriate microtopograph usually necessitates heavy earth-moving machinery. This work inevitably leads to compaction, a condition which must be alleviated before planting. This is achieved by deep tining and recent developments in Britain using a winged tine to lift the soil slightly as the tine moves through it have proved effective (Binns and Fourt 1980).

Improving nutrition

Application of fertilizers may be necessary, especially nitrogen. Heavy applications of organic wastes such as sewage sludge, composts, and slurry are useful for improving the organic matter content, providing some nutrients and as a buffer to toxic metals in lower horizons. Overcoming problems of high acidity are solved partially by heavy applications of lime if it can be well mixed to a depth of 50 cm or more. However, this needs careful management as too high a pH can lead to loss of nitrates through leaching.

Other preparation

Unlike a great many planting sites, restored derelict land will not normally require weed control. The need for adequate protection was noted earlier.

CHOICE OF SPECIES

The nature of reclaimed sites necessitates use of species which are tolerant of exposure, undemanding, or will fix their own nitrogen. Such characteristics are those associated with pioneer species and it is not surprising to find they dominate the species choice. Alders and *Robinia pseudoacacia* are outstandingly valuable in most temperate climates as they fix nitrogen and tolerate moderate compaction as well as acidities down to pH 3.5. Heilman (1982) showed that *Alnus rubra* on opencast mines in Washington, USA, can accumulate nitrogen at rates of between 10 and 80 kg of N ha^{-1} yr^{-1}, and this is sufficient not only to provide for the needs of the species but also to build N levels for use by succeeding tree crops.

In recent years the importance of alders in reclamation planting in Britain has diminished owing to occurrence of deaths and dieback on many sites at the sapling stage. Initially growth is vigorous but after a few years stagnation frequently sets in and 'distress' flowering is exhibited; the reason is thought to be drought and poor water relations generally (Evans 1984).

Many tree species will grow if the pH is at least 4, including larches, many pines, oak and birches; recommendations for Britain classified according to substrate texture are given by Binns and Crowther (1983).

ESTABLISHMENT

Supplementary vegetation

It is common to sow a sward for ground cover, to help build the soil and sometimes to prevent surface erosion. Among grasses for British conditions, *Cynosurus cristatus* and *Agrostis tenuis* are favoured as they are not too competitive with the trees. Legumes include clovers and relatively unpalatable species such as everlasting peas (*Lathyrus sylvestris* and *L. latifolius*), French lilac (*Galega officinalis*), and the prickly gorse (*Ulex europaeus*) (Binns and Fourt 1981). These are receiving increasing attention. Tree lupins (*Lupinus arboreus*) are extremely valuable pioneer plants (Marrs *et al.* 1982) believed to be able to extract some nutrients from sources unavailable to other species.

Planting

Though direct seeding has been successful where conditions are suitable, it is most common to establish trees by planting transplants. The principles do not differ from the establishment of any other crop but because of the more difficult site conditions it is more important that the plants are healthy and have a good store of nutrients, and that they suffer no desiccation or other damage between lifting from the nursery and planting.

11. Short-rotation crops

In temperate regions short-rotation crops may be considered as ones grown on rotations of less than about 30 years. Many such crops are broadleaved and worked as coppice but there are also some short-rotation plantations grown for specialized products, notably poplars for peeled veneer, for packaging material, and matchsticks.

Plantations

Poplars

There are about 30 species of poplar. They occur throughout the northern hemisphere in most of the boreal and temperate zones between the subarctic and subtropical regions. Most poplars are planted for screening, shelter, and/or production of matchwood and chip baskets or vegetable crates (Fig. 11.1). The estimated area of poplar plantations in the EEC countries where they grow best (Germany, Netherlands, Italy, France, and Belgium) is almost 400 000 ha with the equivalent of a further 160 000 ha grown in lines round fields (Crichton 1982). In Britain, where the climate is much less

FIG. 11.1. Line plantings of poplars in the Netherlands as windbreaks and for production of veneer-quality butt logs.

suitable for poplars, the total area is only about 12 000 ha. A comprehensive account of poplar and willow cultivation is in FAO (1980).

Because of the importance of resistance to infection by the bacterial canker *Xanthomonas populi* only a few poplar species and cultivars are planted. These are mostly hybrid black poplars (*P.* × *euramericana*) derived from *P. deltoides* × *P. nigra* crosses, varieties of the north west American black cottonwood (*P. trichocarpa*), or hybrids with this species as one of the parents.

Although poplars will grow on a wide range of sites, to achieve the rapid growth for which they are well known, sheltered sites with base rich loamy soils where the water table is within about 1.0–1.5 m of the surface are required. Almost all poplars are raised by vegetative propagation either by growing forest plants from hardwood cuttings 20–25 cm long or by inserting longer cuttings, called sets, which are usually 2-year unrooted shoots about 2–3 m long. Sets are directly inserted into deep holes at the final planting position.

Poplars grow slowly in competition, and to obtain fast growth are planted at very wide spacings generally ranging from 5 × 5 m to as much as 8 × 8 m. In many plantations no thinning is carried out. Veneer-size logs, for peeling for matchwood or vegetable crates, are reached in 12–25 years depending on site quality. High pruning is essential for veneer quality and it is normally done to 6 m early in the life of the crop. Pruning continues regularly at 2-year intervals throughout the rotation to minimize epicormic growth.

Willows

Short-rotation plantation crops of willows are much less important than poplars though there are many more species in the genus *Salix*. In Britain

FIG. 11.2. Cricket bat willow (*Salix alba* cv 'Coerulea') planted beside rivers and streams in Dedham Vale, Essex.

there are about 2000 ha of planted willow grown for cricket bats (Evans 1984) nearly all of which occurs in Essex (Fig. 11.2). Cricket bat willow is *S. alba* cv 'Coerulea' and individual trees are grown along riverbanks and stream sides where there is constantly flowing water. They are planted using long sets, as in the case of poplar, at spacings of 10–12 m. Utilizable size, greater than 35 cm dbh, is reached in 12–18 years. Absolutely clean boles are essential for bat quality and both disbudding of sets and subsequent high pruning of trees are carried out. Any buds that develop are also rubbed off.

Planted coppices

The production of firewood, poles, and many other types of small and medium-sized material on short, 10–30 year, cutting cycles is one of the oldest forms of management in semi-natural forests. Production is achieved by coppicing and reproduction from stool shoots of species such as oak, ash, sweet chestnut, hazel, poplar, and willow. Nearly all currently worked coppice crops were originally planted, though, in the past, naturally occurring mixed woodland was often coppiced for firewood, primitive building materials, fencing, etc. Coppices of sweet chestnut were planted for firewood and split fencing, osiers for basket-making, and hazel for hurdles.

In Britain and much of Europe the demand for traditional coppice produce declined rapidly from about 1870 until, by the early twentieth century, it almost ceased to exist. The decline started with the industrial revolution when new technology and inventions made available cheaper and better alternatives to the traditional forest produce. For example wire replaced hazel hurdles for fencing and the efficient transport provided by new railways enabled coal to be taken to the countryside, replacing fuelwood. The provision of electricity to rural areas in the 1920s and 1930s caused the final decline.

The energy crisis of the early 1970s stimulated renewed interest in short-rotation crops of coppice in temperate countries. This has resulted in a remarkable expansion of work and literature on the subject which has been reviewed by Anderson *et al.* (1983). Planted crops which are subsequently coppiced on 1–5 year cycles are being economically evaluated as alternative sources of wood, charcoal and liquid fuels, a basis for chemical processes, wood pulp, and sometimes as a fodder supplement. In non-industrial, mostly tropical societies, coppice material is needed for fuel for cooking and heating following widespread deforestation. In many developing countries up to 90 per cent of the total energy used comes from wood.

The main interest in these crops is in countries such as Finland, Sweden, and Ireland where there are no worthwhile supplies of fossil energy resources, making it necessary to import all conventional energy fuels. Forest crops, of course, are not the only sources of biomass for energy, though they are among the most efficient in terms of the ratios of energy contained in the

Table 11.1 *Maximum yields and energy contents of various crops (adapted from Hall 1983)*

Crop	Maximum yield (dry weight) (t ha^{-1} yr^{-1}	Energy content of cultures (GJ ha^{-1})*	Cultural energy ratio[†]
Conventional forestry	15	225	10–20
Short-rotation forestry	12	180	5–15
Algae	60	900	8 to high
Catchcrops	8	120	3–4
Grass	15	225	2.4–5.6
Wheat	5	75	3.4
Sugar beet	10	150	3.6

*1 tonne oil equivalent = 42 GJ.
[†]i.e. harvested crop energy to total energy input.

harvested crop to total energy input (Table 11.1). Field crops such as stubble turnips, rape and sugar beet, crop residues, and animal wastes can also be used for energy production. In Brazil, sugar cane and cassava produce a significant amount of ethanol, used as a fuel for motor vehicles (Monaco 1983).

Coppice has similar mean annual increments to conventional forest crops on comparable sites but for some purposes it can be more attractive than conventional forestry.

1. The material can be reasonably easily handled by inexpensive machinery which can often be attached to a farm tractor. The costly and very specialized equipment for dealing with large trees is not needed.
2. A usable and marketable product is available in a short time. This has many attractions to landowners who are not prepared, or cannot afford to invest in long time scales of normal forestry.
3. Coppice crops can be grown on land which is too wet to grow most agricultural crops, such as surface water gleys in Ireland. These conditions make arable cropping difficult and the successful production and use of grass depends upon high levels of management.
4. Coppice produce air-dries quickly because of its small dimensions. This makes it much more quickly available for use than larger produce.
5. Re-establishment costs following harvesting are very small compared with costs of replanting a conventional tree crop.

Species

Broad-leaved rather than coniferous species are invariably planted for short-rotation crops for two reasons:

1. Costs can be reduced if more than one harvest can be made from one establishment operation. Hence one of the most important attributes

of a species is that it should coppice vigorously. Many broadleaved species coppice well but few conifers do so at all, one exception being *Sequoia sempervirens*. Rapid coppice growth is due to the fact that roots already exploit the soil fully and also contain the carbohydrate reserves which allow the growth.

2. Unlike evergreen conifers, deciduous broadleaved trees invest little assimilated material in their leaves and the leaves are, per unit area, photosynthetically more efficient than those of conifers. Hence a larger amount of assimilate is available from an early age for the growth of stems, branches, and roots. Though evergreen conifers may eventually grow faster, they take many years and a large amount of assimilated carbon to build up an efficient canopy.

Paradoxically, the most favoured trees for short-rotation crops are often species, or close relations of species, which are regarded as weeds in long-rotation plantations. They are often pioneers of natural successions which establish quickly and have vigorous juvenile growth. Species and clones of *Salix* and *Populus* (Fig. 11.3) are most commonly planted but *Platanus* and *Eucalyptus* are increasingly being used, the latter especially in south-west France, northern Spain, and Portugal where many thousands of hectares have been established in recent years for the production of pulpwood (Fig. 11.4). Each clearly has a preferred range of sites on which growth is rapid. There

Fɪɢ. 11.3. One-year-old poplar shoots showing potential for biomass production.

FIG. 11.4. *Eucalyptus globulus* coppice being cleared for pulpwood production in northern Spain. It is grown on a 15-year rotation, and production averages up to $30 \, m^3 \, ha^{-1} \, yr^{-1}$. At felling, trees are about 35 m tall.

is increasing interest in nitrogen-fixing species such as *Alnus* and *Robinia* though yields from these are not expected to be as high as from other species because the process of nitrogen fixation consumes quantities of assimilated carbon.

In most cases the clones used at present are those which have been selected for high-volume production and disease resistance in conventional stands rather than in coppice production.

Yields of short-rotation crops

Though levels of productivity of over $30 \, t \, ha^{-1} \, yr^{-1}$ are sometimes quoted, Cannell and Smith (1980), Cannell (1980), and Pardé (1980) suggest that in most temperate regions it is realistic to base predictions for rotations of 1–5 years on mean annual increments of about $6–8 \, t \, ha^{-1} \, yr^{-1}$ of wood dry weight in stems and branches. Such levels are remarkably consistent between different species and regions and compare with yields of 4–6 t from the traditional but, by standards in Britain, very productive sweet chestnut coppice in southern England (Evans 1982*b*) (Fig. 11.5). Mean annual increments of $10–12 \, t \, ha^{-1} \, yr^{-1}$ quoted for some poplar clones should be regarded as a working maximum and figures substantially higher than this are often suspect because of the bias caused by edge trees in small research

FIG. 11.5. Recently felled sweet chestnut coppice with 14-year-old coppice crop in background.

plots. Yields compare with averages of about $10-11 \, t \, ha^{-1} \, yr^{-1}$ for productive conifers like Norway spruce on long rotations, and more than $15 \, t \, ha^{-1} \, yr^{-1}$ from fast-growing conifers such as Douglas-fir on good sites.

However, potential levels of biomass production as high as $25 \, t \, ha^{-1} \, yr^{-1}$ are thought possible by Hall (1983) through application of site-specific research into crop and tree performance using selected species and clones adapted to varying geographic and climatic conditions. Fundamental investigations into aspects of photosynthesis are also needed.

In temperate regions, including Britain, it is not possible to produce any more wood on short rotations than on long ones. Cannell (1980) stated that vigorous poplar clones, willow and *Nothofagus*, will give mean annual increments of $6-8 \, t \, ha^{-1} \, yr^{-1}$ dry weight on good sites in 1 year if planted at $250\,000$ stems ha^{-1} or 25 years if planted at 2000 stems ha^{-1}.

Silviculture

To achieve reasonably high levels of production, good soils are needed, which often brings energy crops into direct competition with arable agriculture. Most research outside Ireland has been done on arable soils. The land must be reasonably flat for mechanized working and the soils must have a good structure and texture, adequate water, and sufficient nutrients and organic matter. Most of the technical problems on such sites have been solved. Some peatlands may also be suitable but they still pose problems of drainage, cultivation, and nutrition.

The initial establishment of short-rotation crops is intensive and costly. Planting densities are high and are adjusted according to the expected length of rotation and size to which the crop is to be grown before harvesting. Much work on this subject is in progress. Because rotations are short it is important that the available space is occupied quickly, so much greater numbers are planted than in long-rotation crops. Usually no fewer than about 5000 stools ha^{-1} are needed and more commonly between 10 000 and 20 000 for 5-year poplar and willow rotations in the United Kingdom and elsewhere (see McElroy 1982). For traditional sweet chestnut on a 12–15 year cycle (Fig. 11.5), 800–1100 is aimed for (Crowther and Evans 1984).

Plantations of selected poplar and willow clones are usually established as cuttings, rather than bare-rooted plants, and thorough site cultivation and weed control are essential. Adequate protection by fencing and pest and disease management is necessary. Because, like field crops, the total above-ground biomass is harvested, the nutrient cycle is interrupted. Fertilizers, especially nitrogen, must often be applied to replace nutrients removed in the wood to maintain yields. Applications of nitrogen of about 100 kg ha^{-1} yr^{-1} are often recommended (Faber and van den Burg 1982), or irrigation with waste water or liquid animal manure. Irrigation to prevent water stress can also improve yields. Mechanical harvesting is usually carried out in winter, with heavy machinery which may compact the soil and result in poor stool recovery and subsequent growth. The extent to which production levels of first rotations can be maintained in future harvests is still not clear, nor is information about the longevity of stumps (Pardé 1980).

Short-rotation crops, like any intensively managed monoculture, are likely to reduce the diversity of the ecosystem, but less-intensive longer-rotation more traditional coppice systems have the opposite effect and are much favoured by conservationists (Rackham 1976; Peterken 1981).

Uses of coppice material

Apart from sweet chestnut grown for poles and fencing materials, eucalypts for pulpwood, and willow for baskets, the main interest in short-rotation crops is their potential for conversion into useful energy. The most obvious way of doing this is by burning to produce heat. Wood fuel has recently become a practical alternative source of energy for homes and some industrial applications in several areas which formerly relied on fossil fuels. This process has been helped by the development of efficient boiler systems which are now available. Charcoal, gas, and liquid fuels such as methanol can also be produced (Slesser and Lewis 1979). Commercial applications for many purposes are reasonably well developed. Stassen (1982) described the combination of gasifiers and internal combustion engines for generating electricity.

Willow chips have been converted into feeding nuts for cattle (McElroy 1982), and poplar into hardwood pulp (Cannell 1980), both with indifferent success. Many other processes and applications of short-rotation crops are described by Palz *et al.* (1981) and Strub *et al.* (1983).

Economic considerations

The considerable interest in experimenting and developing technologies for short-rotation energy crops has not, so far, been matched by any significant industrial applications in most temperate countries. It seems unlikely that this will happen until the costs of energy from other sources, particularly oil, rise considerably and so cause short-rotation wood crops to become at least equivalent in value to wood produced for other purposes. In many places costs of production are very high in relation to revenues in comparison with, for example, oil, natural gas, and coal. Often the costs of harvesting fuelwood, including transport, are greater than the value of the material itself so that only locally can it sometimes be competitive. The same problem arises with some other residues, such as straw. In addition, in crowded countries like Britain, the provision of a significant area of land would present problems and cause conflict.

Only in countries where political initiatives have been taken has any real progress been made. In Sweden, Koster (1982) records that a start is to be made in 1985 at replacing 20 per cent of the country's oil imports by planting 100 000 ha with short-rotation crops. The European Parliament's view in September 1982 was that it would be desirable to divert some farmland to energy crops rather than continue producing surplus milk, grian, and wine (Seligman 1983).

In most places in temperate regions coppices are likely to play only a minor role in most national energy strategies in the immediate future. In the longer term they may become important. Current research and development will ensure their eventual success and, unlike most tree crops, it will be possible to create productive coppices in a short span of time.

12. Plantations for special purposes

Most plantations are established for the production of wood that can be used for a variety of industrial purposes, though some are grown for a particular specialized use, such as poplars for the match-making and vegetable crate industries which are discussed in Chapter 11. But, as pointed out in Chapter 1, trees are also planted for many other purposes. The economic values of produce other than wood or the environmental benefits of trees and forests can sometimes be more important than timber. Examples of non-wood produce, conventionally called minor forest products, are seed crops from sweet chestnut and oil palms, or exudates like rubber, resins, and maple syrup, the bark of cork oak for cork and that of other species for tannins, and a variety of medicinal and industrial compounds. Products of animals which feed on certain trees may have a considerable economic value including silk, lac, and honey. Fungal associates of specific trees, such as truffles, may be prized for food. Trees are planted for the ornamental value of their foliage, for example species exhibiting rich autumn colouring, and also for the fodder value of their leaves and fruits. They are planted for environmental reasons which can be difficult to value in economic terms: for beauty, shade, and shelter, for soil protection and stabilization, for reclamation of derelict sites, and for their nature conservation and sporting values.

Generally, if trees are grown primarily for a product other than wood, the enterprise becomes associated with agriculture or horticulture. Biologically, the division between agriculture and forestry is unclear. But, in spite of this, it is unfortunate that in many temperate regions a sharp distinction is made for management purposes which greatly hinders good integrated land husbandry.

The main types of plantations established for purposes other than timber are discussed.

Shelter

Using trees to reduce windspeed locally is important in both arable and livestock farming. Most research on the value of trees for shelter has been carried out on the Great Plains of the United States, the Canadian prairies, Russian steppes, Danish heathlands, and Hungarian plains where conditions of soil, climate, and cropping practices are sufficiently uniform over extensive areas to allow for generalization. The main beneficial effects of shelter are in increasing crop yields and reducing or preventing soil erosion, though it should be noted that too much shelter in damp locations can be positively harmful because it causes slow drying of grain and greater incidence of some diseases.

The Great Plains, for example, occupy about one-quarter of the area of the USA. They are in a continental region of climatic extremes, they experience freezing winters and hot dry summers and the wind seldom stops blowing. Wind erosion of the soil is a severe problem on about 30 million hectares of land characterized by fine loose surface soils which become dry (Lyles 1976). When the soil surface is smooth, bare, and dry, it presents ideal conditions for erosion. One benefit of shelter is to reduce the rate of drying of the soil surface; while soil is damp it is more cohesive and much less erodible. Intensive arable agriculture and grassland management have exacerbated potential wind erosion problems. Crumb structure is destroyed, bulk density reduced, and organic matter mineralized. Problems became extremely serious after several years of drought in the 1930s when the area was known as the 'dust bowl'. Though incentives for tree planting have existed in some States since 1865, the most concentrated effort at planting was between 1935 and 1942 when some 30 000 km of 6–8 rows wide shelterbelts were established. these are now declining through age, disease, and the widespread use of herbicides. They are also being removed in many areas by those ignorant of their value, to make more room for arable production and make way for irrigation systems (Griffith 1976). Various authorities estimate that between three and ten times the present length (i.e. up to about 400 000 km) of shelterbelts are needed to prevent the damage by soil removal or deposition which occurs to an average area of about two million hectares each year.

Effects of tree shelterbelts on wind

Windbreaks or shelterbelts reduce soil erosion by decreasing surface wind shear stresses, trapping moving soil, and slowing soil drying. Windbreak design is important and the porosity, height, length, and orientation are the main considerations. When surfaces are highly erodible and windspeeds are above the threshold velocity necessary to initiate particle movement, the erosion rate is proportional to the cube of the windspeed. Thus, even modest reductions in windspeed can cause major reductions in erosion. Caborn (1965), Rosenberg (1974), and Hagen (1976) discuss, in detail, how shelterbelts affect wind.

The higher a shelterbelt, the greater is the distance which is protected downwind and, to some extent, upwind as well. In general, a dense barrier provides some sheltering effect to a distance of 10–15 shelterbelt heights downwind. However, by increasing porosity to about 50 per cent, the downwind influence, though slightly reduced in degree, can be extended over a larger area of 20–25 heights (Fig. 12.1), and also the somewhat greater wind penetration reduces turbulence with important consequences for lodging of crops and incidence of snowdrifts. The longer a windbreak the more constant its influence; if it is too short, or has gaps, jetting effects may increase windspeed at the ends and near gaps. A minimum useful length is generally considered to be 12 times the final shelterbelt height. Ideally shelterbelt density should increase with height in proportion to the logarithmic increase in a windspeed profile with height. Belts of trees are particularly effective in this respect, having dense crowns but, if pruned, can be relatively open nearer the ground. When shelterbelts are numerous enough to increase the overall surface roughness of the landscape the open field windspeeds can also be significantly reduced. A reduction in velocity of about 50 per cent compared with the open sea has been found in Denmark, in areas with many shelterbelts, but only 20 per cent in treeless areas (Olesen 1979).

Effects of shelter on production

Apart from reducing dust storms and soil loss, shelter can have beneficial influences on crop and livestock production by modifying the microclimate to prevent excessive chilling, desiccation, or mechanical injury.

The beneficial and other effects on crop production have been discussed in detail by Rosenberg (1974). Most are attributable to a reduction in the rate of evapotranspiration from the leaves of plants, caused by lower windspeeds and turbulence, and a consequent higher humidity in shelter. This results in greater turgidity in the leaves and a wider stomatal aperture. Plant growth and yields are usually greater in sheltered areas indicating that the

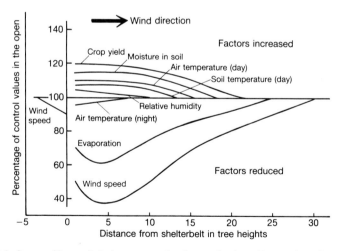

FIG. 12.1. Some effects of shelter on production and microclimate, based on research in Denmark. The curves do not show actual values but illustrate general trends. (From Olesen 1979, based on Marshall 1967.)

net assimilation of carbon dioxide must be increased. This is ascribed partly to the longer period of photosynthetic activity in sheltered plants, owing to the delay or avoidance of wilting, and partly to the lower nocturnal temperatures found in sheltered zones (Fig. 12.1) which results in a reduction in respiration and hence an increase in net assimilation. By contrast, there is a greater water use in exposed areas because there is less resistance to the transport of water vapour. The rate of soil drying is increased, but over long enough periods, soils in both sheltered and exposed sites will reach the same degree of dryness. It is possible that the reduced stomatal resistance in sheltered zones may lead to greater evapotranspiration at times because daytime temperatures are higher and the plants larger.

The generally moist conditions in sheltered areas lead to more rapid seed germination, more vigorous vegetative growth, higher yields, and a reduction in mechanical injury, such as sand blasting to plants. Shelter is also said to result in higher protein contents in wheat and, possibly, in greater oil and sugar yields from sunflower seeds and sugar beet respectively (Labaznikov 1982).

Depending upon the climate, increases in crop yields of 20 per cent to as much as 150 per cent have been quoted in continental sheltered zones. However because growth and yield within one to two shelterbelt heights of a belt are reduced owing to competition for light, water, and nutrients, and the land occupied by the belt itself is unavailable for crop production, the net effect on yields may often be quite small, or negligible (Skidmore 1976) unless the timber production is also included.

In some maritime climates like the British Isles where humidity is generally high and where serious droughts seldom occur, much smaller increases in

FIG. 12.2. Farm shelterbelt plantations used as windbreaks and for encouraging game for sport.

FIG. 12.3. Sheep sheltering and grazing in a larch plantation at Thirlmere in the English Lake District. Even the relatively light trampling of the soil adversely affects tree growth. (Photograph J. H. Williams.)

crop yields, of 5 or 6 per cent, can be anticipated. Indeed, in the lowlands excessive shelter can be harmful, slowing the drying of grain and increasing damage from disease in damp years. The main benefit in upland areas is that shelter can encourage earlier growth of grass in spring, providing a valuable 'early bite' for grazing animals (Figs 12.2 and 12.3). If there is enough protection better species of grasses can be encouraged to grow.

Shelterbelts can also benefit livestock by providing shelter from strong winds. In the British Isles sheep are often lambing, or in the early stages of lactation when grass growth begins on the hills, thus improved growth induced by shelter is of value as is the reduction in lamb losses in cold springs. Cattle are more sensitive to snow and cold winds and will usually seek shelter. By providing it, it is sometimes possible to keep cattle where previously only sheep could be stocked or, in winter, to keep animals on ground not hitherto possible. However, using the woodland itself for livestock shelter may result in problems since too high a stocking over time or in animal numbers can lead to bark stripping, trampling and soil compaction, and browsing of young trees (Fig. 12.3). The usual practice is to allow the animals to shelter beside a fenced wood rather than sheltering inside it.

Sport

For many owners the hunting, stalking, and shooting of wildlife they derive from their woodland is an important return. On estates and farms much planting of trees is done principally for this purpose, and any yield of timber or benefit of shelter is only a secondary consideration.

Exudates

Tree exudates which are of value to man include latex, resins, gums, and sugary saps from which products like maple syrup and rosin are made.

Gums and resins

Gums and resins are important products towards the southern boundaries of temperate regions and in other warmer climates, and their production, properties and uses have been described in detail by Howes (1949).

Gums resemble carbohydrates and are characterized by their ability to dissolve in water or by absorbing water. On losing water they dry to hard clear rather glassy masses. The adhesive properties of gums are their most important feature, especially in the manufacture of paints and pigments. Gum-producing trees are not important in temperate regions, the only species of note being cherry (*Prunus cerasus*).

Resins are in extremely heterogeneous group but a common characteristic is that they are insoluble in water but dissolve in alcohol and some other solvents. With heat, they melt to a more or less clear sticky fluid and burn well. They are resistant to most reagents and to decay. Copals are resins which are characterized by greater hardness and a high melting point. Many species yield turpentine and a rosin residue.

Modern uses of resins are in the manufacture of paint, varnish, and lacquers, as size in papermaking to provide lustre and weight and to hinder the absorption of ink and moisture, and in making soap. Resins were once used widely as torches for their combustible properties, for caulking boats and ships hence they are sometimes called naval stores, and for their medicinal properties or fragrance.

In France the resin industry dates back to the 1700s and was stimulated by the need for land reclamation to prevent severe damage from drifting sand, mostly in the Landes and Gironde areas. Planting started in 1803 using primarily *Pinus pinaster* (see Fig. 1.2, p. 7) which was subsequently tapped, as well as used for timber. Though resin tapping has now declined greatly, significant amounts of tapping (Fig. 12.4) are also done in Spain and Portugal with *P. pinaster*, *P. halepensis*, and *P. nigra*, and in Russia with *P. sylvestris*. In the United States, *P. palustris* and *P. elliottii* are tapped in the coastal states from North Carolina to Texas.

FIG. 12.4. *Pinus pinaster* being tapped for resin production in the Landes region of France. Some pine processionary caterpillars (*Thaumetopoea processionea*) are also on the tree.

In Greece, *Pinus halepensis* is tapped during the period April–September. Trees are first tapped when they reach about 20 cm diameter. At one time fresh cuts had to be made two or three times a week to maintain a continuous flow of resin, but today the use of sulphuric acid paste makes a return visit necessary only every 3 weeks. On average, trees produce about 2.2 kg of resin a year.

Since the early 1970s, the interest in growing trees for energy has led to increasing work on inducing resin production in living trees to obtain a higher calorific content of the wood. The greatest success has been achieved by injecting pines with paraquat. Kossuth *et al.* (1982) showed that *Pinus elliottii* injected with 1 ml of 2 per cent paraquat cation induced resin soaking of the sapwood and reduced the moisture content of the wood. The calorific content of whole trees was increased by 12 per cent, and of the lower 3 m by 33 per cent. Rather similar results were found by Karkkainen (1981) with *Pinus sylvestris* in Finland though increment losses caused by the paraquat treatment made the operation uneconomic, but it may eventually have potential. There was a poor response to similar treatments in Norway spruce.

Aromatic oils

Since early historical times aromatic oils found in parts of various plants have attracted man. They are known as volatile or essential oils. Today, the foliage of various species of eucalypts is a major source of them, accounting for a world trade of 2000–3000 tonnes a year (Small 1981). The oils produced have uses in medicine, as inhalants, embrocations, soaps, and antiseptics, the main therapeutic agent being cineole. Industrial uses are in the manufacture of disinfectants, soaps, and germicidal preparations, where phellandrene is the important constituent. Other constituents are used in perfumery. Most volatile oil production is in China, southern Africa, Portugal, and Spain. In the latter two countries it is obtained from *Eucalyptus globulus* foliage grown in plantations.

Sap

Maple syrup is one of north America's oldest commodities. Its production has always been a farm enterprise and though production has declined steadily since the peak in 1860, it is now very profitable. Lancaster *et al.* (1974) have discussed the management of farm maple groves or 'sugarbushes' for high yields of sugar-rich sap, mostly from *Acer saccharum* in Vermont and New York states. Forest-grown trees are said to produce sap about 30 per cent lower in sugar content than open-grown trees, i.e. 2.25 per cent compared with 3.34 per cent, but there is also much between-tree variation. Identification of the sweeter trees and favouring them can improve the syrup production. Guides have been produced showing recommended basal areas per unit area for different size classes of trees (Smith and Gibbs 1970).

In Russia, birch is tapped in Ukraine forests which are managed primarily for timber production, whereas sugarbushes are managed primarily for sugar production (Sendak 1978). Birch is therefore only tapped for the last 5 or 10 years of the rotation and its sap yields 0.5–2 per cent sugar by weight. The main sugars in birch sap are glucose and fructose with some sucrose, whereas there is only sucrose in maple sap. Maple sap is concentrated to 66 per cent sugar and sold as a syrup while birch sap is converted directly into a drink by adding flavourings.

Nectar

Bee-keeping depends on plentiful flowering within the vicinity for success. Trees are able to augment wild flowers and, in some instances, become a primary source of nectar, e.g. sycamore in parts of Europe and eucalypts, planted specifically for the purpose, in South Africa.

In some instances the selection and breeding has included flowering habit because of the nectar potential; one temperate example is false acacia (*Robinia pseudoacacia*) which is widely grown in Hungary for timber. Varieties have been bred which show both improved timber production and a prolongation of the flowering period to increase nectar yields for bee-keepers. Particular clones have been identified which give good yields of sugar in the nectar. For example, average levels of sugar production are quoted by Keresztesi (1983) as 0.8–1.0 mg in a single flower during a 24 h period whereas levels up to 1.9 mg are found in some clones.

Ornamental foliage and Christmas trees

Methods of production of ornamental foliage and Christmas trees (mainly from young Norway spruce in Europe but Scots pine in north America) range from being lucrative supplements to normal forest practice to highly specialized enterprises in their own right. In some parts of Britain it is possible to dispose profitably of the lower branches of trees such as Lawson's cypress, western hemlock, and western red cedar to florists and to sell the tops of thinned Norway spruce as Christmas trees. Christmas trees are also sometimes interplanted in normal forest stands to provide early financial returns to help offset establishment costs or planted pure on small easily accessible areas.

In many temperate countries there is a long tradition of using decorative foliage. Denmark, for example, produces large quantities of foliage of *Abies procera* and *A. nordmmaniana* from strains with specially selected characteristics such as glaucousness and greenness. Detailed research is carried out in an attempt to combine these attributes with adequate timber production (Barner *et al.* 1980). In recent years an increasingly important foliage used by florists, especially in winter, comes from young eucalypts. In both France and Britain crops are grown specifically for the attractive sprays of glaucous or bluish juvenile foliage produced by blue gums and white gums.

Special attention must be given to the management of stands grown mainly for greenery or Christmas trees. Care must obviously be taken to discourage defoliating insects and nutrition can be difficult. Five to ten tonnes per hectare of foliage may be removed each year, representing a considerable export of nutrients from the site, so there is little recycling of litter. To correct this drain, fertilizers are usually applied to maintain yields (Holstener-Jørgensen 1977).

Bark

The bark of a large number of species is removed prior to using the timber and is pulverized and sold for mulch or as a soil conditioner, and in the manufacture of some kinds of building boards. These can be lucrative means of disposing of what might otherwise be a waste product. The horticultural uses of bark are discussed by Aaron (1982).

Various chemicals, notably tannins (the chemistry of which is described by Halsam 1966), are commercially extracted from bark, and the tan bark industry used at one time to be important in many temperate countries. In much of Europe it was based on oak (*Quercus robur*). Most natural tannins today are produced from tropical species of *Acacia*.

Cork is an important bark product from *Quercus suber* in Mediterranean regions and especially in Portugal. Its cultivation, uses, and properties have been discussed in detail by Faubel (1941). Cork is the outer bark of the tree, and is stripped from the stem and sometimes from the larger lower branches when the trees are 20–30 years old and thereafter every 9 or 10 years during their productive life of about 100 years. Cork oak is often grown in conjunction with raising pigs which thrive on the acorns. It is also planted as a shade tree in vineyards.

Some of the unique properties of cork arise from the structure of the 14-sided cork cells. Each cell contains slightly more than 50 per cent air. The main properties are buoyancy, compressibility, resilience to moisture and liquid penetration, high frictional quality, low thermal conductivity, ability to absorb vibration, and stability. The uses of cork were numerous but many have been overtaken by synthetic materials such as polystyrene and glass fibre. Nevertheless, demand for cork exceeds supply and increasingly cork composites are used, thus improving its utilization.

Food

Fruits, nuts, and fodder

The importance of tree fruits, seeds, and leaves in human and animal diets is enormous in some tropical parts of the world. Few, however, are of major importance in temperate regions, except where cultivated varieties of trees are specially planted in orchards or as single trees in gardens or elsewhere. Among valuable timber species, the common walnut, *Juglans regia*, is an important temperate nut-bearing tree which possibly comes third after almonds and Brazil nuts in world markets (Howes 1958). Though native to the eastern Caucasus and central Asia, they have long been grown in France in the regions between Bordeaux and the Alps, and also in Italy, Romania, California, and China. In Europe, walnuts are mostly cultivated as individual trees in farmyards and occasionally in orchards; numerous varieties exist. The black walnut (*Juglans nigra*) is an important forest timber tree in the USA. Yields of nuts from natural trees are considered an important additional crop but they are not cultivated deliberately for this purpose because other species with thinner shells are more valuable (Knowles 1978).

Several species of chestnut are important sources of food. *Castanea sativa*, in particular, has been cultivated for this purpose for centuries in southern Europe and was one of the staple foods in Roman times. It was introduced to Britain at that time. The nuts are sometimes used as a source of flour and also for feeding animals. They are rich in starch and sugar but contain relatively little oil or fat and are therefore nutritionally akin to cereals. Pine seeds, specially those of the southern European stone pine, *Pinus pinea*, are used for food or dessert nuts in various parts of the world.

Large numbers of trees are used for the fodder value of their leaves or fruits, though only a few are temperate species. The best known examples are oak (*Quercus* spp.) and beech (*Fagus sylvatica*) whose acorns and mast have been used in Europe throughout historical times to feed pigs. There are no multipurpose and highly valued temperate trees similar to the Mediterranean carob (*Ceratonia siliqua*). The pods of this leguminous species have a very high sugar content (40–59 per cent by weight) and are of great value as a supplement to animal feeds. The seeds are sometimes used for such diverse purposes as in the manufacture of chocolate and for making colloidal protection agents for offshore drilling (Winer 1980). The tree is also used for fuelwood and it thrives on land too dry or too infertile or rocky to support most other crops.

Fungi

The cultivation of edible fungi has little influence on normal forest management since many such fungi are mycorrhizal associates of forest trees. Others are saprophytes on rotting wood and a few (e.g. *Armillaria* spp.) are sometimes pathogenic. One of the best known and most valued of fungi is the truffle (*Tuber melanosporum*), a mycorrhizal species on oaks, hazel, hornbeam and sweet chestnut. The value of truffles is so great in France and Italy that techniques have been developed for inoculating tree seedlings in the nursery specifically for truffle production (Anon. 1983*b*) and work is in progress attempting to develop effective associations between members of the shrubby *Cistaceae* (rock rose) and truffles (Giovannetti and Fontana 1982).

An important saprophytic edible fungus in Asia is *Lentinus edodes*. It grows on small diameter hardwood logs, especially oak, which has been felled and inoculated. Leatham (1982) stated that cultivation of shiitake employed 188 000 people in Japan in 1978 and it was Japan's major agricultural export. He considered that there is a potential market for *Lentinus* in the United States, where there are also plentiful supplies of under-used small logs suitable for its culture. *Lentinus* produces large crops of fruiting bodies for a period of 4–6 years, after an incubation period of 2 years. *Suillus luteus* which grows in *Pinus radiata* plantations in Chile is another species which is widely exported.

In much of Continental Europe there is a strong tradition of collecting edible fungi from forests. At the appropriate times of year, mostly in autumn, the woods are full of people gathering them. By contrast, most people in the British Isles consider anything but mushrooms, *Agaricus biosporus*, which originate from the shelves of supermarkets, as deadly poisonous and unsafe even to touch!

Part D

Protection and plantation layout

13. Protection from pests and pathogens

A forest plantation represents a considerable investment and so a concern for its health is an important aspect of silviculture, as discussed in Chapter 2. Though damage to plantations is often unpredictable, irregular and very variable in its severity, fortunately most plantation schemes in temperate regions are successful because serious damage is rare, and adequate protection usually possible.

Stress

Some pests and diseases attack healthy trees but most attacks are facilitated by stress. Among the stresses to which crops and natural forests may be exposed are:

(1) extremes of temperature;
(2) deficits or excesses of water;
(3) high levels of radiation;
(4) chemical stresses induced by a deficiency of nutrients or excess salts or toxic gases;
(5) wind;
(6) attacks by other pests such as defoliators and leaf diseases.

Some plants have adaptations which enable them to avoid or tolerate stresses (the latter is termed 'hardiness' by the layman) and these are discussed in detail by Levitt (1972). The most common stresses found in forestry are caused by drought and freezing, but poor nutrition, waterlogging, wind, and toxic gases associated with pollution may also be important. The absence of an appropriate mechanism for tolerance or avoidance can upset physiological balances in a tree and this leads to conditions which impair vigour. Defensive mechanisms are then lowered, and disorders induced, and pest invasions more likely.

In unstressed natural conditions killing pathogens are most prevalent in phases of development of hosts where they do not greatly affect reproductive vigour, especially seedling and senescent phases. Forest nurseries tend therefore to need more protection than older crops. The most prevalent disease fungi of adult reproductive phases are specialized species which pass greater or lesser periods of symbiotic existence with their hosts and allow them considerable physiological and reproductive vigour (Harley 1971). These species are non-aggressive pathogens. They are commonly found as saprophytes on dead and dying plant tissues and do no damage as long as host vigour is high. Only if vigour is reduced are they able to function as pathogens. The same is true of many insects, which do little damage to healthy trees but can become very harmful to stressed ones. Anything that reduces sap pressure in trees, tends to predispose them to attack by shoot-, bark-, and wood-boring insects. Hence, damage by the wood wasp, *Sirex noctilio*, is more serious in parts of Australia where droughts are common, than in Europe or New Zealand where they are more unusual. Beech bark disease is also induced by stress. It is caused by two organisms; initially the scale insect *Cryptococcus fagisuga* feeds on the inner bark and cambium of beech trees and later the ascomycete fungus *Nectria coccinea* invades attacked areas through wounds caused by the feeding activity of the insect. Large areas of the cambium and bark die. Lonsdale and Pratt (1981) showed that the weakly pathogenic *Nectria* becomes damaging if the trees are severely attacked by *Cryptococcus* or if they are stressed by drought, and this happened widely in Britain after the dry summer of 1976. Nutritional stress arising from inadequate assimilation of iron on some calcareous soils can also increase susceptibility to *Nectria* attack. *Nectria* in turn is a stress-producing factor which lowers a tree's defences and allows the ambrosia beetle *Xyloterus domesticus* to tunnel in the main stems. Windsnap may follow at the boring points to complete the syndrome.

It is important to know which stresses predispose trees to damage by particular pests and pathogens, but the sites most liable to stresses are fairly self-evident and include reclaimed sites (Chapter 10), deep peats, and drought-prone sands.

Maintaining a high level of vigour by planting species which tolerate stress is still the most effective means of *preventing* diseases induced by environmental extremes (Schoenweiss 1981). This, more than anything, emphasizes the need for careful selection of species and provenance for the site in question.

Stress cannot always be avoided since the physical environment is never constant. During the life of a plantation, years with unusually long droughts, low winter temperatures, or severe gales inevitably occur and create the conditions for weakly pathogenic organisms to cause damage. Some examples of these are given in Chapter 2.

An understanding of the factors which cause shifts in the size and structure of pest and pathogen populations can often indicate the best means of protection. Great advances have been made in these respects by theoretical ecologists. Southwood (1981) and Conway (1981) have discussed the relevance of the bionomic characters of organisms such as size, longevity, fecundity, and mobility that have developed to maximize their fitness to their environments. These factors cause selection along the so-called r–K continuum. The term 'r' refers to the rate of increase in numbers of a population and '*K*' to the maximum sustainable number of individuals of that species in a habitat, the carrying capacity.

r- and *K*-strategies

Extreme *r*-strategists, whether pests or not, continually colonize and exploit habitats of an ephemeral nature or respond to variable or unpredictable environmental conditions with an opportunistic 'boom and bust' strategy. Fecundity is high (hence '*r*') and a generation time, or juvenile stage, short but as the habitats are virtual ecological vacuums, a high competitive ability is not required. Migration, or dispersal, often of a very wasteful nature is a major component of their process, so they turn up quickly and breed rapidly in suitable habitats. Some *r*-selected species produce high numbers of sexually derived progeny which ensures a high probability of an appropriate genotype landing on a safe site. Others, such as aphids, reproduce asexually. Populations are unstable and fall rapidly as conditions deteriorate. In the case of insects the fall is often caused by rapid dispersal rather than death or reduced levels of reproduction. The main defences against predators include mobility and a measure of synchrony in reproduction or germination which temporarily satiates predators.

Most of the classic pests such as rats, locusts, and rusts of wheat exhibit typical *r*-strategies. The widespread use of monocultures in agriculture and plantation forestry has greatly increased the availability of favourable habitats for *r*-pests and they include most of the more important pests of foliage and roots. *r*-pests are difficult to control because of their massive damaging outbreaks caused by rapid rises in numbers and high dispersal ability.

K-strategists, by contrast, are specialists which occupy narrow niches in stable crowded habitats. They evolve towards maintaining populations closely to equilibrium levels. Fecundity, or, in the case of trees, recruitment, is not high but *K*-strategists are competitive, typically large in size, with a long period between generations. Survival is good through investment in complex defence mechanisms. There is less tendency towards migration than in *r*-strategists. For the population to persist, the habitat must not be irrevocably disturbed. If mortality does occur, populations need to return quickly to equilibrium levels through a rapid increase in the reproduction rate, or competitors may seize the resources: *K*-strategists are not well adapted to recover from population densities significantly below their equilibrium level and if depressed to such low levels they may become extinct.

K-strategists seldom become pests and, in fact, more often need the concern of conservationists, but when they are pests, they can be both persistent and troublesome. They are often pests of fruit and seeds.

The great majority of pests, and especially forest pests, lie between the extremes of the *r*–*K* continuum. Their most important characteristic is the degree to which numbers are regulated by their own intraspecific mechanisms of competition for food, space, or mates. They are also regulated by natural enemies which are normally present with them in the ecosystem or, by the inbuilt defence mechanisms of trees. This regulation is often sufficient to keep the damage caused to crops below the level at which control is required. They therefore become pests only occasionally, possibly due to stress caused by climatic irregularities.

The best known intermediate pests are those which have been imported to new regions of the world, but their natural enemies are left in the country of origin. Others become important because man has eliminated or reduced the efficiency of their enemies, including hitherto insignificant pests whose natural enemies are killed with pesticides. Man may also have increased the food supply and altered the abiotic environment and hence provided conditions which allows reproduction to increase in reduced competition.

All groups of plants and animals attempt to colonize the range of habitats available and within any group, a portion of the r–K continuum is exposed. Between groups, the most extreme examples of K-selection are found among vertebrates and seed plants and of r-selection among insects and bacteria (Southwood 1981). Among plants, r-strategists are represented by many short-lived weeds which briefly colonize bare ground before being succeeded by other more competitive species. Pioneer trees such as birches and willows, which produce large quantities of wind disseminated seed and colonize recently disturbed sites, show many r-characteristics, as do those which store seed in serotinous cones (p. 191) and release it in great quantities after fires. r-trees are typically intolerant, uncompetitive, and are quite quickly replaced by natural successors which are much more competitive.

Strategies of control

The concept of the r–K continuum provides useful theoretical basis for choosing an appropriate strategy for pest control and has been discussed in detail by Conway (1981). Strategies can include the use of pesticides, biological control, environmental management, the use of resistant varieties, and control of insects by sterile mating. The place of a tree on the continuum might also indicate its possible susceptibility to attack. Thus, those nearer the r-end, trees which are naturally colonizing species such as lodgepole pine, are likely to have fewer defence mechanisms than climax species, and so in some circumstances may be predisposed to more damaging attacks.

r-PESTS

Natural enemies cannot be used effectively against r-pests because their numbers do not build up rapidly enough, so pesticides or herbicides remain the most appropriate means of attack. If food quality and/or quantity for pests can be reduced, the status of the pest can be reduced to something akin to an intermediate pest so that natural enemies or competition may become more important. Resistant varieties or clones may provide some short-term protection but it seldom persists, unless the resistance arises through broad physiological mechanisms, because *r*-pests frequently produce new races or genetic variants which circumvent narrow-based resistance. Breeding for resistance to a pest is therefore fundamentally different from breeding for resistance to frost, drought, salinity, or some other environmental extreme. Many *r*-pests, such as cereal rusts and bacterial cankers of poplars regularly produce new races which overcome narrow-based resistance. Even some *r*-weeds, such as *Senecio vulgaris*, are developing resistance to the herbicide simazine on frequently sprayed sites (Holliday and Putwain 1980).

INTERMEDIATE PESTS

Biological control is most effective against intermediate pests and this should be the preferred means of control. Classic examples of biological control occur when regulation is re-imposed by the deliberate introduction of the original natural enemies of exotic intermediate pests. One of the first successful

FIG. 13.1. Bark-stripping damage by deer to Norway spruce at Grizedale forest in the English Lake District. Adjacent trees have been completely girdled and killed. Deer could have been attracted to the spot by the pocket of windthrow in the background. (Photograph J. H. Williams.)

examples was the introduction to New Zealand and Australia of a parasitic wasp *Rhyssa persuasoria* to control the woodwasp *Sirex noctilio* and its pathogenic fungal symbiont *Amylostereum areolatum* in *Pinus radiata* plantations. More recently other hymenopteran parasitoids *Ibalia leucospoides* and *Megarhyssa nortoni* and the nematode *Deladerius siridicola* have been found more effective (Marks *et al.* 1982). Susceptible trees are usually stressed by competition or drought and produce various volatile substances in the phloem/cambium tissues which attract the woodwasps. Biological control is often combined with strategic placement of trap trees which are deliberately stressed by injection with a herbicide. They are infected with nematodes to ensure that the *Sirex* females are sterilized prior to emergence (Neumann and Minko 1981).

If pesticides have to be applied they should be selective either in their mode of action, or timing of application, or in the way they are applied so that only target pests are affected, and not their enemies or those of other pests.

Among the most troublesome intermediate pests in European plantations are species of deer (Fig. 13.1), because man has effectively eliminated wolves and other carnivores which are their natural enemies. In some areas they can present immense problems of control (p. 204). In a few places, like the Queen Charlotte Islands of British Columbia and New Zealand, deer have been introduced to regions with no native carnivores.

K-PESTS

K-pests are theoretically more susceptible to control and may, in some situations, be totally eradicated. Among insects, they are suitable targets for sterile mating techniques. Pesticides may also be effective when small populations cause high losses. Because *K*-pests occupy narrow niches they may also be vulnerable to strategies aimed directly at reducing, or eliminating, the effective pest niche. In some cases, changes in silvicultural practice can successfully do this. For example, de-barking felled trees (Fig. 13.2) can eliminate the breeding sites for some bark beetles such as *Tomicus piniperda* and the removal of stumps infected with *Heterobasidion annosum* can substantially reduce the risk of infection of the next crop. The use of resistant clones of varieties is also a powerful approach since permanent success can often be achieved with simple monogenic resistance.

When *r*, *K*, and intermediate pests co-exist, successful control of the intermediate pests should be seen as the initial target with which strategies for control of the remaining *r*- and *K*-pests are then integrated. Pesticide applications to the latter must not interfere with biological control of intermediate pests (Conway 1981).

FIG. 13.2. In Belgium felled trees must be de-barked to eliminate potential breeding sites for the bark beetle *Tomicus pinniperda*, unless the logs are sawn almost immediately.

Practical considerations

The general approach to dealing with damage to forests involves four stages: detection, identification, analysis, and deciding what, if anything, to do.

A potentially serious problem can easily pass unnoticed for a long time. Some butt rots, for example *Heterobasidion annosum* and *Phaeolus schweinitzii*, show no visible symptoms of infection until sporophores are present. Reductions in the quantities of protective chemicals in foliage of stressed trees, such as resins and tannins, are not visible yet such reductions may make the trees more palatable to many insects. Even where there is visible damage, it may easily be overlooked for years. This happened in Britain with the great spruce bark beetle, *Dendroctonus micans*, a serious potential hazard native to continental Europe. It was discovered in England and Wales in 1982 but evidence from the callousing of damaged trees indicated that it had been in the country for about nine years before it was first noticed.

Normally, problems are first detected by observation: looking for fruiting bodies of fungi, damaged foliage, fruits or shoots, or more general symptoms such as poor growth, dieback, beetle emergence holes, or discoloured or sparse foliage. Attacks by many species of both fungi and insects are likely to occur at particular stages in the rotation and so can be anticipated to some extent

(Murray 1979; Crooke 1979). Severe outbreaks of some pests can sometimes be predicted from recent climatic patterns and certain sites can be classified as high-risk areas from previous experience.

Once damage to a crop has been detected, the correct identification of the *primary* cause is essential. This can be time-consuming and difficult and is usually the province of specialized forest pathologists and entomologists. Failure to identify the primary cause and treating a secondary infection or attack can lead to a very wasteful use of resources. An example of this may have occurred in Japan in connection with the fatal pine wilt disease of *Pinus densiflora* and *P. thunbergii*. This disease is endemic in the United States (Dropkin *et al.* 1981). It may have been introduced to Japan early in the twentieth century (Kobayashi 1981) and it became epidemic in parts of that country by 1975. In 1978 it caused the loss of two million m^3 of timber, or almost one per cent of the growing stock of pine in Japan (Mamiya 1982). The cause of the wilt has been ascribed by many authors to a nematode, *Bursaphelenchus xylophilus*, which is transmitted by various insects including a pine sawfly, *Monochamus alternatus*. Large sums have been spent on control measures, including insecticide spraying and the use of systematic nematicides. More recently, there is evidence to suggest that the primary cause of wilt may not be the nematode but a fungal pathogen upon which the nematodes merely feed (Tatsuno 1983). Hence, some of the control measures up to now could have been a waste.

It may be necessary to spend time, often years in the case of a 'new' pest, studying its life history, ecology, and the factors which predispose trees to attack, before a wholly appropriate strategy for control can be devised. Frequently damage is not serious enough to warrant any particular control measures or, alternatively, control can, in some cases, be so costly that it cannot be justified. This is true in the case of the green spruce aphid, *Elatobium abietinum*, an *r*-pest, in its periodic non-fatal attacks on Sitka spruce in Britain. In such cases, reductions in yield of a crop are inevitable.

Characteristically densely planted monocultures are usually more at risk than natural forests (see Chapter 2) because, when conditions are suitable for an attack, there are huge excesses of food upon which pests can grow and reproduce rapidly. Speight (1983) states that in virtually all examples, increasing the complexity and diversity of a crop system promotes the survival and success of parasitoids and predators. Diversity may eventually come to be seen as the best first line of defence in reducing the abilities of pests to proliferate. Other pest control techniques should then be required less often and on a smaller scale.

14. Protection from wind

Wind damage to forests is a recurrent hazard in many parts of the world. High winds can uproot trees, break stems, cause malformations, and retard growth. They can also cause major disruptions to planned management, economic losses from higher logging costs, damage during storage, unharvested wood, lowered increment in residual stands, and shortened rotations (Persson 1975).

Among managed forests those in temperate maritime regions suffer most but continental mountainous regions can also be afflicted. In some places wind may be the ecological factor most responsible for the species composition of natural forests through destruction by cyclones. This leads to successions which favour colonizing, rather than climax species.

Storm damage is therefore a constant risk, rather than an unforeseeable event in many places where it occurs. It is regarded as the most important influence affecting the viability of commercial forestry in the British uplands (Atterson 1980).

Damaging winds

Sustained mean windspeeds of $25-29^*$ m s^{-1} or more can cause considerable damage to trees on almost any soil. Gusts over $22-27$ m s^{-1} can uproot individual trees or small groups on soils where rooting is restricted even when the *mean* windspeed is about 18 m s^{-1}, the lower limit of a 'gale' on the Beaufort scale. In more continental regions, the highest winds occur near isolated mountains and especially where airflow is funnelled between mountains or through valleys. High mountains can augment the force of winds towards the bottom of slopes, where serious squalls may occur.

The nature and effects of airflow over plant surfaces have been described by Leyton (1975) and Grace (1977,1983). Normally, windspeeds fluctuate irregularly between lulls and gusts; these fluctuations are caused by turbulence and it is this rather than mean windspeed which is mainly responsible for damage. Turbulence is an extremely complex random phenomenon. But the higher the windspeed and the rougher the forest canopy aerodynamically, the greater the degree of air turbulence. Usually wind has relatively little harmful effect on the canopy, especially when there is crown contact between neighbouring trees, but turbulence readily causes the swaying of stems and

---

*1 m s^{-1} = 2.2 mph, 3.6 km h^{-1} and 2.0 knots.

branches, and also root movements in the soil. If lateral roots are not secure, some movement occurs in the root plate which then rises and falls.

Eventually the trees may be uprooted. The random nature of turbulence is often illustrated by the random directions in which tree stems are thrown by the wind, irrespective of wind direction.

Crops at risk

Winds are obviously the direct cause of damage so the crops most at risk are clearly located in the windier regions of a country, and especially at high elevations. Increased damage, due to increased windspeed and turbulence, is sometimes associated with various topographic features in the landscape, such as the lower leeside slopes of rounded hills (Hütte 1968).

Crops on soils which permit only shallow rooting, especially wet soils and those which have a low sheer strength, are particularly vulnerable as are recently thinned stands which are unable to dissipate the energy of the wind by crown contact.

Damage is also frequently associated with particular genera, especially pines, spruces, and firs whereas broadleaved trees often suffer less. This must be attributed, in part, to the planned regeneration of these genera on selected sites as much as the inherent characteristics of the trees, and the fact that broadleaved species are usually leafless during stormy periods of the year, and so much less at risk.

The precise elements of crop structure which influence energy transfer are not very clearly understood. Obviously crown size, density, and tree height are important, but so too is the spatial distribution of trees in relation to their sizes (Ford 1980). Taller crops are more vulnerable than shorter ones. In extreme conditions, stands of 5 m or more may be at risk, though 10–15 m is more commonly the threshold value. The turning moment exerted by wind of a given velocity on a crown is certainly much greater in a tall than in a short tree. Trees with well-tapered crowns which occupy a larger proportion of their total height have lower bending moments than short-crowned trees of the same height and so are more stable.

It is known that trees are more easily uprooted or broken if they are very slender; that is, if the taper in the stem decreases only slightly with height. This is because the ratio of the bending moment produced by the wind to the resistive moment produced by the elasticity of the stem increases if taper is slight (Petty and Worrell 1981). Slenderness decreases naturally among dominant trees and in thinned crops but increases in unthinned crops once competition has started or in dominated trees (Newnham 1965). Hence crown breakage is more common in co-dominant than dominant spruce trees. Slenderness is one of the factors which is most easily manipulated by foresters, by spacing and thinning.

Anything which injures tree roots or infects them can predispose the crop to risk. This might include soil compaction by machinery during the usual forest operations, root rots and waterlogging.

Damaging effects of winds

The most spectacular and catastrophic form of wind damage occurs as a result of major storms and tropical cyclones. Nothing can be done to prevent losses, for if trees are not uprooted, stems or branches are snapped, usually near the bottom, the most valuable part of the stem (Fig. 14.1). Relatively recent examples of catastrophic damage were the now well documented storms of November 1972 and April 1973 which damaged some 7000 ha of broadleaved trees and 65 000 ha of conifers in Lower Saxony and neighbouring areas of West Germany (Kleinschmit and Otto 1974), the Netherlands, Denmark, and East Germany. Windspeeds of up to $48 \, \text{m s}^{-1}$ (Force 16) were recorded. About 19 million m^3 of timber were damaged in Germany of which 15 million m^3 were in Lower Saxony and amounted to almost 12 times the sustained annual cut of the region (Anon. 1973). The November 1972 storm is considered to be the worst ever recorded in central Europe.

In Britain, return periods for major storms in any one place have been estimated by Shellard (1976) as about 50 years. Longer or shorter intervals

FIG. 14.1. Serious storm damage to spruce, causing widespread windbreak (Ballycastle Forest, Co. Antrim, N. Ireland).

have been calculated for other regions. For example Lorimer (1977) estimated a recurrence interval for large-scale windthrows as 1150 years in north-east Maine, USA, this being much longer than the interval needed to attain a climax, all-age structure. The period may only be about 10 years in parts of the South Island of New Zealand (Hill 1979). Catastrophic storms usually devastate quite small areas which lie in the tracks of the winds.

Less dramatic, but often more serious, is the insidious attritional damage in which individual trees or small groups are uprooted during more frequent but less severe gales. Once this type of 'endemic' windthrow begins, it may extend quite rapidly (Fig. 14.2) and often results in the need for premature clearance of whole crops, long before the desired rotation is reached. In Sweden, 75 per cent of the annual natural mortality is attributed to damage by wind and snow. This amounts to about 8½ million m³ a year, or 11 per cent of the total annual increment of the whole country (Persson 1975).

FIG. 14.2. The start of windthrow in Sitka spruce on a surface water gley. Trees tend to be uprooted along the lines of the plough ridges. Note very shallow rooting.

Endemic windthrow often occurs during the period in the life of a crop when current annual increment is at its highest. If it can be delayed for only a few years, total production can be significantly increased as well as the proportion of larger-sized logs (Fig. 14.3). Apart from losses in production, wind can also damage the wood of the remaining standing trees, as well as the blown ones.

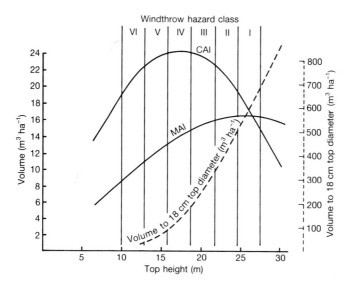

FIG. 14.3. Relationships between growth of yield class 16 m³ ha⁻¹ yr⁻¹ Sitka spruce and top height (from Edwards and Christie 1981). The stage of onset of windthrow in various hazard classes is also shown (from Miller 1985).

In less extreme conditions tree crowns can be damaged by windbreak of tender leading shoots which results in forking and other malformations. Certain species (coastal provenances of lodgepole, and some other pines are notorious examples) do not root well initially and become prone to toppling, which causes undesirable curves in the base of the stem and the development of reaction wood. Later they become even more susceptible to both windthrow and snow damage (Petty and Worrell 1981).

Wind can influence the rate of growth of trees. In controlled environment experiments, Rees and Grace (1980a,b) found that height growth of lodgepole pine was reduced by 20 per cent by wind speeds of up to 8.5 m s⁻¹, though radial growth was not affected. This was ascribed to the shaking effect of wind rather than water stress and was accounted for by differences in cell length rather than cell number.

Silvicultural methods of reducing windthrow risk

There are three approaches to combatting endemic windthrow, (Ford 1980):

(1) improving root development;
(2) designing a form of silviculture appropriate to short rotations;
(3) improving forest design.

In practice more than one of these approaches is usually taken by those afflicted by windthrow problems and they are reviewed by Savill (1983). A further option is to abandon forestry on the worst sites, a choice always worth considering where there is a reasonably profitable alternative form of land use, such as sheep grazing.

IMPROVING ROOT DEVELOPMENT

Ground preparation

An obvious approach to delaying the onset of windthrow is to improve the anchorage of trees by increasing the rooting depth and the radial spread of roots, even by small amounts.

The root form of some species may be determined by the soil type in which it grows. By far the most difficult soils are wet organic ones which impose permanent limitations on rooting depths due to lack of oxygen. On these soils the great majority of tree roots, even in drained areas, are shallow, and severely restricted at about 10 cm below the soil surface. The possibilities for stabilizing crops on such soils must be many fewer than on wet soils which can be drained and aerated.

On some soils, attempts to modify one contributory cause of windthrow, that of waterlogging, through intensive drainage by spaced furrow ploughing, has introduced the new problem of restricting root spread (Chapter 4). Among the most promising of recent techniques for combining good soil drainage with wide root spread and marginally better root depth is the use of mole drainage on gleyed soils and tunnel ploughing on peats (p. 55), methods which are being widely employed in new afforestation schemes in Ireland.

On drier, but compacted soils and those with ironpans there is often a very sharp divide between the upper soil in which the trees root and the compacted soil below. A plane of weakness develops which can make crops very prone to windthrow. Deep ripping can aid deep root development and result in much improved stability on these sites.

In the long-term, breeding trees for improved root ventilation which would enable them to root more deeply in waterlogged soils (Sanderson and Armstrong 1978) or other characteristics, such as root-regenerating capacity (Nambiar 1981) or possibly a flatter cross-section, which is said by Brinar (1972) to confer improved stability, could become important.

Planting stock

Improvements to the rooting qualities of planting stock and methods of planting are an important method of making some species more stable. Some pines, in particular, lose their capacity to initiate first-order lateral roots, which eventually become the main structural elements, early in their first season of growth. Thus, the final configuration of the root system may be established very early in life and remain unchanged with increasing age.

One possibility for overcoming these problems is to use container-grown plants (Chapter 6). If root systems can be developed which grow in a similar way to natural root systems, containers can be of especial value.

Species selection

Some species can escape damage even from cyclones because of their ability to shed leaves and twigs before wind forces are sufficient to cause windthrow or branch or bole fracture. Several tropical eucalypts and species of *Araucaria* have this reputation (Stocker 1976; Brouard 1967). It is an unfortunate fact that the commercially most important forest species in temperate regions are spruces and pines which present large, stiff, and resistant foliage areas to the wind. These trees have much higher drag coefficients than, for example, western hemlock and Douglas fir, with their flexible branches which stream out in the wind (Raymer 1962; Walshe and Fraser 1963), though drag coefficients vary both within species and with windspeed (Mayhead 1973*a*). In many reports of windthrow, spruces and pines are reported as being the most damaged species. However, significant differences in susceptibility to wind damage sometimes occur between provenances. In *Pinus caribaea*, provenances from coastal origins in central America, which experience frequent cyclones, are more resistant than inland provenances (Forestry Dept., Queensland 1981).

There are obvious theoretical advantages in growing species which are likely to be windfirm: trees which root deeply, and have buttressed trunks and wood which is strong and resilient, but the possibilities for doing this *and* maintaining high-volume yields are low. In temperate regions broadleaved deciduous trees, which are leafless during the period of the year when storms are common, have obvious attractions, especially as they frequently root more deeply in wet soils (Gill 1970). Unfortunately, at least in plantation forestry, broadleaved trees are much less commercially attractive because of their lower levels of production.

Root and stem rots

Trees infected with various butt and root rots usually have many dead or dying roots and weakened stems which make them more susceptible to windthrow and windbreak than sound trees. In the case of *Heterobasidion annosum* this was established as early as 1937 by Bornebusch, in Denmark.

First-rotation sites are often free of such diseases and, though freedom is unlikely to last indefinitely, the use of relatively resistant species and at least decaying the onset of infection by careful stump treatment is important.

SHORTENING ROTATIONS

Rotation length

The probability of wind damage can be reduced if rotation lengths are sufficiently short that crops spend little, if any period, at top heights which expose them to risk. Rotations aimed at achieving sawlog-sized material by the time the trees reach 20 m top height have been suggested for parts of Britain through the use of heavy fertilizing, wide spacing, and early pre-commercial thinning.

Spacing

Two mutually incompatible aspects of stability related to spacing and thinning have already been mentioned. On the one hand, damaging wind turbulence is reduced by having a relatively smooth canopy to the forest, implying narrow spacings; on the other, the maintenance of well-tapered stems which bend with the wind rather than break or become uprooted requires wide spacings.

A great deal of continental European and recent Australian literature dwells on the importance of maintaining well-tapered trees, slenderness usually being expressed as a height/dbh ratio (for example Braastad 1978; Brünig 1973; Sheehan *et al.* 1982). Many consider the maintenance of an acceptable ratio to be by far the most important influence on stability. Faber and Sissingh (1975) consider that in the Netherlands an *h/d* ratio of no more than 50 or 60 is necessary for adequate wind resistance. Kramer and Bjerg (1978) suggest that a ratio of about 80 might be acceptable. To maintain a low *h/d* ratio, either very wide spacings with no subsequent thinning or early and heavy thinnings are necessary: if *h/d* ratios are allowed to reach high levels, late thinning is unlikely to reduce them significantly.

Traditional treatments involving thinning, which are enshrined in many yield tables, are criticized by Brünig (1973) as leading to dangerously high *h/d* ratios. The price of greater stability implies a lower stocking than is customary (Table 14.1) and therefore a lower yield has to be accepted. Fewer people take the view that close spacing and maintenance of a relatively smooth

Table 14.1   *Height/diameter ratios at 20 m top height in unthinned Sitka spruce (based on Kilpatrick et al. 1981)*

Stems planted per hectare	Top height/dbh ratio
500	64
1000	72
1500	80
2000	88
2500	96
3000	104

canopy is more important. Richter (1975) in a study on Norway spruce in Sauerland, north west Germany, found a tendency for damage to decrease with increasing stand density as did Etverk (1972) in Estonia who concluded that dense stands of relative slender trees are more stable. Sutton (1970) in New Zealand, Bornebusch (1937) in Denmark, and many British foresters (for example Fraser 1964) advocated rather dense crops especially where conditions are not good for rooting. It is possible that when snow and ice are present in combination with wind, wide spacings are safer, but where the problem is that of wind alone, especially on very wet soils, narrow spacings may be less at risk.

Thinning

The dangers associated with thinning are well understood. Thinned crops are more susceptible to damage during the 2–5 year period when the canopy is reclosing, when they are unable to dissipate the turbulent energy of the wind by crown contact. Cremer et al. (1977), for example, found that with Pinus radiata near Canberra, stands over 30 m tall which had not been disturbed by recent thinning, had only 0.2 per cent of the trees thrown in a gale in July 1974 whereas 22 per cent of the trees in stands thinned in the previous 5 years were damaged.

Forces on trees in thinned plantations can be doubled by removing adjacent trees (Walshe and Fraser 1963). Experience with frequent gales in upland Britain has shown that thinned crops have a decreased height expectancy of about 3 m over unthinned. Furthermore, once 3–4 per cent of a stand is windthrown possibly 50 per cent of the remainder will succumb within the next 3 m of height growth (Mayhead et al. 1975). There are therefore obvious advantages in not thinning at all or giving up thinning early. 'No-thinning' regimes are now widely adopted in the United Kingdom and estimated at 57 per cent of the forests owned by the British Forestry Commission (Ford 1980) and 73 per cent in Northern Ireland (Savill and McEwen 1978).

On high-risk sites which are thinned, regimes which cause large openings in the canopy, such as heavy or systematic thinnings, result in more damage than light or selective thinnings. Delayed thinning and especially heavy thinning in older crops which involves releasing tall slender trees with high h/d ratios is often quoted as being an important contributory cause of damage.

Where thinning is not practised much attention is paid to maintaining timber quality, by adjusting initially rather dense spacings without incurring the risks associated with conventional thinning. Pre-commercial thinning is the main way of doing this: that is thinning when crops are no more than 5 or 6 m tall, well before they are exposed to any serious risk. The use of thinning techniques which are so slow in operating that canopies are never opened sufficiently to endanger the crop are also receiving attention, including the use of self-thinning mixtures of slow- and fast-growing species, or fast- and slow-growing provenances of the same species (Lines 1981), and using arboricides such as glyphosate to inject into unwanted trees (Ogilvie and Taylor 1984).

Pruning

The effects of high pruning on stability, especially the pruning of edge trees, are not clearly known and require more investigation. Some definitely believe that it helps by allowing the wind to filter through the crop and so reduce turbulence.

FOREST DESIGN

Classifying risk

The extent of wind damage can be influenced by plantation layout and local topography. It is however extremely difficult to take these factors into sufficient consideration when establishing large areas of forest.

Several authors have produced hazard classifications. Miller (1985), for example, recognized six hazard classes for Britain based on four site variables: wind zone determined from a map, altitude, exposure, and soil. The system is used for zoning coniferous forests, especially Sitka spruce, of 500 ha or more, and from it top heights at which windthrow may be expected to start are indicated for each hazard class. Adjustments to the system allow for the effects of thinning and method of ploughing.

It provides a basis for delineating broad no-thinning areas. Experience elsewhere may allow much more detailed action. For example from a study in the East German Harz mountains, Hengst and Schulze (1976) proposed measures to increase wind resistance including the creation of new road networks with reconstructed stand margins, the conversion of large plantations to a varied wind-resistant mosaic of different species and ages, and the progression of fellings against the prevailing wind with an elastic time sequence of felling.

Exposed edges

The edges of forests are a particular cause of vulnerability. For reasons discussed below, it is certain that unsuitable edges will predispose crops to damage but the reverse is not necessarily true. There have been many attempts in the past to create windfirm edges in the hope that they will protect the crop behind. Most have been notably unsuccessful: the edges often remain stable, but the part of the crop needing protection behind is as vulnerable as ever, or more so.

The danger from edges arises because relatively large wind eddies and much greater bending moments are produced within 10–15 times the height of the edge. There is a more extended region beyond, up to 40 to 50 times the height, in which wind turbulence gradually declines. Edge trees start the enhancement of turbulence but themselves remain largely intact (Hill 1979). In fact, trees on permanent edges require very high mean windspeeds of about $36 \, \mathrm{m \, s^{-1}}$ to damage them (Papesch 1974).

The treatment of stand margins has therefore received much attention. Kramer (1980) for example stated that a depth of 30–50 m from edges should be specially treated as a shelterbelt. It should be heavily thinned, beginning at 8–10 m, and not thinned after 15 m top height. This will encourage potentially stable well-tapered trees with long crowns. He also emphasized the need for wide spacing, all with the aim of obtaining an edge zone which wind can penetrate, instead of a dense impenetrable border. Fraser (1964) has shown that these treatments have the effect of eliminating the zone of fluctuating forces behind the edge. Internal edges along roads should be along wide breaks of 30–40 m to encourage low h/d ratios of the edge trees. Mitscherlich (1973) similarly emphasized the adverse effect of dense margins and proposed wide spacing and pruning to allow the wind to filter through the edge zone. Hütte (1968) and more recently Neckelmann (1981, 1982) tried cutting the tops off trees within 15–25 m of the edge zone, with lorry-mounted hydraulic shears, to produce a slowly rising zone. While this reduced damage to the edges themselves, the plantation behind still suffered from windthrow, but the topped edge trees often died within a year or two of cutting the crowns and their value was totally lost. Recently cut edges, on the boundaries of clear-fellings, have none of these advantages and are frequently severely damaged. Little can be done about them, though experience in Britain has been that if the temptation to tidy them can be resisted, damage does not always extend too quickly.

Species mixtures

Ford (1982) has stated that the 'classic response to catastrophe is to diversify the forest by planting species which are less vulnerable'. This reaction is very clear in both East and West Germany following the 1972/73 gales where areas of spruce and pine have been markedly reduced in favour of replacement by broad-leaved species.

Intimate mixtures or occasional belts of deep-rooting deciduous trees in crops of shallow-rooting evergreen conifers are also frequently used for stability, with varied and often indifferent success. Experience in Britain has often been that the deciduous component of alder or birch remains stable and the conifer, usually spruce, is at least as vulnerable as before, if not more so because the deciduous trees are usually leafless at the times of major storms and cause pockets in which wind turbulence can increase. However, Konôpka (1975, 1980) considered that 'correct determination of stand composition in mountain regions of Slovakia is the key and first condition for ensuring stability of these forests'. In some situations he recommended no more than 60 per cent of spruce and silver fir in the forests, the remainder being made up of wind-resistant species.

Clear-felling coupes

For equivalent areas of standing and felled trees, damage is consistently less adjacent to large clearfalls than small ones. This is largely explained by the fact that per unit area, small coupes have a greater perimeter length of edge trees at risk than large ones (Gordon 1973; Neustein 1964).

When clear-felling it is usually safest to fell right up to permanent edges or open ground, and as a poor second best, to proceed with felling against the direction of the prevailing wind.

Forest normality

To avoid local catastrophes from windthrow, which can stretch local sawmilling and labour resources beyond their capacity, there is a strong case for deliberately trying to create normal forests. This action could substantially reduce the proportion of stands at risk at any one time. The problem is potentially most serious in countries like Britain and Ireland which have seen new afforestation over the last 30, and especially the last 20 years. Large areas are now entering a stage of serious risk.

15. Fire

Fire can be a spectacular and extremely destructive cause of damage to tree plantations. But, although nearly all such fires are started by man, fire has long been part of natural ecosystems, a point apt to be forgotten though not irrelevant when considering its threat to plantation forestry. A comprehensive account of the nature of forest fires, their significance and their management, including fire fighting, is given by Pyne (1984).

Ecology of fire

In the boreal forests of the northern hemisphere most natural stands that are cut are of post-fire origin. Indeed, much of their diversity in composition, vigour, and character, is due to irregular but periodic fires. Fire acts as a primary nutrient cycling and rejuvenating mechanism, by releasing nutrients bound in organic matter, where otherwise mineralization is slow due to low temperatures, drought or acidity, and stimulating the growth of nitrogen-fixing plants. The importance of fire in forest ecosystems is discussed in detail by Kozlowski and Ahlgren (1974) and Wein and MacLean (1983) and, indeed, the exclusion or fast suppression of fires in managed forests is now believed to have several detrimental effects. In the northern Rocky Mountains, for example, exclusion may encourage dwarf mistletoe infestations, loss of species' diversity, and may predispose forests to damage by such insects as the Douglas-fir tussock moth and Western spruce bud worm because of increases in the proportion of susceptible species (McCune 1983).

Trees react in different ways to fire and some subclimax forests are effectively propagated by it. Rowe (1983) classified trees according to their reactions as invaders, evaders, resisters, endurers, and avoiders of fire. Invaders are typically *r*-selected species (Chapter 13) which produce enormous quantities of wind-disseminated seed. They colonize and grow rapidly in recently burnt sites and include such species as alders, poplars, willows, and birches. Evaders of fire store quantities of strongly dormant seed, either in serotinous cones in the canopy, or in the soil. Germination is triggered by the high temperatures of fires. Thus, in the northern part of their ranges, in Canada and the USA where fires are common, the cones of Jack pine (*Pinus banksiana*), lodgepole pine (*Pinus contorta*), and, to a lesser extent, black spruce (*Picea mariana*) will not open unless the resins which hold the scales shut are subjected to great heat. Cones remain attached to branches for up to 25 years and, although viability may diminish during this time, when fire occurs prolific natural regeneration develops on the exposed soil surface. Subsequent growth is aided by the full overhead light conditions available after a large fire and requisite for such pioneers.

Resisters of fire either exhibit very thick bark, e.g. *Pinus halepensis* and *P. pinaster*, as protection from ground fires or survive through the presence of dormant buds in the stem, for example most oaks and eucalypts, enabling renewal of the crowns of scorched trees. Similar mechanisms are found in fire endurers. Even if totally burnt above ground, several poplars and alders regenerate from root suckers and eucalypts from lignotubers. Only species that normally avoid fire can be eliminated by it. These are mostly climax species, normally strongly shade-bearing, such as many spruces and firs, which occupy unburnt areas and prosper where fires are very rare or absent.

The above adaptations to fire can, from time to time, be both a help and a hindrance when coping with fire damage in plantations. If a young hardwood crop such as oak or sweet chestnut has been burnt, often the vigorous regrowth from the base can be used to advantage to restock the ground. By contrast where a crown fire has burnt through a pole-stage pine plantation the dense natural regeneration that sometimes springs up can create problems of what to do with it — to clean, to respace, or to ignore and replant?

Losses from fires

Annual losses from fires are high at about 0.5 million hectares in Europe (FAO/ECE, 1982), and over 1 million hectares in Canada where losses of wood are valued at about $33 million, or enough to supply 78 newsprint mills for a year (Anon. 1982). Nearly all occur in natural forest and, if there is no danger to life, they may not always be worth extinguishing artificially (Anon. 1983a). This is particularly so in regions remote from forest industries and human habitation. Burning of plantations is small by comparison but, of course, industrial plantations and intensively managed forest are of high economic value and represent a considerable investment.

Apart from losses of wood, destruction of forests by fire can, in some climates, lead to seriously increased water runoff with consequent dangers of flooding, erosion, and siltation. The recreational and amenity values of forests are reduced and fires can endanger agricultural crops and buildings. Contrary to popular belief, most vertebrate wildlife escapes fires by flying, running, or burrowing underground. The main effect of the fire is on the habitat which, after a short period of recovery, is usually enriched in both numbers and diversity of species (Wright and Bailey 1982; Fox 1983).

Susceptibility of forests to fire

It is useful to consider the susceptibility of forest to fire danger in two ways:

(1) the fire hazard, which is the condition of the forest and how easily the vegetation and trees can be burnt; and

(2) fire risk, which is the likelihood of fire actually starting, such as someone lighting it.

FIRE HAZARD

Climate

Conditions of drought, low atmospheric humidity, and high wind all increase the fire hazard. Throughout northern Europe dry polar continental air in spring, accompanied by strong easterly winds and little precipitation make the period from February to May the one of greatest danger, and because there is much dry grass (Fig. 15.1) from the previous season before new growth begins (Parsons and Evans 1977). A second, less serious peak in fire danger occurs in high summer as a result of high temperature and low humidity which makes the undergrowth dry and inflammable.

FIG. 15.1. Hazardous conditions for fire. Dead dry grass, predominantly *Molinia caerulea*, can easily be set alight during dry spells in early spring. (Kielder forest, Northumberland.) (Photograph J. H. Williams.)

Condition of forest

The composition of a forest stand largely determines its susceptibility to fire. This is most easily understood from the idea of fuel loading. A fire will only burn if there is sufficient quantity of material and if such material is reasonably inflammable — lush green vegetation presents a very low hazard. Within a forest inflammable material comes from three sources: the trees themselves, undergrowth, and litter which accumulates on the forest floor; a fourth component can sometimes be added if the plantation is growing on peat in which case the soil itself can burn.

Of the forest stand itself broadleaved species are generally less inflammable than conifers. The total quantity of dry matter per hectare is usually less than for conifers, the stand being generally less dense and the wood and foliage free of resins. There is little difference between different conifer species in fire hazard, though pines are often especially susceptible being planted in drier regions and stands can have much undergrowth. Larches are least susceptible exhibiting rapid initial growth, relatively sparse foliage giving a low fuel load and a deciduous habit.

The undergrowth or weeds that develop among the trees of a plantation are often a great source of danger. In fact young trees growing in dense grass experience one of the most hazardous periods in the life of a stand. In Britain most damage is done to such crops. Such fires are usually called grass fires but are sufficiently hot to kill the trees present; they can move with great rapidity. Once the canopy closes most weeds are suppressed but, as mentioned, under some species a considerable amount of undergrowth can continue to survive. In dry regions this can represent a serious hazard and make a crop more inflammable than one more densely stocked with trees but without the undergrowth — an important role of prescribed burning is to eliminate this material.

The litter on a forest floor is an accumulation of dead foliage and branches. In many parts of the temperate zone breakdown of this litter is slow and up to 10 tonnes per hectare can accumulate. When dry and packed down it is a serious hazard.

FIRE RISK

Fire risk is the other component of fire danger — how likely is a fire to start, and what are the causes?

In nature practically all fires are caused by lightning or volcanic activity. In managed plantations such causes are rare compared with fires started accidentally or deliberately. Only 2 per cent of forest fires in Europe are ascribed to lightning, though the proportion is somewhat higher in some sparsely populated northern countries — Finland 25 per cent, Sweden 12 per cent. Regrettably, most fires are man-made and recognition of this fact is an important step to controlling and preventing fire outbreaks.

A great many fires can be attributed to legitimate activities on neighbouring land. This includes the practice of moor burning to bring on an early grass sward in the spring and, especially in the past, the use of stream trains on railways passing through forest. Both situations identify points of risk and hence where appropriate preventative measures should be taken.

Unfortunately many fires are caused inadvertently or accidentally, in particular by visitors to the forest unaware of the seriousness of a discarded cigarette butt or lighted match. However, even this risk can to some extent be confined since the great majority of visitors will be in car parks, along footpaths and other specific locations and again appropriate steps can be taken.

The most alarming fire risk is from arson where a person deliberately starts a forest fire. Such an act, frequently premeditated, is often done at an unusual and remote place and, all too frequently, at a wholly unpredictable time — even in the early hours of a morning.

Fire prediction

It will be clear from what has been said about hazard and risk that when high hazard and high risk occur together there is extreme fire danger, for example a young conifer stand growing in dense grass (high hazard) close to a picnic site (high risk). This bringing together of the two components of fire danger is the basis of all fire prediction.

Some very sophisticated ways of assessing the fire hazard have been developed which usually employ many climatic parameters such as number of days since heavy rain, air temperature, relative humidities and windspeeds.

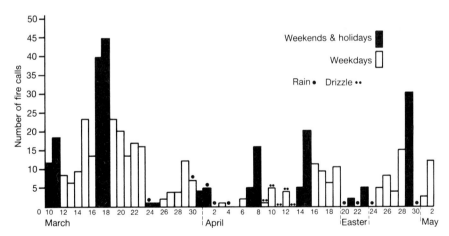

FIG. 15.2. The interaction of weather, the likelihood of forest being visited (weekends/holidays), and number of fire calls in Neath District (south Wales) during March and April 1973. A fire call is a report of fire or smoke which has to be investigated by forest staff. This District is reputed to be one of the most hazardous for fires in Britain. (From Parsons and Evans 1977.)

When predictions of these suggest highly desiccating conditions in the spring, when there is much inflammable vegetation, and on a public holiday, i.e. many people wish to visit the forest, fire danger is extreme. An illustration of the interplay of these factors is provided in Fig. 15.2.

When extreme danger is predicted it is usual to broadcast warnings, activate procedures to reduce access to woodland, and generally publicize the great danger. All these are aimed at lessening the chance of a fire starting by reducing the risk.

Nature of fires

Three stages of development can be identified for a damaging fire (Rothermel 1982).

1. *Ignition and survival.* Most fires die quickly after ignition either because the ground and fuel are too damp or there is too little fuel to burn — the object of a bare firebreak.
2. *Spread through surface fuel.* A fire will develop where there is a plentiful supply of fuel such as dry grass, shrubs, litter, and brushwood. In porous fuels like grass such spread can be very rapid. In compact fuels such as fallen logs spread is slow. At this stage of fire development there may be little or no smoke and, under some conditions, a fire can smoulder for weeks in dense litter or peat.
3. *Crown fires.* In a crown fire the whole tree as well as the undergrowth is alight. Even in a dense stand there is usually insufficient material in the canopy alone to permit a crown fire to spread because it must be continually supplied with heat from a rapidly burning ground fire beneath. This fact is the key to one of the principal means of controlling such devastating fires — prescribed burning as the preventative measure and counter firing as a tactical means of fire fighting.

Few forest fires reach the third stage but those that do mostly occur in coniferous forest. Such fires are extremely dangerous to man and property as well as destructive of valuable plantations. Direct control is difficult, hence the investment in protective measures which prevent fires reaching this stage which are outlined below.

Prevention of forest fires

Prevention has both passive and active components. Measures can be taken to reduce the likelihood of a fire starting such as preventing the encroachment of moor burning with an external firebreak, and measures can be taken to cope effectively once a fire has begun. Traditionally these two aspects are considered under fire prevention and fire fighting, but they overlap and can be usefully considered together.

PREVENTING FIRES FROM STARTING

Since most fires are caused by man the best prevention is to persuade people not to start them. Unfortunately, this is only partially effective, and recourse must be made to other means of prevention. Nevertheless, an important method of reducing the fire risk is to publicize the dangers of forest fires, make the public aware of forest fires when they are in a hazardous location, and, in some instances, even pass laws that will help reduce the danger such as those in Britain which limit grass burning in spring.

Silvicultural methods of preventing fires starting involve generally one of three aspects:

1. increasing diversity of species;
2. design and layout of plantations;
3. reducing fuel loadings.

Diversification involves planting less susceptible species with the main crop and is an important fire protection policy followed, for example, in Lower Saxony (Otto 1982). Typically areas of pine may have broadleaves mixed with them in places of high risk or beech underplanted to suppress grassy undergrowth. In Britain belts of larch were often planted as a fire protection measure next to high-risk boundaries. Diversity can also be achieved by widening the age range of a susceptible species. As was pointed out earlier young crops are most at risk and if the total area of such stands in any one place can be minimized this will help reduce the overall hazard to a forest.

When laying out a plantation it is almost universal practice to make firebreaks and tracks. These are usually located along susceptible boundaries and through a plantation to break up the area of forest into smaller blocks. Although traditionally, such breaks were thought to help prevent fires from spreading, their primary role is not as a fire break as such but as a means of assembly so that men and equipment can be brought to fight a fire. Thus an extremely important aspect of all such protective breaks is good access to them.

For a fire break to stop fires spreading its width generally needs to be more than 100 m. Narrower unplanted breaks within the forest, as well as being unsightly, may actually increase the risk of fire moving across since they act as channels for increasing windspeed and causing turbulence (Cheney 1971).

Because the very wide breaks needed to stop fires occupy much land, at least one hectare per 100 m of length, they are frequently not left simply as fuel-reduced zones with no other function but used for grazing livestock or planted, wholly or partially, with a relatively non-inflammable species such as larch or broadleaves.

Reducing fuel loadings is an important means of fire protection in many forests. Operations to achieve this include low pruning, and removing the pruned branches from the edge of roads and rides so that there is less fuel near where people might be, grazing livestock in a stand to reduce undergrowth, and prescribed burning. This last practice is widely used in north America (Johnson 1984) and parts of Australia and involves the controlled use of fire burning through a pole-stage or older stand to reduce the total amount of inflammable undergrowth and litter to levels unlikely to burn under wild fire conditions. This normally means reducing the quantity of fuel—the litter and undergrowth—to about 1–3 tonnes per hectare.

FIRE-FIGHTING

Effective fire-fighting has two components: (1) detection of a fire, and (2) extinguishing a fire.

Fire detection is primarily a question of good communications. Not only must a fire be observed but it must be reported quickly to the appropriate authority who can initiate action to suppress and extinguish fire. Fire towers, other look-outs, aerial survey, radios, and telephones are all used to detect and report fires rapidly.

Fire suppression methods

A fire will only burn if oxygen, heat, and combustible material are all present; this is the so-called fire triangle. If one element is reduced or eliminated the fire will go out. This is the basis of all fire fighting and the three main methods used against forest fires aim to reduce a different component of the triangle.

Water. Water suppresses fires by lowering the temperature because much heat is needed to vaporize it. It is applied from back packs, portable pumps, direct from vehicles, or from the air. A supply must be available to replenish water dispensing units such as roadside dams, special tankers, perennial streams etc.

Additives are sometimes used to increase the effectiveness of water and they mostly fall into two categories. The first increases the viscosity of the water to enable more to be held on tree foliage. Alginates are often added to water to achieve this. The second group of additives are wetting agents, or surfactants which lower surface tension to overcome the naturally water-repellant characteristics of most leaves and needles.

Beaters. The fire is hit with a flat surface which temporarily excludes oxygen. There are many types of beater, but all are basically a handle with a flap on the end, indeed even birch branches or young trees can be used. Beaters are only suitable for surface fires which are safe to approach within about one metre.

Digging and throwing soil on to a fire fulfils a similar role.

Reducing fuel. Sometimes it is possible to clear combustible material in the path of a fire by bulldozing a break or counter-firing. This may be the only feasible suppression method.

Fire retardants. Retardants provide another way of attacking fires of rather low intensity, by interfering with both the physical and chemical processes of combustion. They generate nonflammable gases and promote glowing rather than flaming and hence reduce the heat output and the rate of spread of a fire. The most widely used retardants are ammonium sulphate and diammonium phosphate. Both are used as fertilizers as well, and are cheap, easily available, and do little environmental damage.

A more complete discussion of the main ways of combating fires is given by Pyne (1984).

16. The layout of plantation forests

In laying out plantations consideration must be given not only to the well-being and economic management of the plantations themselves, but also to wider land-use issues. Forests are no longer seen as places merely having physical, biological, and economic potential for growing wood, which need design features to protect them from fires and wind, and to provide access: public concern and comment is making the plantation manager increasingly aware that he is a tenant on land which has other values and possible uses. This awareness emphasizes the obligation for wise use of the land set aside for forest plantations. Forests have visual and aesthetic values; they are habitats for many species of wild plants and animals, and forests have other economic functions, such as water gathering, hunting and some forms of agriculture. These values can conflict with that of growing wood and, in achieving a balance, compromises must be made.

One of the principal influences affecting these other values is the arrangement of plantations in terms of which areas should be planted and which should not, of how species and ages should be varied to accommodate good landscaping and conservation principles, and to facilitate the management of wild animals. In plantation design, both for new planting schemes and modifications to existing ones during the felling phase surveys are usually carried out so that decisions on these matters have a rational basis.

There is no standard recipe for designing a forest since every case is unique. What may be appropriate in one place, or country, may well not be in another as economics, site, and other conditions change. The main factors to consider are discussed below.

Access

Access routes both to and within forests are needed for road vehicles and vehicles suited to less firm and rougher terrain for establishment, maintenance and harvesting operations. Landing strips for aircraft are sometimes required.

Forest roads

The main function of forest roads is to provide access for timber harvesting vehicles. The construction of the final road network is sometimes delayed until shortly before harvesting begins though in such cases a reduced density of roads, often constructed to a lower specification, is made at the time of planting to allow access for labour and materials.

Detailed considerations in road planning are discussed by Johnston *et al.* (1967) and by Granfield *et al.* (1980). The density required depends on the extraction equipment likely to be used which, in turn, often depends on the terrain. Modern cable cranes, skidders, and forwarders make it feasible to extract over much longer distances than when horses and agricultural tractors were used but the standard of road construction is higher to cope with large modern vehicles. Decisions on desirable road networks cannot be made more than a few years ahead of felling because techniques are constantly changing: for example, where a choice is possible, horse extraction favours roads at the bottom of slopes, whereas, with cable cranes, the top is preferable. Skidders have replaced cable cranes on moderately steep terrain and for them a road at the foot of the slope is ideal, whereas for modern forwarders somewhere in the middle of a moderate slope may be better.

In deciding the spacing of roads the aim is to minimize the total cost of the movement of timber from stump to market. This occurs when extraction costs per cubic metre from the stump to the road equal road construction and maintenance costs. It is therefore difficult to assess the best spacing and positioning of the final road network at the time of planting but an attempt is usually made to do this so that future roadlines can be left unplanted. They are not easy to survey and may expose the forest to windthrow if made later.

Additional factors which influence road planning are the provision of roadside working areas, linking with the public road system and the interests of agriculture, recreation, and amenity. Where possible it may also be desirable to align roads through the least productive land.

The width left unplanted for roads must obviously be enough to accommodate the road itself and any associated drainage. It should also be wide enough to prevent excessive shading of the road surface which will deteriorate rapidly if it remains wet. If windthrow, fire, sport, or conservation are additional considerations, wide road verges may be desirable.

Rides and tracks

Unsurfaced access routes are usually left in forests, in addition to roads. They may be future roadlines or simply routes left for tracked and other off-road vehicles, and for providing easy access on foot. They vary in width from rides 10 m wide to narrow tracks just wide enough for a vehicle.

The desirable density of unsurfaced routes has tended to decrease considerably as operations have become mechanized and the use of aircraft has increased. In the 1960s it was common over much of upland Britain and Ireland to leave one in every 12–14 rows of trees unplanted (Fig. 16.1) to allow access for fertilizing by ground machines and eventual timber extraction (Dallas 1962). Since fertilizing is now normally done from the air, and

Fig. 16.1. Planting pattern commonly used in the United Kingdom in the 1960s. Here, a track is left between every 12 rows of trees to provide access for ground machines, especially for fertilizing. Helicopters have since made this unsightly practice unnecessary. The strip of poorly growing trees in the centre did not receive adequate phosphate at planting.

extraction can be carried out over stumps, these tracks are now obsolete, besides being unsightly and wasteful of ground.

A common practice is to surround compartments of about 25 ha with a ride, with some internal division as well, providing access to blocks of some 5 ha, giving one kilometre of access route, which may include surfaced roads, to about 15 ha of plantations. Many of the narrowest tracks cut obliquely across contours, along the main drains, and facilitate the mechanical maintenance of drains.

Fire

The main features incorporated into plantation design to reduce the risk of fires spreading are the road system which provides access for fire fighting, and zones designed as relatively fuel-free barriers to the spread of fire.

Firebreaks are strips of at least 10 m wide which are kept clear of inflammable vegetation by cultivation, herbicides, burning, mowing, or grazing. Today, they are made mainly on the outer boundaries of forests to prevent fires spreading in. Firebreaks used to be sited within forests as well but they can act as channels, increasing the windspeed and causing severe wind turbulence. They can increase the severity of fires and increase, rather than reduce, the risk of fire moving across. Breaking up large blocks of relatively vulnerable species with trees that do not themselves readily burn is now preferred. Trees along the margins of unavoidable internal breaks for access such as roadlines are sometimes treated specially, for example by brashing, pruning or heavy thinning, to minimize the risk of fire spreading across them. A fire may often burn freely through one species and age of crop but stops once it comes to another, less flammable, species or age class. Where fire risks are high, it may be desirable to avoid planting large homogeneous blocks.

Stability

As already noted on p. 188, where a forest is in an area of high windthrow risk careful design can reduce potential damage. This includes the special treatment of stand margins (p. 189), particularly along internal roadlines. Many of the features incorporated into protective firebelts will also contribute to stability.

Quality of water

The purity of water reaching streams, lakes, and reservoirs can be adversely influenced by nutrient enrichment causing eutrophication and sedimentation. In extreme cases eutrophication can lead to algal blooms which result in reduced oxygen levels in the water and can cause the death of fish and other aquatic life. Algae can block filtering equipment in water treatment plants. High levels of some nutrients in drinking water, such as nitrates, can be dangerous to health. Sediment can reduce water storage in reservoirs, block water courses, and damage aquatic wildlife.

Neither nutrient enrichment nor sedimentation can be completely eliminated but their impact can be reduced by taking care when using fertilizers and giving attention to road alignment and construction methods, and the frequency and slope of drains to prevent erosion (p. 52). A wide fringe of shrubs and suitable trees in a filtration strip next to watercourses can be useful to intercept excess runoff (Peterken 1981). However, the most important step is to avoid treating large areas at any one time. Fertilizers are usually required early in rotation (p. 101) and eutrophication may also occur immediately after clear-felling when there is a rapid release of nutrients from the litter on the felled area. The beginning and end of rotations are also times when sedimentation is most likely to occur. During the long period between canopy closing and clear-felling, forests are effective at retaining nutrients and conserving the soil. If there is a wide distribution of age classes on a catchment, the risk will therefore be minimized.

Conservation of wildlife

When plantations replace natural or semi-natural forests there is usually a decline in the diversity of plants and animals in the woodland. Where plantations are made on previously bare land, the reverse may be true. For example, there has been an increase in the diversity of bird species in Britain where coniferous forests have been established on impoverished moorland, yet some species are also lost. Among birds, buzzards (*Bueto bueto*) use forests for refuge, or to nest in, but they need large areas of open land for hunting. Others like skylarks depend upon open habitats for both food and nest sites; they disappear as a tree cover develops (Moss 1979).

Steele (1972) described the well-marked succession of birds through different stages of British woodlands and he concluded that dense pure conifer plantations are a poor habitat for wildlife generally, between the time when tree canopy closes until conditions become more open again. Open stands which support understorey species are much better habitats.

In the sense that forests, managed primarily for the production of wood, are probably the greatest reservoir of wild plants and animals in a country, foresters have an important part to play in the conservation of wildlife. Quite small modifications to silvicultural practices can have surprisingly large effects (Poore 1972). There are few forests managed for timber production which cannot be improved as wildlife habitats. Steele (1972) and Peterken (1981) have discussed in detail the measures which might be taken to ensure biological diversity under free-living conditions. They include maintaining a good diversity of tree species, a good structural diversity in terms of age classes and layers in the forest canopy, maintaining special habitats and protecting the forest from excessive disturbance.

Deer management

Though forests are the habitat of many animals, the main temperate species which have an impact on the design of plantations are deer. Deer must be managed to control the damage they cause to trees and often to facilitate potential fee-paying hunters. They are also, of course, a form of wildlife enjoyed by the public and the conservation of acceptable numbers is an important aspect of management.

If uncontrolled, many species of deer cause considerable damage by browsing young trees, stripping bark, and fraying. They can prevent satisfactory regeneration and cause diseases. In countries where numbers are excessive, they are regarded as extremely serious pests (König and Gossow 1979; Cooper and Mutch 1979). Attempts are made to keep populations to levels at which damage remains acceptable. It is quite certain that the presence of deer always entails additional costs. They should never, therefore, be introduced to areas where they are not already present. In Britain red deer, roe deer (Fig. 16.2), and, to a lesser extent, fallow deer (*Cervus elaphus*, *Capreolus capreolus*, and *Dama dama* respectively) are probably the second most important influences affecting the viability of forestry, wind being the

FIG. 16.2. A roebuck, a species of deer which can be very damaging in British forests.
(Photograph Ken Taylor.)

first. In very big forests numbers can, to some extent, be predicted by the proportion of forage to cover and its arrangement in space and time. These are the primary factors determining population levels (Thomas *et al.* 1976).

Failure to take account of the ecological needs of deer populations and to design forest layouts which facilitate their management can lead to high and often ineffective expenditure on fencing, and difficult shooting. Good forest design can minimize damage and enable what shooting is necessary to be done relatively easily and even profitably.

Unfortunately, relatively little is known about the population dynamics, social behaviour, and interaction of deer species with their habitats (Chapman and Chapman 1982) so that a detailed understanding of what constitutes effective design of forests is not clear. Deer management is fraught with vested interests, folk lore, and emotion; legislation is frequently controversial, facts are short, and difficult to obtain. It is, for example, extremely difficult to estimate deer numbers with anything approaching accuracy. Andersen (1953) in Denmark and Loudon (1978) in Britain quote cases of annual deer counts, on which culling policies were based, being three or four times too low.

In areas where roe and other species of deer are controlled effectively, provisions include leaving areas of at least 4 ha of favoured grazing unplanted

FIG. 16.3. Part of Eskdalemuir forest in south Scotland where open spaces have been left for roe deer grazing, and to facilitate their control by shooting. (Photograph Ken Taylor.)

and occasionally improving them by fertilizing (Fig. 16.3). These areas may include indigenous woodland, the banks of streams, and roadsides (Prior 1983). Siting such areas on the edges of plantation blocks can be beneficial. Holloway (1967) stated that in Russia, elk damage is much worse in coniferous plantations mixed with aspen than in pure conifers, but willows planted along water courses reduced damage to surrounding blocks of pines. Thinnings timed to coincide with periods of maximum food shortage can provide large quantities of alternative browse from the felled trees. Damage can also be reduced by leaving corridors of unplanted ground, or well brashed young stands, or old stands for deer to move between high and low ground. With some species of deer it can be important to incorporate traditional trails into the forest ride layout. Deliberately planting preferred browse species of shrubs and trees, such as willows, can help if they are sited carefully and the quantities are related to animal density. Also, among crop trees, some species are more able to recover from damage than others. Douglas-fir tends to callous over bark-stripped wounds quickly and the wood does not become rotten, whereas Norway spruce is more susceptible to decay.

Above all, the right animals must be shot. Certain individuals are more prone to strip bark than others. The elimination of these can reduce barking damage out of all proportion to the numbers shot. Dominant territorial bucks are often stabilizing influences on the population as a whole. They deter the immigration of unattached males which can damage trees badly by fraying during displays in the mating season. Selective shooting can therefore result in a spectacular reduction in damage whereas indiscriminate shooting can actually make it worse.

Fencing vulnerable areas is usually a last resort. It is costly and ineffective over long periods. Chemical repellants and individual tree shelters of various kinds can be effective on young trees, to prevent browsing, but are expensive and should be confined to use with small numbers of trees. One new approach to reduce dear browsing being developed in the USA (Boling 1984) involves placing selenium-containing tablets beside each newly planted tree. The selenium taken up by the tree makes the foliage very unpalatable and is said to reduce deer browsing by up to 80 per cent.

In most plantation forests thought given at the design stage to the future management of deer can be a major step in limiting the severity of damage likely to occur. Unfortunately there is not always sufficient information upon which to base sound practices.

Landscape

Most people consider rural landscapes to be timeless. They feel they have been there for a very long time and there often is great resistance to change. Thus, planting a forest on previously bare land can, like subsequent felling of the same forest, arouse public antipathy and, in areas of great natural beauty, can lead to strong criticism. An example of this reaction is that of Symonds (1936) who criticized planting in the English Lake District.

'The planting is continuous, by the square mile. Where there was colour, this is first hidden, then dissolved: grasses, moss, plant-life perishes as the trees form a canopy. Rock and scree, blue, grey or violet are still there, but hidden. What is seen is the rigid and monotonous ranks of spruce, dark green to blackish, goose-stepping on the fell side. Their colour is in effect one steady tone all round the dull year: there are no glories of spring and autumn for the conifer. Sunlight, which a broadleafed, deciduous tree reflects and vivifies, is annihilated on their absorbent texture: on a bright landscape they are so much blotting paper.'

Recognition that ill-considered plantation establishment can mar the landscape led many forest authorities to consult qualified landscape planners from the early 1960s. Foremost among these in Britain was Crowe (1978) whose publications became valuable aids to an appreciation of landscape principles. Though there is a consensus of opinion about what constitutes an attractive landscape, it is less easy to analyse the components of a landscape and then design a forest that will conform to widely held views. Lucas (1983) discussed five major elements in landscape design: shape, visual force, scale, diversity, and unity. The basis of successful integration is to understand the landscape and to design forests and operations within them in sympathy, so they look like natural features.

Landscapes are important in two senses. A forest must fit into the general pattern of the countryside, but the internal view, or immediate foreground, can also be important. The way a forest fits into the countryside increases in its impact as terrain becomes more hilly because the shape and composition of the woodland as a whole is more visible. The foreground view can be important in both flat and hilly country, especially in areas which are used for recreation. Here, diversity adds to the landscape: diversity in terms of species, tree sizes, open areas and dense woodland and views out of the forest.

Evans (1984), in consideration of broadleaved woodland, lists principles of forest design which can influence silvicultural and other decisions:

1. Forests should blend in sympathetically and reflect the form of the land. Thus, obvious things to avoid are unnaturally straight lines and geometric patterns or shapes, for example roads, rides, planting, and felling patterns and even line thinning, which cut across contours (Fig. 16.1), and rigid upper planting lines which follow contours. Roads should instead go diagonally to the contours and planting boundaries should rise in hollows and fall on convexities and ridges.
2. Intrusive effects should be minimized.
3. Visually important natural features such as gullies and crags should be enhanced and not obscured.
4. Forests should be of a scale appropriate to the land form.
5. Forests should integrate visually with adjacent farmland, for example, by planting broadleaved trees near the bottom of slopes to give some continuity from hedgerows and hedgerow trees.
6. Diversity of species, ages, and stand composition should be encouraged. Often careful species selection and matching species to changes in the site can do much to enhance the landscape. If done well, there is little conflict between good landscape and good silviculture.

Recreation

Of all outdoor activities, going into the countryside is the most popular and visiting forests is one of these attractions. There are numerous forms of recreation in forests, ranging from sightseeing, picnicking, walking, and camping, to educational and more energetic pursuits like orienteering and various forms of hunting. Each places different demands on a forest and on its design.

Usually the impact of recreation on timber production is insignificant since only very small areas are needed to accommodate large numbers of people and cars. In general, the features which make forests attractive for recreation are the same as those which make good landscape and a good conservation site: they include a large measure of diversity and the value of edges and water is high. One of the main criticisms of young conifer plantations is their close spacing. At very wide spacings, old conifers are seldom objected to but at close spacings, the dark conditions in relatively young stands are usually considered an eyesore. The answer is to wait and to thin. The constraints on silviculture therefore usually include the need for heavier and earlier thinning than normal, at least immediately adjacent to popular picnic sites and viewpoints and, being more conscious of the need for fire protection. Access may need to be improved and people discouraged from going to certain areas. Ground cover may need to be increased.

Very detailed planning and management of intensively used recreation areas is a subject in its own right and has been discussed in detail by Douglas (1982), among others.

Forest normality

At its simplest the term 'normality' means that a forest has an even distribution of age classes by area, ranging from newly planted crops to stands of rotation age. More precisely, normality implies arranging the forest so that production is the same each year, and can be maintained at a steady sustainable level. The concept can be extended to cover normality of annual production by species and size classes, of annual revenues, and of annual labour requirements.

Normality was considered very important in earlier centuries when local populations and industries depended on sustainable local supplies of wood, because transport over long distances was impossible. However some modern economists (for example Johnston et al. 1967) argue that, today, normality has little relevance in places where cheap and efficient internal transport is available since no one industry or community depends upon a regular supply of material from a single forest. This is clearly true for large forestry enterprises which are able to even out supplies by felling in more distant forests. It is less true for private owners depending upon woodlands for income, and such argument consigns the forests to periods of considerable risk at one time from damage of various kinds, with possible economic consequences.

For many of the aspects of forest design discussed in this chapter and elsewhere, the measure of diversity which normality confers brings advantages, in addition to the conventional one of allowing a steady outturn of produce, accompanied by a steady income and giving continued employment.

1. Normality guarantees that the proportion of the forest at risk from serious damage by wind, fire, pests, and pathogens is at a minimum over the period of a rotation, since stands tend to be vulnerable to any one form of damage only at particular stages in their lives.

2. The creation of a varied forest cover ensures that conservation, amenity, and recreation interests are maintained as far as possible.

The greater risks of a catastrophe occurring in a forest which is not normal could have direct economic consequences, as well as causing less quantifiable damage to the environment. The main disadvantage of too strict an adherence to normality is inflexibility in management, but this is easy to avoid by, for example, considering age classes of 5 years instead of annual ones.

It is often impracticable to spread planting of new areas over a whole, or even a large part of a rotation, but a satisfactory state, approaching normality, can be reached by the end of a second rotation, even in quite small forests. This is achieved by the varying optimum rotation lengths on sites of different levels of productivity, and of different species, the occasional need for some premature felling, windthrow, and the possibilities of some delayed felling.

Managing forests to maintain a mosaic of different age classes and, if possible of species as well, should be an important aim of a silviculturist. As Malcolm (1979) has pointed out, plantations cannot be expected to function as completely stable ecological systems in the face of environmental fluctuations, biological hazards, and changing demands by man. Heterogeneity confers a measure of resilience which enables forests to persist and to continue to be productive, despite such fluctuations, and it also enables them to absorb changes in market demands, social attitudes, and levels of inputs more readily.

References

Aaron, J. R. (1982). Conifer bark: its properties and uses. *Forestry Commission Forest Record* **110**. HMSO, London.

Adams, S. N., Dickson, D. A., and Cornforth, I. S. (1972). Some effects of soil water tables on the growth of Sitka spruce in Northern Ireland. *Forestry* **45**, 129–33.

Aldhous, J. R. (1972). Nursery practice. *Forestry Commission Bulletin* **43**. HMSO, London.

Andersen, J. (1953). Analysis of a Danish roe deer population. *Danish Review of Game Biology* **2**.

Anderson, H. W., Papadopol, C. S., and Zsuffa, L. (1983). Wood energy plantations in temperate climates. *Forest Ecology and Management* **6**, 281–306.

Anderson, M. L. (1961). *The selection of tree species* (2nd edn). Oliver & Boyd, London.

Anon. (1923). Observations on the results of artificial forestry in Germany. *Journal of Forestry* **21**, 718–22.

—— (1973). [The Göttingen Conference on forest and storm damage, February 1973.] *Forstarchiv* **44(3)**, 41–75.

—— (1976). Water balance of the headwater catchments of the Wye and Severn. *Institute of Hydrology Report* **33**. NERC, Wallingford, UK.

—— (1981). Forest planting, seeding and silvical treatments in the United States 1980 report. *USDA Forest Service FS-368*.

—— (1982). Forest fires in north America. In *Forest fire prevention and control* (ed. T. van Nao), pp. 53–61. Martinus Nijhoff/W. Junk Publishers, The Hague.

—— (1983*a*). Forestry Report No. 28 (September 1983). *Northern Forest Research Centre*, Edmonton, Alberta, Canada.

—— (1983*b*). In Research notes and utilization. *Commonwealth Forestry Review* **6?**, 131–2.

Armson, K. A. (1962). The growth of white spruce seedlings in relation to temperature summation indices. *Forestry Chronicle* **38**, 439–44.

Armstrong, W., Booth, T. C., Priestley, P., and Read, D. J. (1976). The relationship between soil aeration, stability and growth of Sitka spruce. *Journal of Applied Ecology* **13**, 585–91.

Ashton, F. M. and Crafts, A. S. (1981). *Mode of action of herbicides*. John Wiley and Sons, New York.

Assmann, E. (1955). Die Bedentung des 'erweiterten Eichhorn'schen Gesetzes' fur die Konstruktion von Fichten-Ertragstafeln. *Forstwissenschaftliches Centralblatt* **74**, 321–30.

—— (1970). *The principles of forest yield study*. Pergamon Press, Oxford.

Atkinson, B. W. and Smithson, P. A. (1976). Precipitation. In *The climate of the British Isles* (eds T. J. Chandler and S. Gregory), pp. 129–182. Longman, London.

Atterson, J. (1980). Gambling with gales. Paper for British Association for the Advancement of Science, Section K* (Forestry). Salford 1980.

Baker, F. S. (1934). *Theory and practice of silviculture.* McGraw-Hill, London.

Baker, H. G. (1974). The evolution of weeds. *Annual Review of Ecology and Systematics* **5**, 1–24.

Balneaves, J. M. (1984). Some aspects of grass control for radiata pine establishment in New Zealand. In *Aspects of Biology* Vol. 5, pp. 69–79. Association of Applied Biologists, Warwick.

Barner, H., Rouland, H., and Qvortrup, S. A. (1980). [*Abies procera* seed supply and choice of provenance.] *Dansk Skovforenings Tidsskrift* **65**, 263–95.

Barnes, R. D. (1984). Genotype–environment interaction in the genetic improvement of fast-growing plantation trees. In IUFRO *Symposium on site and productivity of fast-growing plantations* Vol. 1, pp. 197–213. South Africa Forest Research Institute, Pretoria.

Baule, H. and Fricke, C. (1970). *The fertilizer treatment of forest trees.* BLV · Verlagsgesellschaft mbH, Munich, W. Germany.

Belyi, G. D. (1975). [Stand density and its regulation in the control of *Fomes annosus*.] *Lesovodstvo i agrolesmelioratsiya* **40**, 28–35.

Bengston, G. W. (1977). *Fertilizers in use and under evaluation in silviculture: a status report.* Paper for XVI IUFRO World congress, Oslo 1976. Published by Dorschkamp Research Institute, Wageningen, Netherlands.

Berg, S. (1981). Terrain classification for forestry in the Nordic countries. In *Proceedings of the workshop on land evaluation in forestry* (ed. P. Laban), pp. 152–66. ILRI publication 28, Wageningen, Netherlands.

Bevan, D. (1984). Coping with infestations. *Quarterly Journal of Forestry* **78**, 36–40.

Bigg, W. L. (1982). Some effects of nitrate, ammonium and mycorrhizal fungi on the growth of Douglas-fir and Sitka spruce. Thesis summary in *Forestry Abstracts* **43**, 601–602.

Binns, W. O. (1962). Some aspects of peat as a substrate for tree growth. *Irish Forestry* **19**, 32–55.

—— (1975). Fertilizers in the forest: a guide to materials. *Forestry Commission Leaflet* **63**. HMSO, London.

—— (1983). Treatment of surface workings. In *Forestry Commission Research and Development Paper* **132**, 9–16.

—— and Crowther, R. E. (1983). Land reclamation for trees and woods. *Reclamation* **83**, 23–8.

—— and Fourt, D. F. (1980). Surface workings and trees. *Forestry Commission Occasional Paper* **10**, 60–75.

—— and —— (1981). Reclamation of surface workings for trees. *Forestry Commission Research Information Note* **67**.

—— Mayhead, G. J., and Mackenzie, J. M. (1980). Nutrient deficiencies of conifers in British forests. *Forestry Commission Leaflet* **76**. HMSO, London.

Blatchford, O. N. (ed.) (1978). Forestry practice. *Forestry Commission Bulletin* **14**. HMSO, London.

Boardman, R. (1979). Maintenance of productivity in successive rotations of radiata pine in South Australia. In *Ecology of even-aged forest plantations* (eds E. D. Ford, D. C. Malcolm, and J. Atterson), pp. 543–53. Institute of Terrestrial Ecology, Cambridge.

—— (1984). Fast-growing species—pattern, process and ageing. In *Proceedings of IUFRO Symposium on site and productivity of fast-growing plantations* Vol. 1, pp. 1–49. South Africa Forest Research Institute, Pretoria.

Boggie, R. (1972). Effect of water-table height on root development of *Pinus contorta* on deep peat in Scotland. *Oikos* **23**, 304–12.

—— and Miller, H. G. (1976). Growth of *Pinus contorta* at different water-table levels in deep blanket peat. *Forestry* **49**, 123–31.

Boling, R. (1984). 'The Pill' for seedlings. *American Forests* **90(6)**, 30–32, 56.

Bollen, W. B., Chen, C. S., *et al.* (1967). Influence of red alder on fertility of a forest soil. Microbial and chemical effects. *Research Bulletin Oregon Forest Research Laboratory* **12**.

Bonga, J. M. and Durzan, D. J. (1982). *Tissue culture in forestry*. Martinus Nijhoff/Dr. W. Junk Publishers, The Hague.

Bornebusch, C. H. (1937). [Report on the incidence of storm damage in the spruce thinning plots in Hastrup Plantation.] *Forstlige Forsøgsvaesen i Danmark* **14**, 161–72.

Bowen, G. D. and Nambiar, E. K. S. (ed.) (1984). *Nutrition of plantation forests*. Academic Press, London.

Boyle, K., Farrell, E. P., and Gardiner, J. J. (1982). Harvesting: its effect on the physical properties of soils. *Irish Forestry* **39**, 94–8.

Braastad, H. (1978). [Thinning intensity and frequency of damage. Report on snow and wind damage in research plot 918.] *Norsk Skogbruk* **24(5)**, 20. (From a review.)

Bradley, R. T. (1963). Thinning as an instrument of forest management. *Forestry* **36**, 181–94.

—— Christie, J. M., and Johnston, D. R. (1966). Forest management tables. *Forestry Commission Booklet* **16**. HMSO, London.

Bradshaw, A. D. and Chadwick, M. J. (1980). *The restoration of land*. Blackwell Scientific Publications, Oxford.

Brinar, M. (1972). [Investigation of the hereditary characters of a particular selected spruce.] *Gozderski Vestnik* **30(2)**, 37–45.

Brouard, N. R. (1967). *Damage by tropical cyclones to forest plantations with particular reference to Mauritius*. Government Printer, Mauritius.

Brown, R. M. (1971). Cold storage of forest plants. *Quarterly Journal of Forestry* **65**, 305–15.

Brünig, E. F. (1967). On the limits of vegetable productivity in the tropical rain forest and the boreal coniferous forest. *Journal of Indian Botanical Society* **46**, 314–322.

—— (1973). [Storm damage as a risk factor in wood production in the most important wood-producing regions of the earth.] *Forstarchiv* **44**, 137–140. (English translation by W. Linnard, Commonwealth Forestry Bureau, Oxford 4339).

Bryant, J. P., Chapin, F. S., and Klein, D. R. (1983). Carbon/nutrient balance of boreal plants in relation to vertebrate herbivory. *Oikos* **40**, 357–68.

Bucknell, J. (1964). *Climatology—an introduction*. Macmillan, London.

Burdett, A. N. (1978). Root form and mechanical stability in planted lodgepole pine in British Columbia. In Proceedings of the root form of planted trees symposium. *British Columbia Ministry of Forests/Canadian Forestry service joint Report* **8**. (eds E. van Eerdenan and J. M. Kinghorn), pp. 162–5.

—— (1979). Juvenile instability in planted pines. *Irish Forestry* **36**, 36–47.

Burdon, R. (1982). Monocultures—how vulnerable? *What's new in forest Research* No. **115**. Forest Research Institute, New Zealand.

Burke, M. J., Gusta, L. V., Quamme, H. A., Weiser, C. J., and Li, P. H. (1976). Freezing and injury in plants. *Annual Review of Plant Physiology* **27**, 507–28.

Burke, W. (1967). Principles of drainage with special reference to peat. *Irish Forestry* **24**, 1–7.

—— (1978). Long-term effects of drainage and land use on some physical properties of blanket peat. *Irish Journal of Agricultural Research* **17**, 315–22.

Burley, J. (1965). Genetic variation in *Picea sitchensis*. *Commonwealth Forestry Review* **44**, 47–59.

Busby, R. J. N. (1974). Forest site yield guide to upland Britain. *Forestry Commission Forest Record* **97**. HMSO, London.

—— and Grayson, A. J. (1981). Investment appraisal in forestry. *Forestry Commission Booklet* **47**. HMSO, London.

Butcher, T. B. (1980). Competitive effect of pine regrowth and woody weeds on the growth of *Pinus pinaster*. *Australian Forestry* **43**, 75–80.

Butin, H. and Shigo, A. L. (1981). Radial shakes and 'frostcracks' in living oak trees. · *USDA Forest Service Research Paper NE-478*.

Caborn, J. M. (1965). *Shelterbelts and windbreaks*. Faber and Faber, London.

Cajander, A. K. (1921). Uber Waldtypen in allgemeinen. *Acta Forestalia Fennica* **20**, 1–77.

Callaham, R. Z. (1964). Provenance research: investigation of genetic diversity associated with geography. *Unasylva* **18**, 40–50.

Cannell, M. G. R. (1980). Productivity of closely spaced young poplar on agricultural soils in Britain. *Forestry* **53**, 1–21.

—— and Smith, R. I. (1980). Yields of minirotation closely spaced hardwoods in temperate regions: review and appraisal. *Forest Science* **26**, 415–28.

Chapman, N. G. and Chapman, D. I. (1982). The fallow deer. *Forestry Commission Forestry Record* **124**. HMSO, London.

Chavasse, C. G. R. (1979). The means to excellence through plantation establishment: the New Zealand experience. In *Forest Plantations: the shape of the future*. Proceedings of Weyerhaeuser Science Symposium held at Tacoma, Washington, 30 April–3 May 1978 (ed. D. D. Lloyd), pp. 119–37.

—— Balneaves, J. M., and Bowles, G. P. (1981). Blanking plantations of radiata pine. *New Zealand Journal of Forestry* **26**, 55–69.

Cheney, N. P. (1971). Fire protection of industrial plantations. *FO:SF/ZAM5. Technical Report* **4**. FAO, Rome.

Christie, J. M. and Lines, R. (1979). A comparison of forest productivity in Britain and Europe in relation to climatic factors. *Forestry Ecology and Management* **2**, 75–102.

Clear, T. (1976). Forestry Journey to New Zealand. *Irish Forestry* **33**, 80–93.

Clipsham, I. D. (1984). The effect of oil-surfactant additive on activity and leaf entry of hexazinone and glyphosate. *Aspects of Applied Biology* 5, pp. 143–50. Association of Applied Biologists, Wellesbourne, UK.

Conway, G. (1981). Man versus pests. In *Theoretical ecology* (2nd edn) (ed. R. M. May), pp. 356–86. Blackwell Scientific Publications, Oxford.

Cooke, A. (1983). The effects of fungi on food selection by *Lumbricus terrestris*. In *Earthworm ecology* (ed. J. E. Satchell), pp. 365–73. Chapman & Hall, London.

Cooper, A. B. and Mutch, W. E. S. (1979). The management of red deer in plantations. In *Ecology of even-aged forest plantations* (eds E. D. Ford, D. C. Malcolm, and J. Atterson), pp. 453–62. Institute of Terrestrial Ecology, Cambridge.

Coutts, M. P. and Armstrong, W. (1976). The role of oxygen transport in the tolerance of trees to waterlogging. In *Tree physiology and yield improvement* (eds M. G. R. Cannell and F. T. Last), pp. 361–85. Academic Press, London.

—— and Philipson, J. J. (1978a). Tolerance of tree roots to waterlogging: I. Survival of Sitka spruce and lodgepole pine. *New Phytologist* **80**, 63–9.

—— and —— (1978b). Tolerance of tree roots to waterlogging: II. Adaptation of Sitka spruce and lodgepole pine to waterlogged soil. *New Phytologist* **80**, 71–7.

Craib, I. J. (1939). Thinning, pruning and management studies on the main exotic conifers grown in South Africa. *Department of Agriculture and Forestry Science Bulletin* **196**. Government Printer, Pretoria.

Crawford, R. M. M. (1976). Tolerance of anoxia and the regulation of glycolysis in tree roots. In *Tree physiology and yield improvement* (eds M. G. R. Cannell and F. T. Last), pp. 387–401. Academic Press, London.

—— (1982). Physiological responses to flooding. In *Physiological plant ecology II* (eds O. L. Lange, P. S. Nobel, C. B. Osmond, and H. Ziegler), pp. 454–77. Springer-Verlag, Berlin.

Cremer, K. W., Myers, B. J., Duys, F. van der, and Craig, I. E. (1977). Silvicultural lessons from the 1974 windthrow in radiata pine plantations near Canberra. *Australian Forestry* **40**, 274–92.

Crichton, D. (1982). The future for poplars in Britain. *Proceedings 10th International Forestry Students Symposium*, pp. 60–66. University of Aberdeen.

Critchfield, W. B. (1957). Geographic variation in *Pinus contorta*. *Maria Moors Cabat Foundation Publication* **3**. Harvard University Press.

Crooke, M. (1979). The development of populations of insects. In *Ecology of even-aged forest plantations* (eds E. D. Ford, D. C. Malcolm, and J. Atterson), pp. 209–17. Institute of Terrestrial Ecology, Cambridge.

Crowe, S. (1978). The landscape of forests and woods. *Forestry Commission Booklet* **44**. HMSO, London.

Crowther, R. E. and Evans, J. (1984). Coppice. *Forestry Commission Leaflet* **83**. HMSO, London.

Dallas, W. G. (1962). The progress of peatland afforestation in Northern Ireland. *Irish Forestry* **19**, 84–93.

Daniel, T. W., Helms, J. A., and Baker, F. S. (1979). *Principles of silviculture.* McGraw-Hill, New York.

Davies, E. J. M. (1980). Useless? The case against contorta. *Scottish Forestry* **34**, 110–13 and letter on p. 156.

Davies, R. J. (1984). The importance of weed control and the use of tree shelters for establishing broadleaved trees on grass-dominated sites in England. In proceedings ECE/FAO/ILO Seminar *Techniques and machines for the rehabilitation of low-productivity forest*. Turkey, May 1984.

Dawkins, H. C. (1958). The management of natural tropical high-forest with special reference to Uganda. *Imperial Forestry Institute Oxford Paper* **34**.

—— (1963). Crown diameters: their relation to bole diameter in tropical forest trees. *Commonwealth Forestry Review* **42**, 318–33.

—— (1967). Productivity of tropical rain forests and their ultimate value to man. In *The Ecology of man in the tropical environment*, pp. 178–82. IUCN Publications New Series **4**. Morges, Switzerland.

Day, W. R. and Peace, T. R. (1946). Spring frosts. *Forestry Commission Bulletin* **18**. HMSO, London.

Dickson, D. A. (1971). The effect of form, rate and position of phosphatic fertilizers on growth and nutrient uptake of Sitka spruce on deep peat. *Forestry* **44**, 17–26.

—— (1977). Nutrition of Sitka spruce on peat—problems and speculations. *Irish Forestry* **34**, 31–9.

—— and Savill, P. S. (1974). Early growth of *Picea sitchensis* on deep oligotrophic peat in Northern Ireland. *Forestry* **47**, 57–88.

Dixon, A. F. G. (1971). Effect of aphids on wood formation. *Journal of Applied Ecology* **8**, 165–79.

Dodds, J. H. (ed.) (1983). *Tissue culture of trees*. Croom and Helm, Beckenham, Kent.

Donald, D. G. M. (1984). Silviculture and yield. In IUFRO *Symposium on site and productivity of fast-growing plantations* Vol. 1, pp. 163–80. South Africa Forest Research Institute, Pretoria.

Dørmling, I., Elvenberg, C., and Lindgren, D. (1976). Vegetative propagation and tissue culture. Royal College of Forestry, Department of Forest Genetics, *Research Note* **22**, Stockholm.

Douglas, R. W. (1982). *Forest Recreation*. Pergamon Press, New York.

Drew, J. T. and Flewelling, J. W. (1977). Some recent Japanese theories of yield-density relationships and their application to Monterey pine plantations. *Forest Science* **23**, 517–34.

Driessche, R. van den (1980). Effects of nitrogen and phosphorus fertilization on Douglas-fir nursery growth and survival after outplanting. *Canadian Journal of Forest Research* **10**, 65–70.

—— (1982). Relationship between spacing and nitrogen fertilization of seedlings in the nursery, seedling size and outplanting performance. *Canadian Journal of Forest Research* **12**, 865–75.

—— (1983). Growth, survival and physiology of Douglas-fir seedlings following root wrenching and fertilization. *Canadian Journal of Forest Research* **13**, 270–8.

—— (1984). Relationships between spacing and nitrogen fertilization of seedlings in the nursery, seedling mineral nutrition and outplanting performance. *Canadian Journal of Forest Research* **14**, 431–6.

Dropkin, V. H., Linit, M., Kondo, E., and Smith, M. (1981). Pine wilt associated with *Bursaphelenchus xylophilus* in the USA. *Proceedings Division 2 XVII IUFRO World Congress*, 265–8.

Duryea, M. L. and Landis, T. D. (ed.) (1984). *Forest Nursery Manual*. Martinus Nijhoff/Dr. W. Junk Publishers, The Hague.

Duvigneaud, P. and Denaeyer-de Smet, S. (1970). Biological cycling of minerals in temperate deciduous forests. In *Ecological studies 1: temperate forest ecosystems* (ed. D. E. Reichle), pp. 199–225. Chapman and Hall, London.

Edwards, P. N. (1980). Does pre-commercial thinning have a place in plantation forestry in Britain? *Biologische, technische und wirtschaftliche Aspekte der Jungbestandspflege* (ed. H. Kramer) Vol. 67, pp. 214–23. Schriften Forstlichen Fakultät, Universität Göttingen.

—— and Christie, J. M. (1981). Yield models for forest management. *Forestry Commission Booklet* **48**. Forestry Commission, Edinburgh, UK plus numerous optional loose-leaf tables.

Eerden, E. van and Kinghorn, J. M. (eds). (1978). Proceedings of the root form of planted trees symposium. *British Columbia Ministry of Forests/Canadian Forestry Service Joint Report* **8**.

Eis, S. (1978). Natural root forms of western conifers. In *Proceedings of the root form of planted trees symposium. British Columbia Ministry of Forests/ Canadian Forestry Service Joint Report* **8** (eds E. van Eerden and J. M. Kinghorn), pp. 23–7.

Etverk, I. (1972). [Factors affecting the resistance of stands to storms.] *Metsanduslikud Uurimused, Estorian SSR9*, 222–36.

Evans, J. (1976). Plantations: productivity and prospects. *Australian Forestry* **39**, 150–63.

—— (1982*a*). *Plantation Forestry in the Tropics.* Clarendon Press, Oxford.

—— (1982*b*). Sweet chestnut coppice. *Forestry Commission Research Information Note* 770/82.

—— (1982*c*). Silviculture of oak and beech in northern France: observations and current trends. *Quarterly Journal of Forestry* **76**, 75–82.

—— (1983). Choice of *Eucalyptus* species for cold temperate atlantic climates. In *Frost resistant eucalypts.* IUFRO/AFOCEL Symposium, Bordeaux, France.

—— (1984). Silviculture of broadleaved woodland. *Forestry Commission Bulletin* **62**. HMSO, London.

Everard, J. E. (1974). Fertilizers in the establishment of conifers in Wales and southern England. *Forestry Commission Booklet* **41**. HMSO, London.

Evert, F. (1971). Spacing studies—a review. Canadian Forest Service. *Forest Management Institute Information Report* FMR-X-37.

Faber, P. J. and Burg, J. van den. (1982). [The production of woody biomass]. *Nederlands Bosbouw Tijdschrift* **54(7/8)**, 198–205.

—— and Sissingh, G. (1975). Stability of stands to wind. I. A theoretical approach. II. The practical viewpoint. *Nederlands Bosbouw Tijdschrift* **47(7/8)**, 179–93.

Fairbairn, W. A. (1968). Climatic zonation in the British Isles. *Forestry* **41**, 115–30.

FAO (1967). Actual and potential role of man-made forests in the changing world pattern of wood consumption. In *World Symposium on man-made forests and their industrial importance.* Vol. 1, pp. 1–51. FAO, Rome.

—— (1980). Poplars and willows in wood production and land use. *FAO Forestry Series No.* **10**. FAO, Rome.

FAO/ECE (1982). Information on forest fires. In *Forest fire prevention and control* (ed. T. van Nao), pp. 1–19. Martinus Nijhoff/W. Junk Publishers, The Hague.

Farrell, P. W. (1984). Radiata pine residue management and its implications for site productivity on sandy soils. *Australian Forestry* **47**, 95–102.

—— Flinn, D. W., Squire, R. O., and Craig, F. G. (1981). On the maintenance of productivity of radiata pine monocultures on sandy soils in south-east Australia. *Proceedings division 1, XVII IUFRO world congress*, Japan, pp. 117–28.

Faubel, A. L. (1941). *Cork and the American cork industry.* Cork Institute of America.

Faulkner, R. (ed.) (1975). Seed orchards. *Forestry Commission Bulletin* **54**. HMSO, London.

Fauss, D. L. and Pierce, W. R. (1969). Stand conditions and spruce budworm damage in a western Montana forest. *Journal of Forestry* **67**, 322–5.

Feeny, P. (1976). Plant apparency and chemical defense. In *Recent advances in phytochemistry* (eds J. W. Wallace and R. L. Mansell) Vol. 10, pp. 1–40. Plenum Press, New York and London.

Fenton, R. T. (1967). Rotations in man-made forests. *FAO World symposium on man-made forests and their industrial importance*, Canberra, Australia. Vol. 1, pp. 600–3.

Ford, E. D. (1980). Can we design a short rotation silviculture for windthrow-prone areas? In *Research strategy for silviculture* (ed. D. C. Malcolm), pp. 25–34. Institute of Foresters of Great Britain, Edinburgh.

—— (1982). Catastrophe and disruption in forest ecosystems and their implications for plantation forestry. *Scottish Forestry* **36**, 9–24.

Ford-Robertson, F. C. (1971). Terminology of forest science, technology, practice and products. *Multilingual Forestry Terminology Series* No. **1**. Society of American Foresters, Washington, D.C.

Forestry Department, Brisbane (1963). *Technique for the establishment and maintenance of plantations of Hoop pine*, pp. 22–8. Government Printer, Brisbane.

Forestry Department, Queensland (1981). Exotic conifer plantations. In *Research Report 1981*, pp. 37–41. Department of Forestry, Brisbane, Queensland.

Fox, J. E. D. (1984). Rehabilitation of mined lands. *Forestry Abstracts* (Review Article) **45(9)**, 565–600.

Fox, J. F. (1983). Post-fire succession of small-mammal and bird communities. In *The role of fire in northern circumpolar ecosystems* (eds R. W. Wein and D. A. MacLean), pp. 155–80. John Wiley and Sons, New York.

Fraser, A. I. (1964). Wind tunnel and other related studies on coniferous trees and tree crops. *Scottish Forestry* **18**, 84–92.

French, D. W. and Schroeder, D. B. (1969). The oak wilt fungus, *Ceratocystis fagacearum*, as a selective silvicide. *Forest Science* **15**, 198–203.

Frissel, M. J. (ed.) (1977). Cycling of mineral nutrients in agricultural ecosystems. *Agro-Ecosystems* **4**.

Fryer, J. D. and Makepeace, R. J. (1977). *Weed control handbook Volume 1: Principles* (6th edn). Blackwell Scientific Publications, Oxford.

—— and —— (1978). *Weed control handbook Volume II: Recommendations* (8th edn). Blackwell Scientific Publications, Oxford.

Fujimori, T. (1980). Pruning techniques in Japan. *Biologische technische und wirtschaftliche Aspekte der Jungbestanspflege* (ed. H. Kramer) Vol. 67, pp. 77–81. Schriften Forstlichen Fakultät, Universität Göttingen.

Funk, D. T. (1979). Stem form response to repeated pruning of young black walnut trees. *Canadian Journal of Forest Research* **9**, 114–16.

Gerischer, G. F. R. and de Villiers, A. M. (1963). The effect of heavy pruning on timber properties. *Forestry in South Africa* **3**, 15–41.

Gibson, I. A. S. and Jones, T. (1977). Monoculture as the origin of major forest pests and diseases. In *Origins of pest, parasite, disease and weed problems* (eds J. M. Cherritt and G. R. Sagar), pp. 139–61. Blackwell Scientific Publications, Oxford.

—— Burley, J., and Speight, M. R. (1982). The adoption of agricultural practices for the development of heritable resistance to pests and pathogens in forest crops. In *Resistance to diseases and pests in forest trees* (eds H. M. Heybroek, B. R. Stephan, and K. von Weissenberg), pp. 9–21. Centre for Agricultural Publishing and Documentation, Wageningen, Netherlands.

Giertych, M. M. (1976). Summary results of the IUFRO 1938 Norway spruce provenance experiment height growth. *Silvae Genetica* **25**, 154–64.

Gilchrist, W. (1872). On the soils best suited for the different kinds of forest trees, as indicated by the plants that grow naturally upon them. *Transactions of the Scottish Arboricultural Society* **6**, 293–303.

Gill, C. J. (1970). The flooding tolerance of woody species—a review. *Forestry Abstracts* (Review Article) **31**, 671–688.

Giovannetti, B. and Fontana, A. (1982). Mycorrhizal synthesis between *Cistaceae* and *Tuberaceae*. *New Phytologist* **92**, 533–7.

Goor, C. P. van (1970). Fertilization of conifer plantations. *Irish Forestry* **27**, 68–80.

Gordon, G. T. (1973). Damage from wind and other causes in mixed white fir–red fir stands adjacent to clear cuttings. *Research Paper Pacific Southwest Forest and Range Experiment Station PSW-90. USDA Forest Service.*

Grace, J. (1977). *Plant responses to wind*. Academic Press, London.

—— (1983). *Plant-atmosphere relationships*. Chapman and Hall, London.

Granfield, E. F., MacMahon, C. D., and Mithen, D. A. (1980). Developments in forest road planning. *Forestry Commission Research and Development Paper* **127**. Edinburgh.

Gregory, S. (1976). Regional climates. In *The climate of the British Isles* (eds T. J. Chandler and S. Gregory), pp. 330–42. Longman, London.

Grene, S. (1978). Root deformations reduce root growth and stability. In Proceedings of the root form of planted trees symposium. *British Columbia Ministry of Forests/Canadian Forestry Service Joint Report* **8** (eds E. van Eerden and J. M. Kinghorn), pp. 150–5.

Grieve, I. C. (1978). Some effects of the plantation of conifers on a freely drained lowland soil, Forest of Dean, U.K. *Forestry* **51**, 21–28.

Griffith, P. W. (1976). Introduction of the problems. In Shelterbelts on the great plains (ed. R. W. Tinus). *Great Plains Agricultural Publication* **78**, pp. 3–7.

Griffiths, J. D. (1966). *Applied climatology*. Oxford University Press.

Gryse, J. J. de (1955). Forest pathology in New Zealand. *New Zealand Forest Service Bulletin*, **11**.

Guillaume, C. A. (1982). The use of chemicals in forest fire suppression. In *Forest fire prevention and control* (ed. T. van Nao), pp. 159–63. Martinus Nijhoff/ W. Junk Publishers, The Hague.

Habjørg, A. (1972). Effects of photoperiod on temperature growth and development of three longitudinal and three altitudinal populations of *Betula pubescens*. *Meldinger fra Norges landbrukshogskole* **51(2)**.

Hagen, L. J. (1976). Windbreak design for optimum wind erosion control. In Shelterbelts on the Great Plains (ed. R. W. Tinus), *Great Plains Agricultural Publication* **78**, 31–6.

Hagglund, B. (1981). Evaluation of forest site productivity. *Forestry Abstracts* (Review Article) **42**, 515–27.

Hagner, S. (1983). *Pinus contorta*: Sweden's third conifer. *Forest Ecology and Management* **6**, 185–99.

Hall, D. O. (1983). Food versus fuel, a world problem. In *Energy from Biomass* (eds A. Strub, P. Chartier, and G. Schleser), pp. 43–62. Applied Science Publishers, London.

Hall, R. L. (1978). The analysis and significance of competitive and non-competitive interactions between species. In *Plant relations and pastures* (ed. J. R. Wilson), pp. 263–74. CSIRO, Melbourne, Australia.

Halsam, E. (1966). *Chemistry of vegetable tannins*. Academic Press, New York.

Hamilton, G. J. (1976a). The Bowmont Norway spruce thinning experiment 1930–1974. *Forestry* **49**, 109–19.

—— (ed.) (1976b). Effects of line thinning on increment. In *Aspects of thinning. Forestry Commission Bulletin* **55**, 37–45. HMSO, London.

—— (1980). Line thinning. *Forestry Commission Leaflet* **77**. HMSO, London.

—— (1981). The effect of high intensity thinning on yield. *Forestry* **54**, 1–15.

—— and Christie, J. M. (1971). Forest management tables (metric). *Forestry Commission Booklet* **34**. HMSO, London.

Handley, W. R. C. (1963). Mycorrhizal associations and *Calluna* heathland afforestation. *Forestry Commission Bulletin* **36**. HMSO, London.

Harley, J. L. (1971). Fungi in ecosystems. *Journal of Applied Ecology* **8**, 627–42.

Harper, J. L. (1977). *Population biology of plants*. Academic Press, London.

—— (1982). The concept of population in modular organisms. In *Theoretical ecology* (2nd edn) (ed. R. M. May), pp. 53–77. Blackwell Scientific publications, Oxford.

Hawkins, J. C. (1962). The effects of cultivation on aeration, drainage and other soil factors important in plant growth. *Journal of the Science of Food and Agriculture* **13**, 386–91.

Heal, O. W., Swift, M. J., and Anderson, J. M. (1982). Nitrogen cycling in United Kingdom forests: the relevance of basic ecological research. *Philosophical Transactions of the Royal Society Ser. B* **296**, 427–44.

Heilman, P. (1982). Nitrogen and organic-matter accumulation in coal mine spoils supporting red alder stands. *Canadian Journal of Forest Research* **12**, 809–13.

—— Dao, T., Cheng, H. H., Webster, S. R., and Harper, S. S. (1982*a*). Comparison of fall and spring applications of ^{15}N-labelled urea to Douglas-fir: I. Growth responses and nitrogen levels in foliage and soil. *Soil Science Society of America Journal* **46**, 1293–9.

—— —— —— —— and Christensen, L. (1982*b*). Comparison of fall and spring applications of ^{15}N-labelled urea to Douglas-fir: II. Fertilizer nitrogen recovery in trees and soil after two years. *Soil Science Society of America Journal* **46**, 1300–4.

Helliwell, D. R. (1982). *Options in forestry*. Packard Publishing Ltd, Chichester, UK.

Hellum, A. K. (1978). The growth of planted spruce in Alberta. In Proceedings of the root form of planted trees symposium. *British Columbia Ministry of Forests/Canadian Forestry Service Joint Report* **8** (eds E. van Eerden and J. M. Kinghorn). pp. 191–6.

Hendrick, E., O'Carroll, N., and Pfeifer, A. R. (1984). Effect of ploughing direction and method on stem form of south coastal lodgepole pine. *Irish Forestry* **41**, 66–76.

Hengst, E. and Schulze, W. (1976). [Examples of spatial organisation as a means of increasing the security of production in *Picea abies* forests.] *Wissenschaftliche Zeitschrift der Technischen Universität*, Dresden 25, 313–14.

Henman, D. W. (1963*a*). Forest drainage. *Forestry Commission Research Branch Paper* **26**. HMSO, London.

—— (1963*b*). Pruning conifers for the production of quality timber. *Forestry Commission Bulletin* **35**. HMSO, London.

Heybroek, H. M. (1981). Possibilities of clonal plantations in the 1980s and beyond. *Commonwealth Forestry Institute Occasional Paper* **15**. (ed. K. A. Longman), pp. 21–2.

—— Stephan, B, R., and Weissenberg, K. von (eds) (1982). *Resistance to diseases and pests in forest trees*. Centre for Agricultural Publishing and Documentation, Wageningen, Netherlands.

Hill, H. W. (1979). Severe damage to forests in Canterbury, New Zealand resulting from orographically reinforced winds. In *Symposium of forest meteorology*.

World meteorological organisation 527 (published by Canadian Forest Service). pp. 22–40.

Hill, M. O. (1979). The development of a flora in even-aged plantations. In *Ecology of even-aged forest plantations* (eds E. D. Ford, D. C. Malcolm, and J. Atterson), pp. 175–92. Institute of Terrestrial Ecology, Cambridge.

Hillel, D. (1971). *Soil and water: Physical principles and processes*. Academic Press, New York.

Hinson, W. H., Pyatt, D. G., and Fourt, D. F. (1970). Drainage studies. In *Report on forest research* 1970. Forestry Commission, HMSO, London. pp. 90–1.

Holliday, R. J. and Putwain, P. D. (1980). The development of resistance to simazine, in frequently sprayed orchards, in *Senecio vulgaris*. *Journal of Applied Ecology* **17**, 779–91.

Holloway, C. W. (1967). The protection of man-made forests from wildlife. In *FAO World Symposium on man-made forests and their industrial importance*, Canberra, Australia. Vol. 1, pp. 697–715.

Holmes, G. D. (1980). Weed control in forestry—achievements and prospects in Britain. In *Proceedings of the conference on weed control in forestry*, 1–2 April 1980. University of Nottingham. pp. 1–11.

Holmsgaard, E., Holstener-Jørgensen, H., and Yde-Andersen, A. (1961). [Soil formation, increment and health of first—and second—generation stands of Norway spruce.] *Forstlige Forsøgsvaesen i Danmark* **27(1)**.

Holstener-Jørgensen, H. (1977). Plant nutrient balance in decoration greenery cultivation. *Silvae fennica* **11(3)**, 230–3.

Howes, F. N. (1949). *Vegetable gums and resins*. Chronica Botanica Co., Waltham. MA, USA.

—— (1958). *Nuts*. Faber and Faber, London.

Hutchinson, C. E. (1965). *The ecology theater and the evolutionary play*. Yale University Press, Newhaven, CT, USA.

Hütte, P. (1968). Experiments on windthrow and wind damage in Germany: site and susceptibility of spruce forests to storm damage. *Forestry* (supplement) **41**, 20–6.

Huuri, O. (1978). Effect of various treatments at planting and of soft containers in the development of Scots pine. In Proceedings of the root form of planted trees symposium. *British Columbia Ministry of Forests/Canadian Forestry Service Joint Report* **8**. (eds E. van Eerden and J. M. Kinghorn). pp. 101–18.

Insley, H. (1982). The influence of post planting maintenance on the growth of newly planted broadleaved trees. In *Proceedings of Conference of Horticultural Education Association*, 5–8th April 1982 Bridgewater, UK. pp. 74–80.

Jack, W. H. (1965). Experiments on tree growing on peat in N. Ireland. *Forestry* **38**, 220–40.

Jahn, G. (ed.) (1982). *Handbook of vegetation science*. W. Junk Publishers, The Hague.

Jarvis, P. G. (1981). Production efficiency of coniferous forest in the UK. In *Physiological processes limiting plant production* (ed. C. B. Johnson), pp. 81–107. 30th University of Nottingham Easter School, UK.

—— and Leverenz, J. W. (1983). Productivity of temperate, deciduous and evergreen forests. In *Physiological Plant Ecology IV* (eds O. L. Lange, P. S. Nobel, C. B. Osmond, and M. Ziegler), pp. 233–80. Springer-Verlag, Berlin.

Johnston, D. R., Grayson, A. J., and Bradley, R. T. (1967). *Forest planning*. Faber and Faber, London.

Johnson, V. J. (1984). Prescribed burning. *Journal of Forestry* **82(2)**, 82–90.

Jones, E. W. (1945). The structure and reproduction of the virgin forest of the north temperate zone. *New Phytologist* **44**, 130–48.

—— (1965). Pure conifers in central Europe—a review of some old and new work. *Journal Oxford University Forestry Society* **13**, 3–15.

Karkkainen, M. (1981). [Increasing resin content in pine and spruce stemwood for higher by-product yield.] *Communications Institute Forestalais Fenniae* **96(8)**.

Keeves, A. (1966). Some evidence of loss of productivity with successive rotations of *Pinus radiata* in the south-east of South Australia. *Australian Forestry* **30**, 51–63.

Kendrew, W. G. (1953). *Climates of the continents* (4th edn). Clarendon Press, Oxford.

Keresztesi, B. (1983). Breeding and cultivation of black locust in Hungary. *Forest Ecology and Management* **6**, 217–44.

Khanna, P. K. (1981). Soil analyses for evaluation of forest nutrient supply. In *Proceedings of Australian forest nutrition workshop: Productivity in perpetuity*, Australia, 10–14 August 1981. CSIRO Division of Forest Research. pp. 231–8.

Kilian, W. (1981). Site classification systems used in forestry. In *Proceedings of the workshop on land evaluation for forestry* (ed. P. Laban), pp. 134–51. International Institute for Land Reclamation and Improvement, Publication 28, Wageningen, Netherlands.

Kilpatrick, D. J., Sanderson, J. M., and Savill, P. S. (1981). The influence of five early respacing treatments on the growth of Sitka spruce. *Forestry* **54**, 17–29.

Kinghorn, J. M. (1978). Minimising potential root problems through container design. In Proceedings of the root form of planted trees symposium. *British Columbia Ministry of Forests/Canadian Forestry Service Joint Report* **8** (eds E. van Eerden and J. M. Kinghorn), pp. 311–18.

Kira, T. (1975). Primary production in forests. In *Photosynthesis and productivity in different environments* (ed. J. P. Cooper), pp. 5–40. Cambridge University Press, UK.

—— and Shidei, T. (1967). Primary production and turnover of organic matter in different forest ecosystems of western Pacific. *Japanese Journal of Ecology* **17**, 80–7.

Kleinschmit, J. and Otto, H-J. (1974). [Rehabilitation of the gale-damage of forests of Lower Saxony.] *Forst und Holzwirt* **29**, 1–12.

—— and Schmidt, J. (1977). Experiences with *Picea abies* cuttings propagation in Germany and problems conected with large scale application. *Silvae Genetica* **26**, 197–203.

Knowles, R. L. (1978). Black walnut: what can New Zealand learn from the United States? *New Zealand Journal of Forestry* **23**, 224–39.

Kobayashi, F. (1981). Review on the pine mortality and its research in Japan. *Proceedings division 2, XVII IUFRO world congress*, 261–3.

König, E. and Gossow, H. (1979). Even-aged stands as habitat for deer in central Europe. In *Ecology of even-aged forest plantations* (eds E. D. Ford, D. C. Malcolm, and J. Atterson), pp. 429–51. Institute of Terrestrial Ecology, Cambridge.

Konôpka, J. (1975). [Assessing the wind resistance of forest stands on the basis of their basic mensurational values and of forest-type groups.] *Lesnicke Studie, Vyskumny Ustav Lesneho Hospodarstra*, Zvolen, No **23**.

—— (1980). Forest protection against abiotic harmful forces. In *Stability of spruce ecosystems*, pp. 321–34. University of Agriculture, Brno, Czechoslovakia.

Köppen, W. (1923). *Die Klimate der Erde*. de Gruyter, Berlin.

Kossuth, S. V., Roberts, D. R., Huffman, J. B., and Wang, S. C. (1982). Resin acid, turpentine and calorific content of paraquat-treated slash pine. *Canadian Journal of Forest Research* **12**(3), 489–92.

Koster, R. (1982). [The cultivation of 'energy forest' in Sweden]. *Nederlands Bosbouw Tijdschrift* **54**(7/8), 206–13.

Kozlowski, T. T. and Ahlgren, C. E. (eds) (1974). *Fire and ecosystems*. Academic Press, New York.

Kramer, H. (1980). Tending and stability of Norway spruce stands. In *Stability of spruce ecosystems*, pp. 121–33. University of Agriculture, Brno, Czechoslovakia.

—— and Bjerg, N. (1978). [Biological aspects of tending young stands of Norway spruce.] Forestry Faculty, University of Göttingen, West Germany, No. **55**.

—— and Spellmann, H. (1980). Beitrage zur Bestandesbegrundung der Fichte. Forestry Faculty University of Göttingen, No. **64**.

Kreutzer, K. (1979). How do physical classifications contrast with site type classifications. In *Ecology of even-aged forest plantations* (eds E. D. Ford, D. C. Malcolm, and J. Atterson), pp. 39–56. Institute of Terrestrial Ecology, Cambridge.

Kroth, W., Loffler, H. D., Plochman, R., and Rader-Roitch, J. E. (1976). Forestry problems and their implications for the environment in member states of the E.C. *Study P.E. 168 volume III*, Munich, West Germany.

Labaznikov, B. V. (1982). [Geographical variation in the protein content of grain crops in fields protected by shelterbelts.] *Lesnoe Khozyaistvo* No. **8**, 30–32. Cited from *Forestry Abstracts* (1983) **44**, FA6786.

Lähde, E. (1969). Biological activity in some natural and drained peat soils with special reference to oxidation–reduction conditions. *Acta Forestalia Fennica* **94**.

Lancaster, D. F., Walters, R. S., Laing, F. M., and Foulds, R. T. (1974). A silvicultural guide for developing a sugarbush. USDA Forest Service *Research Paper NE-286*.

Leaf, A. L., Rathakette, P., and Solan, F. M. (1978). Nursery seedling quality in relation to plantation performance. In Proceedings of the root form of planted trees symposium. *British Columbia Ministry of Forests/Canadian Forestry Service Joint Report* **8**. (eds E. van Eerden and J. M. Kinghorn). pp. 45–51.

Leatham, G. F. (1982). Cultivation of shiitake, the Japanese forest mushroom, on logs; a potential industry for the United States. *Forest Products Journal* **32**(8), 29–35.

Leek, N. A. (1979). Techniques of stand establishment in the Netherlands. Paper for IUFRO symposium on stand establishment techniques and technology, Wageningen, Netherlands.

Lees, J. C. (1972). Soil aeration response to drainage intensity in basin peat. *Forestry* **45**, 135–43.

Leith, H. (1975). Primary production of the major vegetation units of the world. In *Primary production of the biosphere* (eds H. Leith and R. H. Whittaker), pp. 203–15. Springer-Verlag, Berlin.

Levitt, J. (1972). *Responses of plants to environmental stress*. Academic Press, New York.

Lewis, H. T. (1982). A time for burning. *Occasional publication* **17**. Boreal Institute for Northern Studies, University of Alberta.

Leyton, L. (1958). The mineral requirements of forest plants. *Handbuch der Pflanzenphysiologie* **6**, 1026–39.

—— (1972). Forests, flooding and soil moisture. In *Proceedings Piene: Loro Previsione e difesa del suolo*. Rome, 23–30 November 1969. Accademia Nazionale dei Lincei 1972. pp. 327–37.

—— (1975). *Fluid behaviour in biological systems*. Oxford University Press.

Li, C. Y., Lu, K. C., Trappe, J. M., and Bollen, W. B. (1967). Selective nitrogen assimilation by *Poria weiru*. *Nature (London)* **213**, 814.

Lines, R. (1967). The planning and conduct of provenance experiments. *Forestry Commission Research and Development Paper* **45**. HMSO, London.

—— (1979*a*). The IUFRO experiments with Sitka spruce in Great Britain. In *Proceedings of the IUFRO joint meeting of working parties*, Vancouver, Canada, Vol. 2. pp. 211–25.

—— (1979*b*). The IUFRO experiments with *Pinus contorta* in Britain—results after six years in the forest. In *Proceedings of the IUFRO joint meeting of working parties*, Vancouver, Canada. Vol. 2. pp. 125–35.

—— (1980). *Pinus contorta*—another viewpoint. *Scottish Forestry* **34**, 114–16.

—— (1981). 'Self-thinning' mixtures. In *Forestry Commission Report on Forest Research* 1981. HMSO, London.

—— (1984). Species and seed origin trials in the industrial Pennines. *Quarterly Journal of Forestry* **78**, 9–23.

Locke, G. M. L. (1978). The growing stock of regions. *Forestry* **51**, 5–8.

Lonsdale, D. and Pratt, J. E. (1981). Some aspects of the growth of beech trees and the incidence of beech bark disease on chalk soils. *Forestry* **54**, 183–95.

Loomis, R. S. and Gerakis, P. A. (1975). Productivity of agricultural ecosystems. In *Photosynthesis and productivity in different environments* (ed. J. P. Cooper), pp. 145–72. Cambridge University Press.

Lorimer, C. G. (1977). The presettlement forest and natural disturbance cycle of northeastern Maine. *Ecology* **58**, 130–48.

Loudon, A. S. I. (1978). The control of roe deer populations: a problem in forest management. *Forestry* **51**, 73–83.

Low, A. J. (1975). Production and use of tubed seedlings. *Forestry Commission Bulletin* **53**. HMSO, London.

Lucas, O. W. R. (1983). Design of landform and planting. *Forestry Commission Research and Development Paper* **132**, 24–36.

Lyles, L. (1976). Wind patterns and soil erosion on the Great Plains. In Shelterbelts on the Great Plains (ed. R. W. Tinus). *Great Plains Agricultural Publication* **78**, 22–30.

MacLaren, P. (1983). Chemical welfare in the forest: a review of allelopathy with regard to New Zealand. *New Zealand Journal of Forestry* **28**, 73–92.

Malcolm, D. C. (1979). The future development of even-aged plantations: silvicultural implications. In *Ecology of even-aged forest plantations* (eds E. D. Ford, D. C. Malcolm, and J. Atterson), pp. 481–504. Institute of Terrestrial Ecology, Cambridge.

Mamiya, Y. (1982). Pine wilt and pine wood nematode: histopathological aspects of disease development. In *Resistance to diseases and pests in forest trees* (eds H. M. Heybroek, B. R. Stephan, and K. von Weissenberg), pp. 153–60. Wageningen, Netherlands.

Marks, G. C., Fuhrer, B. A., and Walters, N. E. M. (1982). Tree diseases in Victoria. *Handbook* **1**, Forests Commission, Victoria, Australia.

Marrs, R. H., Owen, L. D. C., Roberts, R. D., and Bradshaw, A. D. (1982). Tree lupin: an ideal nurse crop for land restoration and amenity plantings. *Arboricultural Journal* **6**, 161–74.

Marshall, J. K. (1967). The effect of shelter on the productivity of grassland and field crops. *Field Crops Abstracts* (Review Article) **20(1)**, 1–14.

Mayhead, G. J. (1973*a*). Some drag co-efficients for British forest trees derived from wind tunnel studies. *Agricultural Meteorology* **12**, 123–30.

—— (1973*b*). The effect of altitude above sea level on the yield class of Sitka spruce. *Scottish Forestry* **30**, 231–37.

—— Gardiner, J. B. H., and Durrant, D. W. (1975). A report on the physical properties of conifers in relation to plantation stability. *Forestry Commission Research and Development Division Paper* (unpublished).

McAllister, J. S. V. and Savill, P. S. (1977). Effects of pig and cow slurry on the growth of Sitka spruce on oligotrophic peat and gley soils in Northern Ireland. *Irish Forestry* **34**, 77–84.

McCune, B. (1983). Fire frequency reduced by two orders of magnitude on the Bitterroot Canyons, Montana. *Canadian Journal of Forest Research* **13**, 212–18.

McElroy, G. H. (1982). Energy from biomass/novel sources of cellulose. *Annual Report Loughall Horticultural Centre* 1981. Department of Agriculture, Northern Ireland. pp. 68–71.

McIntosh, R. (1983). In *Forestry Commission Report on Forest Research* 1983. HMSO, London.

McKinnell (1979). Silviculture of *Pinus radiata* in an agroforestry management system. *Research Paper* **51**, Forests Department, Western Australia.

McMahon, T. A. (1975). The mechanical design of trees. *Scientific American* **233(1)**, 92–102.

Mengel, K. and Kirkby, E. A. (1978). *Principles of plant nutrition*. International Potash Institute, Bern, Switzerland.

Mergen, F. (1981). Sowing forests from the air. National Academy Press, Washington, D.C. *Library of Congress Catalog No: 80-83796.*

Mexal, J. and Burton, S. (1978). Root development of planted loblolly pine seedlings. In Proceedings of the root form of planted trees symposium. *British Columbia Ministry of Forests/Canadian Forestry Service Report* **8** (eds E. van Eerden and J. M. Kinghorn). pp. 85–90.

Miles, J. (1981). Effects of trees on soils. In *Forest and Woodland Ecology*, pp. 85–8. Institute of Terrestrial Ecology, Cambridge.

Miller, H. G. (1979). The nutrient budgets of even-aged forests. In *Ecology of even-aged forest plantations* (eds E. D. Ford, D. C. Malcolm, and J. Atterson), pp. 221–56. Institute of Terrestrial Ecology, Cambridge.

—— (1981*a*). Nutrient cycles in forest plantations, their change with age and the consequence for fertilizer practice. In *Proceedings of Australian forest nutrition workshop: Productivity in perpetuity*, Canberra, Australia, 10–14 August 1981. CSIRO Division of Forest Research. pp. 187–99.

—— (1981*b*). Forest fertilization: some guiding concepts. *Forestry* **54**, 157–67.

—— (1981*c*). Aspects of forest fertilization practice and research in New Zealand. *Scottish Forestry* **35**, 277–88.

—— (1984). Nutrition of hardwoods. In *Report of fifth meeting of National Hardwoods Programme*, pp. 17–19. Commonwealth Forestry Institute, Oxford.

—— Cooper, J. M., and Miller, J. D. (1976). Effect of nitrogen supply on nutrients in litter fall and crown leaching in a stand of Corsican pine. *Journal of Applied Ecology* **13**, 233–48.

—— Miller, J. D., and Cooper, J. M. (1981). Optimum foliar nitrogen concentration in pine and its change with stand age. *Canadian Journal of Forest Research* **11**, 563–72.

—— Williams, B. L., Millar, C. S., and Warin, T. R. (1977). Ground vegetation and humus nitrogen levels as indicators of nitrogen status in an established sand-dune forest. *Forestry* **50**, 93–101.

Miller, K. F. (1985). *Windthrow hazard classification*. Forestry Commission Leaflet **85**. HMSO, London.

Mills, D. H. (1980). *The management of forest streams*. Forestry Commission Leaflet **78**. HMSO, London.

Mitscherlich, E. A. (1921). Das wirkungsgesetz der Wachstumfaktoren. *Landwirtschaft Jahrbuch Bog*, 11–15.

Mitscherlich, G. (1973). [Forest and wind.] *Allgemeine Forst-und Jagdzeitung* **144(4)**, 76–81.

Mohrdiek, O. (1983). Discussion: future possibilities for poplar breeding. *Canadian Journal of Forest Research* **13**, 465–71.

Møller, C. M. (1960). The influence of pruning on the growth of conifers. *Forestry* **33**, 37–53.

Monaco, L. C. (1983). Bioenergy in the north–south dialogue. In *Energy from Biomass* (eds A. Strub, P. Chartier, and G. Schleser), pp. 36–42. Applied Science Publishers, London.

Moore, P. D. (1984). Why be an evergreen? *Nature (London)* **312**, 703.

Morrison, I. K. (1984). Acid rain. A review of literature on acid deposition effects in forest ecosystems. *Forestry Abstracts* (Review Article), **45(8)**, 483–506.

Moss, D. (1979). Even-aged plantations as a habitat for birds. In *Ecology of even-aged forest plantations* (eds E. D. Ford, D. C. Malcolm, and J. Atterson), pp. 413–27. Institute of Terrestrial Ecology, Cambridge.

Mullin, R. E. (1974). Some planting effects still significant after 20 years. *The Forestry Chronicle* **50**, 191–3.

Murphy, G. (1982). Soil damage associated with production thinning. *New Zealand Journal of Forestry Science* **12**, 281–92.

—— (1984). *Pinus radiata* survival, growth and form four years after planting off and on skidtrails. *New Zealand Journal of Forestry* **28**, 184–93.

Murray, J. S. (1979). The development of populations of pests and pathogens in even-aged plantations — fungi. In *Ecology of even-aged forest plantations* (eds E. D. Ford, D. C. Malcolm, and J. A. Atterson), pp. 193–208. Institute of Terrestrial Ecology, Cambridge.

Nambiar, E. K. S. (1981). Ecological and physiological aspects of the development of roots: from nursery to forest. In *Proceedings of the Australian forest nutrition workshop*, Canberra, ACT, Australia. pp. 117–29.

Neckelmann, J. (1981). [Stabilization of edges and internal shelter zones in stands of Norway spruce on sandy soil.] *Dansk Skovforenings Tidsskrift* **66**, 196–314.

—— (1982). [Stabilizing measures in Norway spruce — and the hurricane of November 1981.] *Dansk Sckovforenings Tidsskrift* **67**, 77–86.

Neuman, F. G. and Minko, G. (1981). The *Sirex* wood wasp in Australian radiata pine plantations. *Australia Forestry* **44**, 46–63.

Neustein, S. A. (1964). Windthrow on the margins of various sizes of felling area. In *Forestry Commission Report on Forest Research* 1964. HMSO, London. pp. 166–71.

Newnham, R. M. (1965). Stem form and the variation of taper with age and thinning regime. *Forestry* **38**, 218–24.

Nicholls, P. H. (1981). Spatial analysis of forest growth. *Occasional Paper* **12**. Forestry Commission, Edinburgh.

O'Carroll, N. (1978). The nursing of Sitka spruce: 1. Japanese larch. *Irish Forestry* **35**, 60–5.

—— Carey, M. L., Hendrick, E., and Dillon, J. (1981). The tunnel plough in peatland afforestation. *Irish Forestry* **38**, 27–40.

O'Driscoll, J. (1980). The importance of lodgepole pine in Irish forestry. *Irish Forestry* **37**, 7–22.

Ogilvie, J. F. (1983). The first hundred thousand. *Scottish Forestry* **37**, 264–81.

—— and Taylor, C. S. (1984). Chemical silviculture (chemical thinning and respacement). *Scottish Forestry* **38**, 83–8.

Olesen, F. (1979). [Planting Shelterbelts.] Laeplanting, Denmark. Landhusholdnings-selskabet, Copenhagen.

Otto, H.-J. (1976). [Forestry experience and conclusions from the forest catastrophes in Lower Saxony.] *Forst und Holzwirt* **15**, 285–295. (British Lending Library Translation RTS 11890).

—— (1982). Measures to reduce forest fire hazards and restoration of damaged trees in Lower Saxony. In *Fire prevention and control* (ed. T. van Nao), pp. 173–9. Martinus Nijhoff/W. Junk Publishers, The Hague.

Ovington, J. D. and Madgwick, H. A. I. (1959). The growth and composition of natural stands of birch. *Plant and Soil* **10**, 271–83, 389–400.

Palz, W., Chartier, P., and Hall, D. O. (eds) (1981). *Energy from biomass*. Applied Science Publishers, London.

Papesch, A. J. G. (1974). A simplified theoretical analysis of the factors that influence windthrow of trees. *5th Australasian Conference on Hydraulics and Fluid mechanics*, pp. 235–42. University of Canterbury, New Zealand.

Pardé, J. (1980). Forest biomass. *Forestry Abstracts* (Review Article) **41(8)**, 343–62.

Parry, W. H. (1982). The role of the environment in host-interactions. In *Resistance to diseases and pests in forest trees* (eds H. M. Heybroek, B. R. Stephan, and K. von Weissenberg), Centre for Agricultural Publishing and Documentation, Wageningen, Netherlands. pp. 22–31.

Parsons, A. D. and Evans, J. (1977). Forest fire protection in the Neath district of south Wales. *Quarterly Journal of Forestry* **71**, 186–98.

Pawsey, C. K. (1972). Survival and early development of *Pinus radiata* as influenced by size of planting stock. *Australian Forestry Research* **5**, 13–24.

Peace, T. R. (1952). Poplars. *Forestry Commission Bulletin* **19**. HMSO, London.

Perry, D. A. (1979). Variation between and within tree species. In *Ecology of even-aged forest plantations* (eds E. D. Ford, D. C. Malcolm, and J. Atterson), pp. 71–98. Institute of Terrestrial Ecology, Cambridge.

Persson, A. (1980). In *Pinus contorta* as an exotic species. Swedish University of Agricultural Sciences. Department of Forest Genetics, Garpenberg. *Research Notes* **30**. p. 15.

Persson, H. (1982). The importance of fine roots in boreal forests. In *Root Ecology and its practical applications* (eds W. Bohm, L. Kutschera, and E. Lichtenegger), pp. 595–608. Irdning: Bundenstalt fur alpenlandische Landwirtschaft.

Persson, P. (1975). [Windthrow in forests: its cause and the effect of forestry measures]. *Rapporter och Uppsater, Institutionen för Skogsproduktion* No. **36**.

Peterken, G. F. (1981). *Woodland conservation and management.* Chapman and Hall, London.

Petty, J. A. and Worrell, R. (1981). Stability of coniferous tree stems in relation to damage by snow. *Forestry* **54**, 115–28.

Philipson, J. J. and Coutts, M. P. (1978). The tolerance of tree roots to waterlogging: III. Oxygen transport in lodgepole pine and Sitka spruce roots of primary structure. *New Phytologist* **80**, 341–9.

—— and —— (1980). The tolerance of tree roots to waterlogging. IV. Oxygen transport in woody roots of Sitka spruce and lodgepole pine. *New Phytologist* **85**, 489–94.

Poore, M. E. D. (1972). *Forestry Commission Booklet* **29**. HMSO, London. p. 3.

Prebble, M. L. and Morris, R. F. (1951). The spruce budworm problem. *Forestry Chronicle* **27**, 14–22.

Preest, D. S., Davenhill, N. A., Sanderson, H., and Cranswick, A. (1978). Controlling bracken in forests. *What's new in forest research* No. **58**.

Prichett, W. L. (1979). *Properties and management of forest soils.* John Wiley and Sons, New York.

Prior, R. (1983). *Trees and deer.* B. T. Batsford, London.

Pyatt, D. G. (1970). Soil groups of upland forests. *Forestry Commission Forest Record* **71**. HMSO, London.

—— and Craven, M. M. (1979). Soil changes under even-aged plantations. In *Ecology of even-aged forest plantations* (eds E. D. Ford, D. C. Malcolm, and J. Atterson), pp. 369–386. Institute of Terrestrial Ecology, Cambridge.

Pyne, S. J. (1984). *Introduction to wildland fire: fire management in the United States.* John Wiley and Sons, New York.

Quimby, P. C. (1982). Impact of diseases on plant populations. In *Biological control of weeds with plant pathogens* (eds R. Charudattan and H. L. Walker), pp. 47–60. John Wiley and Sons, New York.

Rackham, O. (1976). *Trees and woodland in the British landscape.* J. M. Dent and Sons, London.

Raymer, W. G. (1962). Wind resistance of conifers. Report 1008, National Physical Laboratory aerodynamics Division, UK.

Read, D. J., Armstrong, W., and Weatherall, J. (1973). The effects of cultivation treatment on water potential and soil aeration in wet heathland with special reference to afforestation. *Journal of Applied Ecology* **10**, 479–87.

Reed, F. L. C. (1983). Forest renewal in Canada. *Commonwealth Forestry Review* **62**, 169–77.

Rees, D. J. and Grace, J. (1980*a*). The effects of wind on the extension growth of *Pinus contorta. Forestry* **53**, 145–53.

—— and —— (1980*b*). The effects of shaking on extension growth of *Pinus contorta. Forestry* **53**, 155–66.

Reineke, L. H. (1933). Perfecting a stand-density index for even-aged forests. *Journal of Agricultural Research* **46**, 627–38.

Richter, J. (1975). [Gale damage to spruce in Sauerland.] *Forst-und Holzwirt* **30(6)**, 106–8.

Ritchie, G. A. (1982). Carbohydrate reserves and root growth potential in Douglas-fir seedlings before and after cold storage. *Canadian Journal of Forest Research* **12**, 905–12.

—— and Dunlap, J. R. (1980). Root growth potential: its development and expression in forest tree seedlings. *New Zealand Journal of Forestry Science* **10**, 218–48.

Rollinson, T. J. D. (1983). In *Forestry Commission Report on Forest Research* 1983. HMSO, London.

Rosenberg, N. J. (1974). *Microclimate: The biological environment*. John Wiley and Sons, New York.

Ross, S. M. and Malcolm, D. C. (1982). Effects of intensive forestry ploughing practices on an upland heath soil in south east Scotland. *Forestry* **55**, 155–71.

Rothermel, R. C. (1982). Modelling the development of fire in a forest environment. In *Forest fire prevention and control* (ed. T. van Nao), pp. 77–84. Martinus Nijhoff/W. Junk Publishers. The Hague.

Roulund, H. (1981). Problems of clonal forestry in spruce and their influence on breeding strategy. *Forestry Abstracts* (Review Article) **42(10)**, 457–71.

Rowan, A. A. (1977). Terrain Classification. *Forestry Commission Forest Record* **114**. HMSO, London.

Rowe, J. S. (1983). Concepts of fire effects on plant individuals and species. In *The role of fire in northern circumpolar ecosystems* (eds R. W. Wein and D. A. MacLean), pp. 135–54. John Wiley and Sons, New York.

Sanders, C. J. (1974). Spruce budworm in Ontario and Prairie provinces. *USDA Forest Service Miscellaneous Publication* **1327**, 21–4.

Sanderson, P. L. and Armstrong, W. (1978). Soil waterlogging, root rot and conifer windthrow: oxygen deficiency or phytotoxicity? *Plant and soil* **49(1)**, 185–90.

Savill, P. S. (1976). The effects of drainage and ploughing of surface water gleys on rooting and windthrow of Sitka spruce in Northern Ireland. *Forestry* **49**, 133–41.

—— (1983). Silviculture in windy climates. *Forestry Abstracts* (Review Article) **44(8)**, 473–88.

—— and McEwen, J. E. (1978). Timber production from Northern Ireland 1980–2004. *Irish Forestry* **35**, 115–23.

—— and Sandels, A. J. (1983). The influence of spacing on the wood density of Sitka spruce. *Forestry* **56**, 109–20.

—— Dickson, D. A., and Wilson, W. T. (1974). Effects of ploughing and drainage on growth and root development of Sitka spruce on deep peat in Northern Ireland. In *Proceedings IUFRO Symposium on Forest Drainage*, Helsinki.

Schlich, W. (1899). *Manual of forestry*, Vol. I. Bradbury, Agnew and Co., London.

Schoenweiss, D. F. (1981). The role of environmental stress in disease of woody plants. *Plant Diseases* **65**, 308–14.

Schulze, E.-D. (1982). Plant life forms and their carbon, water and nutrient relations. In *Physiological plant ecology II* (eds O. L. Lange, P. S. Nobel, C. B. Osmond, and H. Ziegler), pp. 615–76. Springer-Verlag, Berlin.

Selby, C. and Seaby, D. A. (1982). The effect of auxins on *Pinus contorta* seedling root development. *Forestry* **55**, 125–35.

Seligman, R. M. (1983). Biofuels in the European Community—a view from the European Parliament. In *Energy from biomass* (eds A. Strub, P. Chartier, and G. Schleser), pp. 16–22. Applied Science Publishers, London.

Sendak, P. E. (1978). Birch sap utilization in the Ukraine. *Journal of Forestry* **76(2)**, 120–1.

Shea, S. R., Gillen, K. J., and Kitt, R. J. (1978). Variation in sporangial production of *Phytophthora cinnamomi* on jarrah forest sites with different understorey compositions. *Australian Forest Research* **8**, 219–26.

Sheehan, P. G., Lavery, P. B., and Walsh, B. M. (1982). Thinning and salvage strategies in plantations prone to storm damage. *New Zealand Journal of Forestry Science* **12**, 269–80.

Shellard, H. C. (1976). Wind. In *The climate of the British Isles* (eds T. J. Chandler and S. Gregory), pp. 39–73. Longman, London.

Shirley, H. L. (1945). Reproduction of upland conifers in the Lake States as affected by root competition and height. *American Midland Naturalist* **33**, 537–612.

Simpson, J. (1900). *The new forestry*. Pawson and Brailsford, Sheffield.

Skidmore, E. L. (1976). Barrier-induced microclimate and its influence on growth and yield of winter wheat. In Shelterbelts on the Great Plains (ed. R. W. Tinus). *Great Plains Agricultural Publication* **78**, 57–63.

Slesser, M. and Lewis, C. (1979). *Biological energy resources*. E. and F. N. Spon, London and New York, Halsted Press.

Small, B. E. J. (1981). The Australian eucalyptus oil industry—an overview. *Australian Forestry* **44**, 170–77.

Small, D. (1982). Reproduction of even-aged high forest oak—with special reference to the New Forest Statutory Inclosures. In *Broadleaves in Britain: future management and research* (eds D. C. Malcolm, J. Evans, and P. N. Edwards), pp. 65–71. Institute of Chartered Foresters, Edinburgh.

Smith, H. C. and Gibbs, C. B. (1970). A guide to sugarbush stocking. *USDA Forest Service Research Paper NE-171*.

Southwood, T. R. E. (1981). Bionomic strategies and population parameters. In *Theoretical ecology* (2nd edn) (ed. R. M. May), pp. 30–52. Blackwell Scientific Publications, Oxford.

Speight, M. R. (1983). The potential of ecosystem management for pest control. *Agriculture, Ecosystems and Environment* **10**, 183–99.

—— (1985). Environmental influences on host plant susceptibility to insect attack. *Proceedings of Linnean Society* (eds B. Juniper and T. R. E. Southwood).

Stassen, H. E. M. (1982). [Energy from wood and wood waste; technologies and perspectives]. *Nederlands Bosbouw Tijdschrift* **54(7/8)**, 172–8.

Steele, R. C. (1972). Wildlife conservation in woodlands. *Forestry Commission Booklet* **29**. HMSO, London.

Stein, W. I. (1978). Naturally developed seedling roots of five western conifers. In Proceedings of the root form of planted trees symposium. *British Columbia Ministry of Forests/Canadian Forestry Service Joint Report* **8** (eds E. van Eerden and J. M. Kinghorn) pp. 28–35.

Stewart, A. J. A. and Lance, A. N. (1983). Moor-draining: a review of impacts on land use. *Journal of Environmental Management* **17**, 81–99.

Stoakley, J. T. (1979). Pine beauty moth. *Forestry Commission Forest Record* **120**. HMSO, London.

Stocker, G. C. (1976). Report on cyclone damage to natural vegetation in the Darwin area after cyclone Tracey, 25 December 1974. *Leaflet Forestry and Timber Bureau Canberra* **127**.

Streets, R. J. (1962). *Exotic forest trees in the British Commonwealth*. Clarendon Press, Oxford.

Strub, A., Chartier, P., and Schleser, G. (eds) (1983). *Energy from biomass*. Applied Science Publishers, London.

Sutton, R. F. (1979). Planting stock quality and grading. *Forest Ecology and Management* **2**, 123-32.

Sutton, W. R. J. (ed.) (1970). Pruning and thinning practice. In *Proceedings of New Zealand Forest Service, Forest Research Institute Symposium* Vol. 2.

—— (1984). Economic and strategic implications of fast-growing plantations. In IUFRO *Symposium on site and productivity of fast-growing plantations* Vol. 1, pp. 417-31. South Africa Forest Research Institute, Pretoria.

Sweet, G. B. and Waring, P. F. (1966). The relative growth rate of large and small seedlings in forest tree species. *Forestry* (supplement) **39**, 110-17.

Symonds, H. H. (1936). *Afforestation in the Lake District*. J. M. Dent and Sons, London.

Tabbush, P. M. (1984). Scandinavian scarifiers and their potential for site preparation in British Forestry. *Forestry Commission Research Information Note* 84/84.

Tadaki, Y. (1966). Some discussions on the leaf biomass of forest stands and trees. *Bulletin of the Government Forest Experiment Station, Meguro* **84**, 135-61.

Tatsuno, T. (1983). *Journal Antibacterial and Antifungal Agents* **11**(7), 423-31.

Taylor, G. G. M. (1970). Ploughing practice in the Forestry Commission. *Forestry Commission Forest Record* 73. HMSO, London.

Taylor, J. A. (1976). Upland climates. In *The climate of the British Isles* (eds T. J. Chandler and S. Gregory), pp. 264-87. Longman, London.

—— and Yates, R. A. (1967). *British weather in maps*. Macmillan, London.

Templeton, G. E. (1982). Status of weed control with plant pathogens. In *Biological control of weeds with plant pathogens* (eds R. Charudattan and H. L. Walker), pp. 29-44. John Wiley and Sons, New York.

Thomas, J. W., Miller, R. J., Black, H., Rodiek, J. E., and Maser, C. (1976). Guidelines for maintaining and enhancing wildlife habitat in forest management in the Blue Mountains of Washington and Oregon. *Transactions of the North American Wildlife and Natural Resources Conference* **41**, 452-76.

Thompson, D. A. (1978). Forest ploughs. *Forestry Commission Leaflet* 70. HMSO, London.

—— (1979). Forest drainage schemes. *Forestry Commission Leaflet* 72. HMSO, London.

—— (1984). Ploughing of forest soils. *Forestry Commission Leaflet* 71. HMSO, London.

—— and Neustein, S. A. (1973). In *Forestry Commission Report on Forest Research* 1973, pp. 67-68. HMSO, London.

Thornthwaite, C. W. (1948). An approach toward a rational classification of climate. *Geographical Review* **38**, 55-94.

Tinus, R. W. (1978). Root form: what difference does it make? In Proceedings of the root form of planted trees symposium. *British Columbia Ministry of Forests/Canadian Forestry Service Joint Report* 8 (eds E. van Eerden and J. M. Kinghorn). pp. 11-15.

Toda, R. (1974). Vegetative propagation in relation to Japanese forest tree improvement. *New Zealand Journal of Forestry Science* **4**, 410-17.

Toleman, R. D. L. and Pyatt, D. G. (1974). Site classification as an aid to silviculture in the Forestry Commission of Great Britain. *Paper for 10th Commonwealth Forestry Conference*, UK, 1974.

Tranquillini, W. (1979). *Alpine timberline*. Springer-Verlag, Berlin.

Tribun, P. A., Gavrilyuk, M. V., Yukhimchuk, G. V., and Lopareva, E. B. (1983). [Biochemical features of young spruce trees in stands of different density.] *Lesnoi Zhurnal* **3**, 23-6.

Troedsson, T. (1980). Long-term changes of forest soils. *Annales Agriculturae Fenniae* **19**, 81-4.

Troup, R. S. (1955). *Silvicultural systems* (2nd edn revised by E. W. Jones). Clarendon Press, Oxford.

Tuley, G. (1983). Shelters improve the growth of young trees. *Quarterly Journal of Forestry* **77**, 78-87.

Walshe, D. E. and Fraser, A. I. (1963). Wind tunnel tests on a model forest. *Report 1078*, National Physical Laboratory Aerodynamics Division, UK.

Wang, T.-T., Pai, N.-Y., Peng, P. L. F., Lin, T.-S., and Shih, C.-F. (1980). The effect of pruning on the growth of *Cryptomeria. Biologische, technische und wirtschaftliche Aspekte der Jungbestandspflege* (ed. H. Kramer) Vol. 67, pp. 92-106. Schriften Forstlichen Fakultät, Universität Göttingen, W. Germany.

Waring, R. H. (1983). Estimating forest growth and efficiency in relation to canopy leaf area. *Advances in ecological research* **13**, 327-54.

Watts, S. B. (1983). *Forestry Handbook for British Columbia*. University of British Columbia, Canada.

Wein, R. W. and MacLean, D. A. (eds) (1983). *The role of fire in northern circumpolar ecosystems*. John Wiley and Sons, New York.

Whitehead, D. (1982). Ecological aspects of natural and plantation forests. *Forestry Abstracts* (Review Article) **43(10)**, 615-24.

Whiteside, I. D. and Sutton, W. R. J. (1983). A silvicultural stand model: implications for radiata pine management. *New Zealand Journal of Forestry* **28**, 300-13.

Wiedemann, E. (1923). [Regress in increment and growth interruptions of spruce in middle and lower altitudes of the Saxon State forests]. Translation No. 302, United States Forest Service, 1936.

Will, G. M. (1981). Fertilizer applications to New Zealand's exotic forests in 1980. In *Proceedings of Australian forest nutrition workshop: productivity in perpetuity*, Canberra, Australia, 10-14 August 1981. CSIRO Division of Forest Research.

Wilson, C. L. (1969). Use of plant pathogens in weed control. *Annual Review of Phytopathology* **7**, 411-34.

Winer, N. (1980). The potential of the carob. *International Tree Crops Journal* **1**, 15-26.

Wingate-Hill, R. and Jakobsen, B. F. (1982). Increased mechanisation and soil damage in forests—a review. *New Zealand Journal of Forestry Science* **12**, 380-93.

Wood, P. J. (1975). The world situation as it will affect the UK. *Scottish Forestry* **29**, 25-38.

Woods, R. V. (1976). Early silviculture for upgrading productivity on marginal *Pinus radiata* sites in the south-east region of South Australia. *Bulletin* **24**, Woods and Forests Department, South Australia.

World Bank (1978). Forestry sector policy paper. *World Bank*, Washington DC.

World Wood (1982). Country reports. *World Wood* **23(5)**, 16 August 1982, 9-71.

Worsham, A. D. (1982). Discussion of topics. In *Biological control of weeds with plant pathogens* (eds R. Charudattan and H. L. Walker), p. 220. John Wiley and Sons, New York.

Wright, H. A. and Bailey, A. W. (1982). *Fire ecology*. John Wiley and Sons, New York.

Yoda, K., Kira, T., Ogawa, H., and Hozumi, K. (1963). Self-thinning in overcrowded pure stands under cultivated and natural conditions. *Journal of Biology Osaka City University* **14**, 107–29.

Young, H. E. (ed.) (1967). Symposium on primary production and mineral cycling in natural ecosystems. 13th Annual meeting, American Association for the Advancement of Science, New York.

Zehetmayr, J. W. L. (1954). Experiments in tree planting on peat. *Forestry Commission Bulletin* **22**. HMSO, London.

Zobel, B. J. (1982). The world's need for pest resistant trees. In *Resistance to diseases and pests in forest trees* (eds H. M. Heybroek, B. R. Stephan, and K. von Weissenberg), pp. 1–8. Centre for Agricultural Publishing and Documentation, Wageningen, Netherlands.

—— Campinhos, E., and Ikemori, Y. (1983). Selecting and breeding for desirable wood. *Tappi* January 1983, 70–4.

Index

This index includes the scientific names of plants mentioned in the text, the authorities for naming them, and their local names.

plantations (*cont.*)
  stocking, *see* spacing
  uses/values of 6, 157
Platanus 152
ploughing 28, 50–8, 145
  direction 54
  and root growth 54, 184
  and tree growth 54
ploughs 184
  double mouldboard 53, 54
  mole 56, 184
  single mouldboard 53, 54
  tunnel 55, 184
podzols, *see* soils
Poland 11
polar front 5, 32
pollution, *see* atmospheric pollution
pondorosa pine, *see Pinus pondorosa*
poplars, *see Populus*
Populus 5, 11, 28, 47, 64, 68, 70–1, 74, 75, 92, 148, 192
  deltoides Marh 149
  x *euramericana* (Dode) Guinier 149
  nigra L. 149
  tremula L. 18, 25
  trichocarpa Torrey & Gray ex Hook 149
Poria spp. (fungus) 25
porosity, *see* soil
Portugal 164, 166
potassium 22, 103
  fertilizers 108–10
  deficiencies 104–5
precipitation 30, 32, 35, 48, 64
pre-commercial thinning 9, 128–9, 187
predation 24, 173
prescribed burning, *see* burning
pressure systems, *see* atmospheric pressure systems
prickly pear, *see Opuntia*
primary production 15–20, 98
  gross 15–16
  in managed forests 19–20, 115, 159
  net 15–17
produce 12
production 11, 15–20
  in natural forests 9
  in plantations 11, 19–20, 28, 63
propyzamide (herbicide) 95
productivity, long-term 20–9
protection
  from fire 191–9
  from pests and pathogens 26, 171–7
  from wind 179–89; *see also* wind
provenance 12, 67–71
  and climate 67
  mixtures of 28
  of *Picea sitchensis* 69

of *Pinus contorta* 69
of *Pinus radiata* 68
pruning 125, 129–31
  practice 128, 129–31, 133, 149, 203
  responses to 129–31
  and wind 188
  wounds 131
Prunus
  avium L. 89
  cerasus L. 162
Pseudotsuga menziesii (Mirb.) Franco 8, 19, 20, 25, 26, 64, 68, 76, 98, 104, 129, 154, 206
Pteridium acquilinum (L.) Kuhn (fern) 40, 89
puddling 61
pulverized fuel ash 137, 142
Pyrenees 32
pyrite (FeS$_2$) 142

Queen Charlotte Islands 69, 176
Queensland 127
Quercus 4, 7, 10, 19, 94, 98, 167
  petraea (Mattuschka) Liebl. 86
  robur L. 166
  suber L. 166

rabbits 65, 92
radiata pine, *see Pinus radiata*
radiation, *see* solar radiation
raindrops 48
rainfall, *see* precipitation
reafforestation, *see* establishment; planting; replanting
reclamation of mined sites 137–47
recreation 192, 208–9
red alder, *see Alnus rubra*
red deer, *see Cervus*
red pine, *see Pinus resinosa*
red spruce, *see Picea rubra*
reforestation, *see* establishment; planting; replanting
regrowth 88
replacing dead plants, *see* beating up
replanting 3, 9, 60, 82
resins 162
  stimulating production of 163
  tapping 163
resistance to pests and diseases 28, 175, 176
respacing, *see* pre-commercial thinning
respiration 16, 122, 127; *see also* root respiration
restoration of sites 143–7
Rhododendron ponticum L. (shrub) 91, 94